About Island Press

Since 1984, the nonprofit organization Island Press has been stimulating, shaping, and communicating ideas that are essential for solving environmental problems worldwide. With more than 1,000 titles in print and some 30 new releases each year, we are the nation's leading publisher on environmental issues. We identify innovative thinkers and emerging trends in the environmental field. We work with world-renowned experts and authors to develop cross-disciplinary solutions to environmental challenges.

Island Press designs and executes educational campaigns in conjunction with our authors to communicate their critical messages in print, in person, and online using the latest technologies, innovative programs, and the media. Our goal is to reach targeted audiences—scientists, policymakers, environmental advocates, urban planners, the media, and concerned citizens—with information that can be used to create the framework for long-term ecological health and human well-being.

Island Press gratefully acknowledges major support of our work by The Agua Fund, The Andrew W. Mellon Foundation, The Bobolink Foundation, The Curtis and Edith Munson Foundation, Forrest C. and Frances H. Lattner Foundation, The JPB Foundation, The Kresge Foundation, The Oram Foundation, Inc., The Overbrook Foundation, The S.D. Bechtel, Jr. Foundation, The Summit Charitable Foundation, Inc., and many other generous supporters.

The opinions expressed in this book are those of the author(s) and do not necessarily reflect the views of our supporters.

SUBURBAN
REMIX

SUBURBAN
REMIX

Creating the Next Generation of Urban Places

Edited by
Jason Beske and David Dixon

Washington | Covelo | London

Island Press is a trademark of The Center for Resource Economics.

Library of Congress Control Number: 2017942242

All Island Press books are printed on environmentally responsible materials.

Manufactured in the United States of America
10 9 8 7 6 5 4 3 2 1

Keywords: commercial strip, density, drivable sub-urban, the great reset, locally serving retail, regionally significant retail, shopping mall reuse, suburban poverty, suburban sprawl, suburban town center, urbanizing suburbia, walkable urban

CONTENTS

ACKNOWLEDGMENTS

We'd like to thank our wonderful families for supporting (and humoring) us while we created *Suburban Remix*. They remain the focus of our respective worlds.

We feel deep gratitude for a team whose work and guidance helped us conjure a book out of a mutual interest in the walkable urban places transforming North America's suburbs: Steve Wolf, our remarkable editor at Stantec's Urban Places (who deserves a credit on half the chapters in this book); Heather Boyer, our equally remarkable, and remarkably patient editor at Island Press, whose thoughtful direction never failed to improve the book; Stantec's Kasey Grzyb, our image wrangler extraordinaire; Stantec's Anushree Nallapaneni, our data-visualization wizard; Justin Falango, our placemaking and graphics guru; and map-making experts Ma Shuyun and Xumengqi. We also recognize our special debt to many generous colleagues who filled in for us on multiple occasions so that we could complete this book.

We're particularly grateful for Stantec's unwavering support for this project, which does not benefit its bottom line but does reflect a firm-wide commitment to and focus on all things urban. It would be hard to overstate the value of the chapters written by Michael J. Berne, Terry Foegler, Mark Hinshaw, Linda E. Hollis, Christopher B. Leinberger, Harold Madi, Simon O'Byrne, Stewart Schwartz, Chris Snyder, Tianyao Sun, Laurie Volk, Christopher Volk-Zimmerman, Sterling Wheeler, Sarah Woodworth, Christopher Zimmerman, and Todd Zimmerman. We deeply respect their knowledge and their commitment to helping us describe the emergence of walkable suburban centers, and remain grateful both for the time they took to shape their chapters and for the way they took this task to heart. Their complementary perspectives add a depth and richness that elevate *Suburban Remix*—but we expected nothing less from these accomplished practitioners who care deeply about the communities in which they live and for which they work.

Several developers who have pioneered the field of walkable suburban places offered valuable reports. In particular, we thank Federal Realty Investment Trust for its willingness to provide photographs of its projects; Crawford Hoying for making so many materials from Bridge Park available to us; and the Reston Town Center Association for its insight, cooperation, and images.

Finally, we dedicate this book to Samuel, Benji, Giacomo, and all the other kids who will inherit the world we are creating.

Jason and David

May 2, 2017

SUBURBAN
REMIX

Figure 0.1. In the six decades after World War II, the classic suburban dream meant homogeneity, a growing middle class, two-parent families with children, and a single-family house. That era has ended. *Suburban Remix* describes how suburbs can invent and make real a suburban dream for today.

INTRODUCTION

David Dixon

"North America is a suburban continent with an urban population."[1]

Roughly two-thirds of North Americans live in suburbs, and two-thirds live in single-family houses (see Figure 0.1). The traditional suburban dream that built this world—promulgated widely in the decades following World War II—was about homogeneity represented by a growing middle class and symbolized by a single-family house with a white picket fence and a car in the driveway. That dream is dead. It simply no longer describes the places in which most North Americans aspire to live or for which they are willing to pay. Today—as they grow steadily older and younger, richer and poorer, and more racially and ethnically varied—North Americans and their dreams are far more diverse. A 2016 survey even found that affluent Americans, whose default lifestyle has been suburban for decades, do not list suburban living among their top terms to describe the "American Dream."[2]

So Why Not Join the "End of Suburbs" Chorus?

Suburbs are not destined to suffer the fate of the traditional suburban dream. Today suburbs face an era of unparalleled, albeit far more urban, opportunity. This book views suburbs as an ongoing experiment in trying out new forms of development to respond to social, economic, and technological change (a notion introduced by Charles Marohn, founder and president of Strong Towns)—and over the long history of human settlement, a very recent experiment. In fact, since suburbs first emerged as a recognizable form, with the advent of commuter railroads and then streetcars, they have represented a continuous experiment, evolving in response to the interplay of fundamental demographic, economic,

Figure 0.2. Very different demographics, economy, and personal values are reshaping suburbia.

and technological changes. The considerable social, economic, and environmental costs of suburban sprawl have been widely reported, but criticism of sprawl does not equate to a failure of suburbs. Instead, it represents the wrapping up of one era as we prepare to open a new, more resilient one—marked by resilience defined by adapting to and drawing renewed vigor from the rapid changes that mark our world today (see Figure 0.2).

Suburban Remix tells the story of this next era. This book is about an optimistic future in which suburbs can make a conscious choice, followed by concrete action, to become as current and central to our society today as they were for much of the latter half of the twentieth century. Without damaging a blade of grass on a single lawn, suburbs across North America can seize opportunities to transform tens of millions of acres of "grayfields"—outmoded predominantly single-use shopping centers and office parks—into a new generation of compact, dense, walkable, mixed-use—urban—places that accommodate multiple dreams. By expanding the traditional suburban model to embrace a new generation of urban places, these communities can enhance quality of life not just for residents of these new urban centers but for their entire communities.

These urban places create more than social value. They attract knowledge workers, employers, and high-value jobs along with people who prefer urban living and seek places with urban amenities. In the process they offer new futures for tired strip retail centers

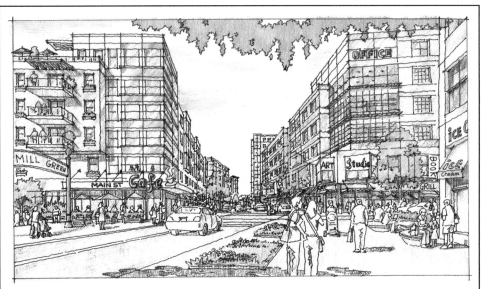

Figure 0.3a, b. A new generation of walkable urban places is replacing outmoded suburban retail centers and office parks. This rendering shows a mixed-use, walkable "urban village" that will replace a strip retail center in Newton, Massachusetts. (Both images: Stantec)

and obsolete office parks. They greatly intensify development on these sites and don't just increase, but multiply fiscal value (see Figure 0.3a, b).

Nor can North America's cities accommodate the demand for urban places to live, work, study, and play over the next couple of decades. The best measure? Rising urban property values represent a direct measure of the reality that cities cannot meet the demands created by changing demographics and an expanding knowledge economy by themselves. Suburbs can tap these trends by building a new generation of urban places. And as demonstrated by the case studies in this book, suburban governments, along with neighborhood and business leaders, have disproved the notion that they won't consider moving their communities along a post-sprawl path.

Few organizations have worked as hard to keep the traditional suburban dream alive as the National Association of Realtors. Yet few organizations now offer such a succinct vision of how suburbs can innovate going forward. Introducing the association's 2015 American Communities Survey, its president Chris Polychron said, "Realtors don't only sell homes; they sell . . . communities." These communities are no longer "one size fits all"; instead, their future is about becoming walkable, mixed-use, transit-accessible "urban centers."[3]

The Challenge Is the Opportunity

Fundamental, long-term trends are shaping demand for more urban lifestyles in cities and suburbs alike. Termed by Richard Florida "the Great Reset," coming out of the Great Recession America's growth has essentially reversed from the predominant pattern that characterized the six decades following World War II. Headlines abound about how rapidly many cities are changing. Whether the accompanying stories focus on renaissance, gentrification, or start-ups, the theme is the same: following a decades-long decline after World War II, cities reflect growing affluence and self-confidence, and the pace of this change is accelerating. Less widely reported is the fact that suburbs are changing too, and the pace of this change is also accelerating. The demographic, social, and economic dynamics that for roughly six decades made suburbs the default destination as a place to live and work for a growing middle class have eroded.

To start, while the traditional suburban demographic base—households with children—will remain an important suburban constituency, it will also continue to represent a declining share not just of North American housing markets but also of suburban housing markets. By 2030 the US population will have grown by 170 million people since 1970, while adding all of two million school-age children[4] (see Figure 0.4). Singles and couples and aging baby boomers will play a much more significant role in shaping housing markets, development patterns, and suburbs well into the 2030s.

Nor are the changes just about household size. The Great Reset also applies to a shift in values in which walkable urban places are now viewed as healthier and more environmentally responsible places to live and work. In fact, the very word "urban," long a derogative term that called up images of the worst of crime and crowding, today is far more likely to call up images of bustling cafés and expensive condominiums.

New households shape housing markets, and these markets are telling the story of this dramatic transition. As of 2017 more than two-thirds of all US housing units are

School-Age Children as a Proportion of the U.S. Population

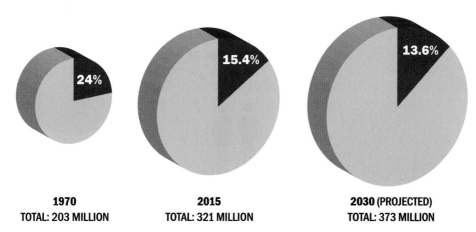

1970	**2015**	**2030** (PROJECTED)
TOTAL: 203 MILLION	TOTAL: 321 MILLION	TOTAL: 373 MILLION

Figure 0.4. Post–World War II suburbs were designed for families with school-age children. The proportion of those households within the United States has been shrinking steadily since the 1970s. (Stantec graphic, based on data from the US Census Bureau)

single-family, and due to the preponderance of singles and couples over the next two decades more than two-thirds of the demand is likely to be for multifamily housing. This imbalance together with changed values and a growing preference for walkable environments is making itself felt across US housing markets. Using Zillow data, Richard Florida notes that in 2000 urban and suburban housing values were roughly comparable (measured on a per-square-foot basis). Over the next 15 years, however, values for urban housing rose almost 60% faster than suburban values.[5]

The Great Reset is also relocating the center of North America's economy from suburban office parks back to urban centers. Jed Kolko—chief economist at the employment website Indeed.com, formerly chief economist at Trulia, and a prolific interpreter of urban data—has pointed out that not all millennials are moving into cities—just those with more education (see Figure 0.5). As growth in higher education attendance levels off, North America faces a long-term, increasingly acute shortage of knowledge workers (and slowing US immigration will make the shortage worse). Knowledge industries—the most important source of economic growth across North America—follow scarce knowledge workers to the places where they choose to live and work, which, as Kolko's work demonstrates, are urban.

The impact on regional office economies, and the tax base of many suburbs, has been dramatic. Since the late 1980s, office rents have risen more than twice as fast in downtowns as they have in suburban locations. More concerning from a tax base perspective, real estate values for office space have appreciated five times faster in downtowns than in

Millennials Self-Sort by Education

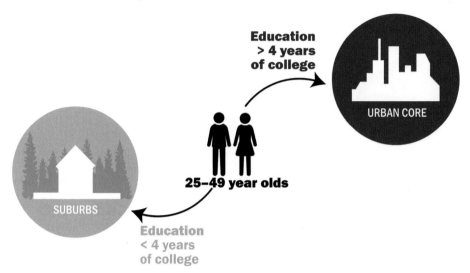

Figure 0.5. Not all millennials are moving to cities—just those with four or more years of higher education. (Stantec graphic, based on data for 2000–2014 from Trulia.com)

suburbs during the same period[6] (see Figure 0.6). Retail rents have followed a similar trajectory. These divergent trends show no sign of abating.

The pace of these changes has been as dramatic as their extent. Joe Cortright of City Observatory, a nonprofit website devoted to urban analytics, reports that in 1980 people aged 25 to 34 were just 10% more likely than the rest of us to live in "close-in," walkable, urban settings. By 2010, that figure had increased to 51%. More notable, while the urban preferences of the current crop of 25- to 34-year-olds, termed "millennials," captures media attention, a similar shift had occurred across the entire housing market. Housing analyst Laurie Volk reports that in the 1990s proximity to golf courses and large backyards topped the priorities cited by people searching for a house; by 2016 very different qualities led the list—proximity to a Main Street and walkability.[7]

Suburbs can capitalize on these "urban" trends—and emerging "disruptive" forces are adding urgency to moving forward. The trends described above carry as much opportunity for suburbs as they do for cities. As market values for denser, mixed-use, walkable—urban— environments rise relative to strip retail centers and outmoded office parks, suburbs will have plenty of opportunities to tap these market shifts and benefit. Suburbs will have one distinct advantage over core cities—the ability to respond to changing markets without being encumbered by fragmented landownership. Developers in suburbs will be in a far better position to assemble large, contiguous sites with a single or a few owners to create vibrant new districts. This said, suburbs also face emerging demographic, social, and fiscal pressures that add a note of urgency to launching a generation of urban places.

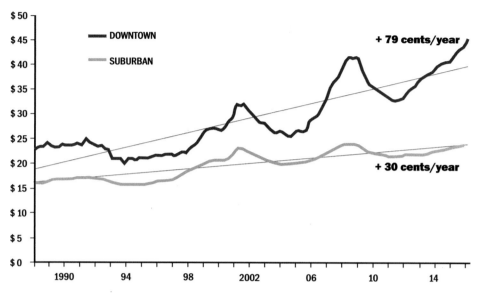

Office Rents, 1998-2016

Figure 0.6. As knowledge-economy employers follow knowledge workers to urban environments, suburban office rents have lagged. (Stantec graphic, based on data from CBRE Econometric Advisor)

To an extent that goes underreported, suburbs are ground zero for some of the most disruptive changes stemming from accelerating wealth inequities, a rapidly aging population, and growing racial and ethnic diversity. As a result, they face mounting pressure to create urban centers that enhance their tax base, expand their housing options, and provide common grounds that bring together increasingly diverse populations. The most dramatic change has been the rise of suburban poverty. In 2012, for the first time in America's history, more people in poverty lived in suburbs than in cities, and, driven in part by the rising cost of urban housing, the number of poor people living in suburbs swelled 65% between 2000 and 2014.[8] This sharp rate of growth shows no sign of abating as housing costs in cities continue to grow faster than those in suburbs. While there are significant moral and social implications to this dramatic trend, the impacts on suburban schools, social and health services, transportation systems, and similar functions that shape suburban budgets have been particularly severe and come at a time when many suburban communities are already struggling with flat or slow growth in their real estate tax base—their primary source of revenue.

At the same time, while people over age 65 will represent more than half of all US population growth to 2030, they will represent a still larger share of suburban population growth. As people reach their mid-60s they become net sellers of single-family houses

Figure 0.7. Shared autonomous vehicles will boost the prospects of higher-density, walkable centers that offer a critical mass of riders and destinations. (Local Motors)

in favor of rental multifamily housing in more walkable settings. Studies suggest many of these older residents love their suburban communities and want to remain, but they need workable housing choices. It is not unusual to find suburbs for which people over 65 represent all the projected growth to 2030 and for which most of the net new demand will be for multifamily housing. And layered across these changes is a rapid surge in racial and ethnic diversity. People of color represented more than 90% of the growth in suburban population between 2000 and 2010. Given current trends, suburbs are likely to be more racially and ethnically diverse than cities by 2040. Greater diversity brings a greater variation in lifestyles, values, cultural preferences, and other lines of difference, and a correspondingly greater importance to creating places like traditional downtowns where everyone can come together to find and celebrate community.

An autonomous-mobility revolution is about to give a big boost to walkable urban places in cities and suburbs (see Figure 0.7). Congested suburban arteries and lack of transit access have long complicated efforts to accommodate, and build community support for, denser suburban development. The arrival of autonomous vehicles (AVs) over the next five years will begin to shift this equation dramatically. Although some observers have predicted that AVs would encourage a new generation of suburban sprawl, it seems likely that the primary impact for at least the first decade and probably for many more years will be precisely the opposite. The real disruption will come from "autonomous transit" in the form of shared autonomous vehicles (SAVs)—6- to 12-passenger electric vehicles that run on schedule or on demand (ordered on a mobile device). Thanks to not having to pay a driver, SAV transit will cost less than half of what shared services like Uber/Lyft cost today—and offer the same advantage of almost never needing to park.

The first generation of SAVs, arriving in large numbers in the early 202s, will not be equal-opportunity disruptors. Built to navigate compact, dense urban settings (both city and suburb) and connect urban places to transit, they will spread rapidly where a critical mass of people and varied activities combine to generate lots of trips. Because they pick up and drop off passengers then move on, they will begin to decrease parking requirements. Within a decade, large numbers of SAVs designed to operate in mixed traffic at conventional speeds will join this first generation. "Urban" will increasingly signify places where vehicles are shared, not owned. In lower-density suburbs, privately owned automated vehicles, although far more expensive to own and operate, will make more phase but will phase in more slowly.

Rod Schebesch, who leads Stantec's SAV research program, calls SAVs the "ultimate mobile device for urban connectivity." The rise of universal car ownership drained vitality from cities. The rise of SAVs will unlock opportunities for urban places to grow simultaneously denser, more livable, and greener.

Moving Forward

The stage is set for suburbia to write its next chapter—suburbs whose proudest feature is not a new mall but a new downtown. No specific formula exists for creating these suburban downtowns, but they tend to share certain threshold characteristics.

Whether they grow from historic village centers (Dublin, Ohio) or emerge de novo in communities with no historic center (Tysons, Virginia), the **process** of creating these downtowns requires a confluence of three dynamics:

- **Civic leadership**—an official, property owner, or community leader—who steps forward to take responsibility for launching a downtown initiative and building the public support and partnerships to move it forward
- **Planning**—shaped around information, analysis, vision, and implementation that translate diverse perspectives, values, market realities, and other factors into an achievable strategy for moving forward

- **In-depth, community-wide engagement**—a community-wide conversation built on education, communication, and trade-offs

For this process to succeed, a new urban place requires a **foundation** marked by the following:

- **Market-driven demand**—backed by fiscal opportunities that support public/private partnerships
- **The right site**—one or more contiguous parcels with owners who want to partner
- **A compact, critical mass**—often 3 to 5 million square feet or more, developed on largely contiguous sites of at least 50 acres
- **A commitment to equity**—housing, retail, public space, and mobility choices that invite diversity and make the promise of inclusivity real
- **Flexibility to adapt to rapid technological change**—particularly a transition to automated mobility

To achieve their promise, these urban places not only meet high environmental and design standards, they also embody core principles often ascribed to downtown and Main Street and that together bring them to life as the civic, economic, and social heart of community life:

- **Above all, they're walkable**—distinguished by lively sidewalks, animated by a wide variety of shops, food, entertainment, and other amenities that invite people to walk.
- **They connect to their community on every level**—by bike, on foot, by bus (and sometimes to the larger region by transit), and, of course, by car—these are suburbs, after all.
- **They enjoy a multilayered public realm**—from "active" squares to places of quiet reflection and often including a "town green" and other civic spaces.
- **They offer a diverse mix of choices**—for living, working, shopping, and playing, geared to residents' increasingly diverse lifestyles.
- **They are authentic**—rarely as defined by a long history (these are essentially new places) but more often by unique traditions, arts, innovation, culture, diversity, landscapes, or other qualities that define a community and its setting today.

Map of the Book

Unlike Caesar's Gaul—another tale of transformation—this book is divided into four parts. Together they tell the story of suburban reinvention—a society that has crossed a demographic, economic, and social Rubicon and is well on its way to adding a far richer, more urban sensibility to what it means to be suburbia.

Part I sets the stage. Christopher Leinberger provides a broad overview of the origin and essential importance of walkable urban places for suburbs. David Dixon then takes the reader through a rapid history of suburbia, from before the Civil War through the Great Recession, and tells the story of how dramatic demographic, economic, and social changes are setting the stage today for a generation of walkable urban places in suburbia.

Part II tells the story from the perspective of markets. Real estate economists Laurie Volk, Todd Zimmerman, and Christopher Volk-Zimmerman; Sarah Woodworth; and Michael J. Berne explain why market forces have reversed course to favor urban environments and how this dynamic is playing out across housing, office and research, and retail markets.

Part III tells the story from the perspective of civic leaders, planning and design consultants, and local officials. Stewart Schwartz, Sterling Wheeler and Linda E. Hollis, Chris Snyder, Tianyao Sun, Harold Madi and Simon O'Byrne, Terry Foegler, Christopher Zimmerman, and Mark Hinshaw describe how these actors are making new walkable urban places happen in diverse suburbs across North America (and in one case, China).

In Part IV David Dixon draws out the strategies and principles that represent the core building blocks for these and other successful walkable urban places. Jason Beske concludes the story, describing how to build on all these perspectives to design walkable urban places that people love.

Notes

1. A community member commenting on planning for redevelopment of the 419 corridor in suburban Roanoke County, Virginia, into a walkable "town center," March 23, 2017.

2. Matthew Schiffman, "SURVEY: The American Dream is 'no longer in reach,'" Business Insider, April 20, 2016, accessed February 22, 2017, http://www.businessinsider.com /american-dream-is-no-longer-in-reach-2016-4.

3. National Association of Realtors, news release, July 28, 2015, accessed February 22, 2017, http://nacto.org/wp-content/uploads/2016/02/1_Natl-Assoc-of-Realtors-2015-Com munity-Preference-Survey.pdf.

4. US Census projections.

5. Richard Florida, "The Incredible Rise of Urban Real Estate," CityLab, February 25, 2016, accessed August 6, 2017, https://www.citylab.com/equity/2016/02/rise-of-urban -real-estate/470748/.

6. CBRE Global Investors, "U.S. Urbanization Trends: Investment Implications for Commercial Real Estate," January 2015, accessed February 22, 2017, http://www.cbreglobal investors.com/research/publications/Documents/Special%20Reports/US%20Urbani zation%20Trends_JAN%202015.pdf.

7. Conversation with Laurie Volk, Zimmerman Volk Associates, January 10, 2018.

8. Elizabeth Kneebone, "Suburban Poverty Is Missing from the Conversation about America's Future," Brookings Institution, September 15, 2016, accessed February 21, 2017, https: //www.brookings.edu/articles/suburban-poverty-is-missing-from-the-conversation -about-americas-future/.

PART I SETTING THE STAGE

Part I sets the stage with an overview on the origin and essential importance of walkable urban places followed by a rapid history of suburbia from before the Civil War to the Great Recession. It describes how the demographic, social, and economic forces collectively termed the "Great Reset" will create a far more urban future for suburbia.

1

Urbanizing the Suburbs
The Major Development Trend
of the Next Generation

Christopher B. Leinberger

The Built Environment

The dawning of the twenty-first century in the United States has seen a structural shift in how the country creates its built environment (defined as infrastructure and real estate). The suburbs have played the major role for a century, but that role is fundamentally changing. Understanding the implications of this structural shift requires the introduction of a few basic concepts.

First, it is important to understand that the built environment takes two basic forms: walkable urban and drivable sub-urban. There are many variations, but broadly speaking there are just these two.

Walkable Urban Development

Walkable urban development is the oldest form employed in building cities and metropolitan areas. This type of development has been the basis for how we have built our cities since Çatalhöyük (in present-day Turkey) was built around 9,500 years ago—the oldest city known to date. Walking is the primary means of getting to and getting around a walkable urban place. The distance that most people feel comfortable walking is about 1,500 to 3,000 feet, which limits the geographic size of a walkable urban place. Research conducted at George Washington University has shown that the average walkable urban place in metropolitan Washington, DC, is 408 acres, about the size of three regional malls, including their parking lots.

Beyond that distance, most people will use another means of transport if it is available. Historically that has meant a horse, a horse-drawn wagon, a bike, public transit (rail or bus), or a car. Within that defined and confined walkable urban place, walking provides access to many if not all everyday needs—shopping, social life, education, civic life, and maybe even work. This mixed-use character means the walkable urban place has a relatively high density; measured by gross floor area ratios (FARs, measuring all land within the area being evaluated, including right of way), between 1.0 and 30. The lowest walkable urban density, such as a small town, could be 1.0, whereas high walkable urban density, like Midtown Manhattan, is about 30 FAR. However, most walkable urban places developed today, particularly those in the suburbs, range between 2.0 and 4.0 FAR, assuming they are employment, destination retail, or civic places (defined later as regionally significant places).

Drivable Sub-urban Development

The second form of built environment is drivable sub-urban development (the hyphen is used to indicate that it is a fundamentally different from and less dense than walkable urban). Drivable sub-urban development segregates the various needs of everyday life one from the other—retail is in a shopping center, work is in a business park, housing is in a subdivision—and the only way to connect these is by car. Walking is generally not a safe or viable option, nor is generally any other form of transportation, such as public transport or biking. The early twentieth-century introduction of cars as a means of transportation was the obvious prerequisite for the drivable sub-urban form of development, enabling a never-before-known alternative form of building and living.

Drivable sub-urban has extremely low-density development compared to walkable urbanism, generally less than 20% of the density as measured by FAR. FAR tends to range between 0.005 and 0.40. Its various land uses—for-sale housing, rental housing, office, industrial, retail, civic, educational, medical, hotel, and more—spread out across vast swaths of land. In other words, sprawl. Most real estate developers and investors, government regulators, and financiers have come to understand this model extremely well, turning it into a successful development formula and economic driver for the mid- and late twentieth century. Drivable sub-urban development provided a foundation for the economy and "fueled" the dominant industry of the industrial era—the building of automobiles and trucks, including the support industries of road building, finance, insurance, and oil. Drivable sub-urban development was essential to American economic growth in the mid- to late twentieth century.

Economic Functions of the Built Environment

Metropolitan land use supports either regionally significant or local-serving functions.

Regionally Significant Locations

Regionally significant locations, sometimes referred to as submarkets by commercial brokers, are used for the following purposes:

- Concentrations of jobs
- Civic centers
- Institutions of higher education
- Major medical centers
- Regional retail
- One-of-a-kind cultural, entertainment, and sports facilities

Regionally significant land constitutes less than 5% of all metropolitan landmass, according to George Washington University School of Business (GWSB) research, yet it is where the region's wealth is created, where many one-of-a-kind facilities prefer to locate, and where regionally significant retail outlets locate (e.g., malls, concentrations of specialty stores, big box stores, flea markets, and major farmer's markets). GWSB research in metropolitan Boston has shown that regionally significant walkable urban places account for 1.2% of the metro landmass and regionally significant drivable sub-urban locations represent 2.5% of the metro landmass.

Regionally significant places are generally net fiscal contributors for local jurisdictions; that is, the tax revenues they produce (income, sales, property, and other taxes) exceed the costs of the government services they receive (transportation, police, fire, regulatory, legal, etc.). This land use function is generally the reason a metropolitan economy—and therefore the metropolitan area—exists.

Local-Serving Locations

Local-serving locations are bedroom communities dominated by residential development and complemented by local-serving commercial uses (e.g., grocery stores) and civic uses (e.g., primary and secondary schools, police and fire stations, etc.). The vast majority of the local-serving land is residential, either for-sale or rental properties, whereas the minority of the land supports commercial development, generally for retail (e.g., grocery stores).

Local-serving drivable sub-urban land use accounts for the vast majority (~ 92%) of the total metropolitan landmass. Local-serving locations are generally net financial losers for local jurisdictions; that is, they produce less in tax revenues (income, sales, property, and other taxes) than they cost in terms of public services (transportation, police, fire, regulatory, and legal services, but especially education). In other words, most local-serving jurisdictions have to be subsidized by regionally significant land uses within the jurisdiction or they would have to raise their taxes substantially to pay for these services.

Generally speaking, regionally significant locations are where the metropolitan area earns its living, and local-serving places are where most residents spend their nonwork lives and the income and surplus generated by regionally significant locations.

Form Meets Function

The two forms and two functions of metropolitan land use produce a simple four-cell matrix, shown in Figure 1.1. This matrix outlines the land use options available for any metropolitan land and includes an estimate of the metropolitan land used for each form/function combination. The upper-left cell, regionally significant walkable urban places, are called WalkUPs. They are the focus of the urbanization of the suburbs, as will be shown here.

The "Foot Traffic Ahead" research from the Center for Real Estate and Urban Analysis at GWSB surveys the walkable urbanism of three real estate products (office, retail, and rental apartments) of the 30 largest metropolitan areas in the United States. It demonstrates that there are eight types of regionally significant WalkUPs[12]:

1. Downtown—the traditional center of the metro's central city
2. Downtown adjacent—surrounding the downtown, such as Dupont Circle in Washington, DC, Capitol Hill in Seattle, and Uptown in Dallas
3. Urban commercial—local-serving commercial districts that went into decline in the late twentieth century but have experienced a recent revival as regionally significant WalkUPs, such as Columbia Heights in Washington, DC, Lincoln Park in Chicago, and West Hollywood in Los Angeles
4. Urban university—institutions of higher learning that have embraced their community, such as UCLA in Los Angeles, Penn and Drexel in West Philadelphia, and Columbia in New York
5. Innovation district—described by the Brookings Institution as "geographic areas where leading-edge anchor institutions and companies cluster and connect with start-ups, business incubators, and accelerators," such as Kendall Square Innovation District in Cambridge, Massachusetts (sponsored by MIT and the developer Forest City), University City Science Center in West Philadelphia (sponsored by the colleges and universities in the region, led by the University of Pennsylvania and Drexel), and Cortex in St. Louis (sponsored by Washington University and various health care and civic institutions)
6. Suburban town center—eighteenth- and nineteenth-century towns that the metro area grew to include and that have also enjoyed a recent revival, such as Evanston in metro Chicago, Bellevue in metro Seattle, and Pasadena in metro Los Angeles

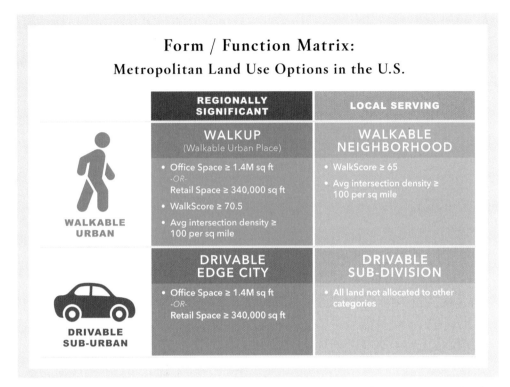

Figure 1.1. Types of WalkUPs: Central City versus Suburb. (Center for Real Estate and Urban Analysis at the George Washington University School of Business)

7. Redeveloped drivable sub-urban—strip and regional malls that have urbanized, such as Belmar in metro Denver, Tysons in metro Washington, DC, and Perimeter in metro Atlanta

8. Greenfield/brownfield development—complete walkable urban developments built from scratch, such as Reston Town Center in metro Washington, DC, Atlantic Station in metro Atlanta, and Easton Town Center in metro Columbus

The first five WalkUP types tend to locate in the central city. The last three types tend to be in the suburbs.

The same research shows that the most walkable urban metropolitan areas, particularly metro Washington, DC, (ranked no. 2 most walkable urban) and Boston (no. 3), earned their high rankings because they contained 49% and 41%, respectively, of total rental office and multifamily walkable urban inventory in their suburbs (see Figure 1.2). These are places like Clarendon and Bethesda in metro Washington, DC, and Harvard Square and Assembly Row in metro Boston. The Washington, DC, and Boston metros are models of development for the future. Boston is an older metro area with a legacy rail system that has redeveloped formerly depressed walkable urban places to accept the majority of new

WALKABLE URBANISM OF THE
30 LARGEST U.S. METROPOLITANS:

Current Ranking

RANK	METRO AREA	# OF WALKUPS	POPULATION			OFFICE, RETAIL & MULTI-FAMILY RENTAL OCCUPIED SPACE			
			Total in Metro Area	Per WalkUP	Rank Pop per WalkUP	% Office Located in WalkUPs	% Retail Located in WalkUPs	% Multi-Family Located in WalkUPs	% Total Located in WalkUPs
1	New York City	67	20,942,101	312,569	21	55%	13%	39%	38%
2	Washington, DC	44	5,037,427	114,487	2	53%	20%	23%	33%
3	Boston	54	5,035,729	93,254	1	45%	17%	31%	32%
4	Chicago	38	8,509,657	223,938	13	43%	15%	33%	30%
5	San Francisco Bay	56	7,360,487	131,437	4	37%	21%	19%	25%
6	Seattle	25	3,810,651	152,426	6	42%	12%	17%	22%
7	Portland	16	2,017,438	126,090	3	39%	15%	12%	19%
8	Pittsburgh	11	2,575,124	234,102	15	35%	6%	15%	18%
9	Denver	18	2,962,508	164,584	7	29%	8%	15%	17%
10	Philadelphia	17	5,302,186	311,893	20	25%	10%	14%	17%
11	Atlanta	27	5,020,710	185,952	10	33%	9%	11%	16%
12	Charlotte	8	1,340,886	167,611	8	26%	8%	12%	15%
13	Minneapolis-St. Paul	11	2,920,637	265,512	17	30%	6%	10%	15%
14	Cleveland	10	2,064,517	206,452	11	36%	5%	7%	14%
15	St. Louis	10	2,580,896	258,090	16	26%	4%	9%	12%
16	Kansas City	9	1,928,582	214,287	12	25%	6%	6%	12%
17	Los Angeles	53	18,413,866	347,431	22	23%	7%	8%	11%
18	Cincinnati	7	2,007,335	286,762	18	27%	6%	5%	11%
19	Baltimore	15	2,704,957	180,330	9	18%	9%	8%	11%
20	Houston	16	6,175,417	385,964	24	29%	6%	4%	11%
21	Detroit	32	4,706,797	147,087	5	22%	6%	7%	10%
22	Miami	20	5,771,020	288,551	19	18%	8%	8%	10%
23	Sacramento	6	2,328,199	388,033	25	22%	5%	4%	9%
24	San Diego	14	3,183,143	227,367	14	13%	7%	6%	7%
25	Dallas	18	6,694,445	371,914	23	10%	9%	5%	7%
26	Las Vegas	2	2,014,260	1,007,130	29	7%	8%	3%	5%
27	Tampa	6	3,326,846	554,474	26	11%	2%	2%	4%
28	San Antonio	2	1,863,530	931,765	28	10%	3%	1%	3%
29	Phoenix	4	4,204,089	1,051,022	30	11%	1%	1%	3%
30	Orlando	3	1,921,825	640,608	27	11%	1%	2%	3%

Metropolitan areas are ranked according to their current levels of walkable urbanism.

The walkable urbanism of each metro is determined to be the share of office, retail, and multi-family rental occupied space located in its WalkUPs in 2015.

Rankings are divided into four levels of walkable urbanism, which are described on the following pages.

KEY:
Levels of Current Walkable Urbanism

■ LEVEL 1:
HIGHEST WALKABLE URBANISM

■ LEVEL 2:
UPPER-MIDDLE WALKABLE URBANISM

■ LEVEL 3:
LOWER-MIDDLE WALKABLE URBANISM

■ LEVEL 4:
LOWEST WALKABLE URBANISM

Figure 1.2. Walkable urbanism levels for the 30 largest US metro areas, 2016.

development in recent years. Metro Washington, DC, behaved like a Sunbelt boom town in the late twentieth century, akin to Atlanta, Dallas, or Phoenix, but more recently it has begun building the majority of its development in walkable urban places immediately adjacent to stations on the 1970s Metrorail system. The Metro system has grown to meet demand over the last few decades (see Figure 1.3).

Arlington, Virginia, as the National Urbanizing Suburb

The most important suburban jurisdiction in the region, and in fact in the country, is Arlington County, just across the Potomac River from Washington, DC. Part of the original District, it was "de-annexed" in 1846 back to Virginia and eventually became Arlington County. At 26 square miles it is the second smallest county in the country.[3] The county has seven WalkUPs, representing 11% of its landmass. A generation ago, most of these places were declining as drivable sub-urban strip commercial, including the first regional mall in metro Washington, DC, known as Parkington (lots of parking), and car

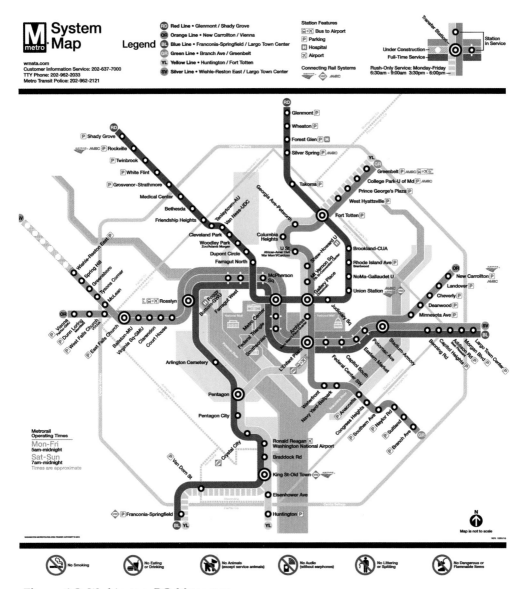

Figure 1.3. Washington, DC, Metro map.

dealerships were gradually moving to freeway locations farther out. This land was generating roughly 20% of county tax revenue, and falling, in the 1980s.

Fast-forward to 2016. Redevelopment of these dying strip commercial and car lots has seen a near quadrupling of square footage. Parkington Mall became Ballston Commons in the 1980s, an urban regional mall that is about to be redeveloped yet again as a mixed-use, open-air element of the complex fabric of the Ballston WalkUP. The seven walkable urban places in Arlington County now generate more than 50% of county tax

Figure 1.4a, b. The 1985 photo (a) shows the closed Sears store in Clarendon, Arlington County, to the left, with the closed garden center on the right; the shot was taken from the closed tire and car-repair center. The 2017 photo (b) shows the same location, with high-end retail beneath upper-floor condominiums that sell for $600 per square foot. (Chris Zimmerman)

revenues and rising. Counterintuitively, absolute car counts on the major boulevards have fallen (10–25%) since the 1980s in spite of the remarkable growth in square footage and vitality. The building of a major Metrorail line in the 1980s and its placement underground, beneath Wilson and Clarendon Boulevards, is a major reason for the success of Arlington, coupled with the enlightened leadership of the county and zoning (see Figure 1.4a, b).

Urbanizing-Suburb Walkable Urban Rankings

A ranking of the 30 largest US metro areas by level of suburban urbanism appears in Figure 1.2. Metro Washington, DC, and Boston both sit near the top and have some of the highest rates of suburban urbanization. Other metros that rank highly for their urban areas in Figure 1.5 do not fare so well when the scope expands to include their suburbs.

METRO AREA	WALKUP SPACE IN SUBURBS		METRO AREA	WALKUP SPACE IN SUBURBS	
	RANK	% SHARE Q1 2010		RANK	% SHARE Q1 2010
Las Vegas	1	53%	Portland	16	13%
Washington, DC	2	49%	San Diego	17	12%
Houston	3	48%	Denver	18	11%
Miami	4	46%	San Francisco Bay	19	11%
Boston	5	41%	Dallas	20	10%
Phoenix	6	40%	Orlando	21	9%
Los Angeles	7	38%	Cleveland	22	7%
Atlanta	8	32%	Chicago	23	7%
Detroit	9	29%	New York City	24	6%
St. Louis	10	26%	Tampa	25	6%
Baltimore	11	22%	Sacramento	26	3%
Kansas City	12	18%	Pittsburgh	27	1%
Seattle	13	17%	Minneapolis-St. Paul	28	1%
Charlotte	14	17%	Cincinnati	29	0%
Philadelphia	15	16%	San Antonio	30	0%

Figure 1.5. Urbanizing suburbs in the 30 largest US metros, 2016. Green-highlighted metros are the top metros, which measure urban-center walkability. Las Vegas's position here is a statistical fluke, since the metro area ranks very low on walkable urbanism (no. 26 in the current rankings) and has only two WalkUPs, one of which, The Strip, sits just outside the city boundaries for political reasons.

In terms of urbanization of their suburbs, these metro areas face different realities. The first category includes walkable urban metros where the bulk of walkable urbanism is located in the central city, highly ranked metros like New York, and Chicago, but also more modestly ranked Philadelphia, Pittsburgh, Minneapolis–St. Paul, Denver, and, surprisingly, Portland, Oregon. Most of these metro areas have legacy rail transit or are building new rail systems, yet most of their urbanism still focuses on the central city. This means that the next great opportunity for economic and real estate development in these metros will lie in urbanizing the suburbs, many times taking advantage of the existing or new rail transit infrastructure. These metros could be on the path toward building substantially more walkable urban places in suburban locations. However, all of them suffer from extreme attitudes of "not in my back yard" (NIMBYism) or self-satisfaction (Portland, Minneapolis, Denver), basking in an image of walkable urban character that doesn't fully match reality.

One of the best examples of a drivable sub-urban suburb transforming into a walkable urban place is Belmar in Lakewood, a first-ring suburb of Denver. The first regional mall in the metro area, Villa Italia, occupied the Belmar site beginning in the early 1960s and provided the tax base for the jurisdiction and a shopping destination for two generations of Denverites. By the late 1990s, the mall was nearly empty and the town's tax base had shrunken dramatically. Continuum Partners, in a joint venture with the town, bulldozed the bulk of the mall and built a grid of walkable streets, focused on urban entertainment (restaurants, a 14-screen movie theater, specialty shopping), high-density housing, and some offices in the first phases. It became a stunning success for the city and the developer as a new WalkUP emerged from the dust of the bulldozed mall (see Figure 1.6). Many more examples are planned in suburban Denver.

The second group comprises three metropolitan areas that have been infamous for sprawl over the past 60 years but are making an impressive structural change from drivable sub-urban to walkable urban development patterns. Although Miami, Atlanta, and Los Angeles ranked as moderate or low on the current rankings, their futures look much different. In the real estate cycle that began in 2010, most rental office and multifamily absorption has taken place in the suburbs in these three metro areas: 46% in Miami, 32% in Atlanta, and 38% in Los Angeles. Suburban WalkUPs like Ft. Lauderdale and Coral Gables in Miami; Roswell and Decatur in Atlanta; and Pasadena and Long Beach in metro Los Angeles have propelled the emergence of walkable urbanism in these sprawling metros. Most of these places, particularly in Miami and Los Angeles, were where the metro area was founded, based on late nineteenth- and early twentieth-century rail systems. This is certainly a Back to the Future outcome for these once-declining sub-urban town centers that are now seeing a real estate boom and the rise of vital, mixed-use suburban places.

Figure 1.6. Belmar has become a success as a walkable urban place in suburban Denver.

The third category comprises metro areas whose development remains predominantly drivable sub-urban in character, generally the bottom half of metros in the largest-30 current ranking of the "Foot Traffic Ahead" analysis. In these metros, the few WalkUPs and walkable urban developments that exist tend to be concentrated in the central city, whereas the suburbs are classically drivable sub-urban in character. These metros tend to be in the Midwest (Kansas City, Columbus, and Cincinnati) or the Sunbelt (Houston, Dallas, Tampa, and Las Vegas). They continue to follow the car-driven economic development model of the late twentieth century. There are some instances of suburban WalkUPs in this third category, like Easton Town Center in Columbus, The Woodlands in Houston, and Plano Town Center in Dallas, but they tend to be few and far between.

Why Does the Market Want to Urbanize the Suburbs?

The pent-up demand for walkable urbanism has been primarily satisfied in gentrifying places in our central cities. The turnaround of many downtowns, the emergence of downtown-adjacent places, urban universities rising in academic rankings partially due to their embrace of formerly poor and dangerous neighborhoods, the emergence of innovation districts,[4] and the transformation of burned-out 1960s commercial urban corridors into regionally significant destinations have contributed to the spread of WalkUPs in center cities over the past 15–20 years.

However, not all market demand can be satisfied in city centers. A market exists for walkable urban places that are not as gritty as most center cities. Not everyone wants to walk past homeless people on the street, share heavily used sidewalks, look up at tall buildings, and experience other aspects of center city walkable urbanism. Suburban walkable urbanism tends to be less gritty and can be nearly Disneyesque in its cleanliness and newness. WalkUPs like Reston Town Center in Virginia, Avalon north of Atlanta, and Sugarland in metro Houston all represent examples of "just-add-water instant urbanity" that has significant appeal to certain market segments.

Another major factor in suburban urbanization, especially in inner suburbs, is the quality of schools. Although many center city school districts are slowly turning themselves around, many young couples are not willing to wait or work hard to effect change in their city schools, and they bolt to suburban systems as soon as they have children. However, many of these same couples choose walkable urban suburbs with outstanding schools in order to have the best of two worlds: good schools and walkable urbanism. Suburban WalkUPs like Santa Monica and Palo Alto in California; Bellevue, Washington; Evanston, Illinois; Bethesda, Maryland; and, of course, Arlington, Virginia, offer both.

A lesson that can be learned from Arlington is that most new development in the past decade has been multifamily residential, both for rent and for sale. The typical reaction of a suburban jurisdiction to the idea of multifamily development is to ban it, especially rental housing: If all those units contain families with children, educating them would impose substantial new costs (how did the country's concern for our next generation evaporate?). However, Arlington has found that the school participation rate for residents of multifamily developments in their seven WalkUPs is one-thirteenth the rate found in neighborhoods of for-sale single-family homes. The new multifamily households are paying school taxes but barely sending any kids to the schools—a huge benefit to a school district.

There is another reason for the urbanization of the suburbs: it improves the quality of life of the single-family neighborhoods immediately adjacent to growing WalkUPs. This is also counterintuitive. Generally, these dense walkable urban places have faced vigorous NIMBY opposition, particularly from the immediate neighborhood. However, experience and research show this need not be the case. Great walkable urbanism, particularly with the thoughtful management of side effects, such as noise, overflow parking, and cut-through traffic, improves quality of life for the immediate neighborhoods by providing households with the best of two worlds: suburban living within walking distance of restaurants, shopping, transit, and maybe work. Preliminary research shows 40% to 100% increases in prices per square foot for nearby for-sale housing in comparison to similar housing in the same school district but not within walking distance of a WalkUP. As a result, suburban Washington, DC, and Long Island, New York, have begun to see NIMBYs turn into YIMBYs (yes in my back yard), advocating for increased density and walkable urban place development, assuming it is well managed.

Neither research nor our experience has delivered a final verdict, but it appears likely that at least 50% of the demand for walkable urbanism will be satisfied in the suburbs, as it is in metro Washington, DC, the leading urbanizing suburban metro. It may be even higher. Yet it is important to note that the demand for walkable urbanism, both in the center city and in suburbs, will be concentrated in less than 10% of the landmass. The rest of the drivable sub-urban locations in the suburbs will stay the same, just a little less well-off, as will be explored next.

Economic Benefits for Urbanizing Suburbs

Research has shown that the participants in the knowledge economy, both companies and their "creative class" workers, have moved to and are demanding walkable urban places today. Many downtown turnarounds have been led by knowledge-based companies, such as Twitter, Yelp, Dropbox, and Square, among many others, south of Market in San Francisco; Google, WeWork, and other high-tech firms in New York's Meatpacking District (also known as Silicon Alley); and Compuware and Quicken in downtown Detroit.

The same benefits are beginning to occur in the urbanizing suburbs, such as Cambridge and Somerville in metro Boston and Redmond in metro Seattle. Even the Research Triangle of Raleigh–Durham–Chapel Hill, North Carolina, is planning to urbanize what has been the quintessential drivable sub-urban business park.

Many studies have shown a causal link between increased education and increased economic performance of an individual, household, and metropolitan gross domestic product (GDP) area. In 2013 the Milken Institute released a study of GDP performance of 261 US metros that concluded the following: "The overall explanatory power of the relationship [between higher education and GDP per capita] is strong and robust. Over 70 percent of the variation in real GDP per capita across the 261 metros from 1990 to 2010 is explained [by higher educational attainment]."

Our GWU research also shows a significant correlation between the most walkable urban metros and both higher education (measured by the percentage of the population over 25 years of age with a college degree) and metropolitan GDP per capita. There is an r^2 of 0.55 between walkable urbanism and higher education. There is an r^2 of 0.49 between walkable urbanism and GDP per capita in the 30 largest metro areas.

The six highest-ranked walkable urban metropolitan areas in the current ranking chart in Figure 1.2 have an average GDP per capita of $72,110. The ten lowest-ranked metros have an average GDP per capita of $48,313. These most walkable urban metros have a 49% premium in GDP per capita. This is the same premium Germany has over economically poorly performing Russia, Latvia, and Croatia.

There is no indication in this research as to whether walkable urbanism causes highly educated people to move to or stay in a metro or whether more highly educated people cause a metro area to add more walkable urban places. Either way, educated people seem to prefer walkable urban places.

It will probably take another decade to prove or disprove a causal link between walkable urbanism and increased higher education of the workforce and GDP per capita. However, any county executive or mayor of a suburban city would want to pay attention to these correlations. Although not proven, it appears that building walkable urban places will improve a community's economic development and wealth.

Future of Suburbs That Don't Urbanize

As mentioned, the bulk of the suburbs in the United States will be left undisturbed. Their culs-de-sac and multilane arterials will remain for decades, serving the market for drivable sub-urban living, shopping, and working. However, the United States can expect to experience a "tale of three suburbs." The first suburb will be walkable urban and prosperous, as described earlier. The other two will likely be less prosperous, and one could actually suffer decline.

Drivable sub-urban locations in high-income and many moderate-income sections of metro areas will do fine, though they will probably experience weaker economic growth than urbanizing suburbs. Why? The overbuilding of drivable sub-urban business parks, regional and strip malls, and large-lot housing. The shift in demand toward walkable urban office and retail spaces has produced significant price premiums over business parks and regional and strip malls. In addition, the method of evaluating the capitalized worth of commercial assets, "cap rates," has shifted in recent years so that walkable urban office and retail enjoy a 50 to 60% price premium. Lower rents and lower capitalized values (which result in higher valuations) represent a double whammy for drivable sub-urban office and retail space, harming underlying valuation and occupancy. In addition, forecasts project an oversupply of large-lot, single-family homes. One estimate suggests that current existing supply eliminates the need for *any* new large-lot, single-family house to be built until 2030.[5] There is just not enough demand for the huge supply of existing housing, even in upscale suburbs, such as McLean, Virginia; Westchester County, New York; Dunwoody, Georgia; and Scottsdale, Arizona. These communities will do just fine economically and socially, but they will not maintain their relative values. Moving to a house in these communities will offer a great value for the money, but that house will be difficult to sell and will probably not appreciate very much.

A second group of suburbs faces a troubled future: the moderate- to low-income suburbs on the "wrong side" of the metropolitan area face the danger of becoming "The Next Slum," the title of an *Atlantic* article I wrote in 2008.[6] The overbuilding of large-lot, single-family homes will particularly affect these communities, as was first demonstrated by the 2007–2008 housing crash, which hit these communities far harder than other locations in their metropolitan areas. These communities have a monoculture of tax revenues, almost all of which come from residential property taxes. With prices low and weak, these revenues are flat and may be dropping in real dollar terms. Meanwhile, as the Brookings Institution has shown, the growth of poverty is now more of a suburban phenomenon than a center city fact, as it was in the mid- to late twentieth century.[7] As Elizabeth Kneebone of Brookings has said: "The 2000s saw suburbs become home to the largest and fastest-growing poor population in the nation. Today the number of poor residents in suburbs outstrips the number in big cities by 3.4 million."[8] Increasing poverty and the requirement of more social-service spending, while quality of life declines and tax revenues remain flat or fall, serves as a useful definition of an emerging suburban slum.

This future is already emerging in the southeast of metro Washington, DC; in suburban Prince George's County; south of Chicago; and infamously in the northern St. Louis suburb of Ferguson. This depressing model has been common in Europe for decades as well; the slums of Paris lie in its northern suburbs; the slums of London are to the east of the city limits.

The only historic parallel from which we can learn about probable slums emerging in selected suburbs is the experience of American cities abandoned to the poor from the 1950s through the 1980s. White flight led to housing-price depreciation and a growing need for social services. Like it did then, it is playing out on the ground as market prices for houses fall below replacement cost, but now in drivable sub-urban areas. This means that, although an owner may get a great value buying a property, there is no financial incentive for the owner to keep that property up. Any investment in the property will not be recouped upon resale. Slowly—or quickly, should social unrest occur as it did in American cities in the 1960s and in suburban Ferguson, Missouri, in 2015—property values decline, lowering taxes; crime and poverty increase; and schools deteriorate. Unlike central cities in the 1960s, which had more diverse tax bases and effective lobbyists in their mayors for state and federal assistance, suburbs rely largely on one form of revenue (property taxes) and rarely get the spotlight, except when there is a riot. This "out of sight, out of mind" perception of faltering suburbs is almost invisible and is not getting much attention at the moment. This will make addressing their challenges even more difficult.

Future Impacts of the Urbanization of Suburbs

The urbanization of the suburbs will affect less than 10% of landmass in the United States yet represent the bulk if not the vast majority of new real estate development over the next generation. The highest-ranked walkable urban metros, New York, Washington, DC, and Boston, already have between 93 and 115% of their office and multifamily development being built in walkable urban places, taking up a few percentage points of their metro landmass.[9] Although much of this chapter has focused on regionally significant walkable urban development, substantial local-serving walkable urban development will also occur, especially immediately adjacent to the regional walkable urban places.

We have discussed the economic and fiscal benefits of making suburbs more walk-able and more urban. Yet benefits that have not been explored here (social equity if managed, public health benefits of unintended exercise, reduced infrastructure costs due to concentrated development, and possibly the most effective method of reducing green-house gas emissions to address climate change) will make urbanizing suburbs well worth the effort as well.

This trend will place an economic foundation under metropolitan economies, similar to the way the building of drivable sub-urban locations did in the late twentieth century. It is crucial to provide the vision, leadership, regulatory changes, infrastructure investment, and place management to make the coming walkable urban future happen in a suburb near you.

Notes

1. Christopher B. Leinberger and Michael Rodriguez, "Foot Traffic Ahead: Ranking Walkable Urbanism in America's Largest Metros 2016," accessed June 21, 2016, http://business.gwu.edu/wp-content/uploads/2016/06/CREUA_Foot-Traffic-Ahead_2016.06.14.pdf.

2. Center for Real Estate and Urban Analysis (CREUA), accessed June 21, 2017, http://business.gwu.edu/about-us/research/center-for-real-estate-urban-analysis/research/walkable-urban-places-research/.

3. The smallest county in the country is New York County, otherwise known as the Borough of Manhattan, which covers 23 square miles. Arlington is about 15% larger than Manhattan.

4. Bruce Katz and Rebecca Rosen, *The Rise of Innovation Districts: A New Geography of Innovation in America* (Washington, DC: Brookings Institution, May 2014).

5. Arthur C. Nelson, *Reshaping Metropolitan America: Trends and Opportunities to 2030* (Washington, DC: Island Press, 2013).

6. Christopher B. Leinberger, "The Next Slum," *The Atlantic*, March 2008, accessed June 22, 2016, www.theatlantic.com/magazine/archive/2008/03/the-next-slum/306653/.

7. Elizabeth Kneebone, "The Growth and Spread of Concentrated Poverty, 2000 to 2008–2012," Washington, DC: Brookings Institution, July 31, 2014, accessed June 21, 2016, www.brookings.edu/research/interactives/2014/concentrated-poverty#/M10420.

8.   Rebecca J. Rosen et al., "Will Inequality Ever Stop Growing?" *The Atlantic*, December 29, 2015, accessed June 21, 2016, www.theatlantic.com/business/archive/2015/12/hope-despair-inequality/421806/.

9.   Christopher B. Leinberger and Michael Rodriguez, "Foot Traffic Ahead: Ranking Walkable Urbanism in America's Largest Metros 2016," accessed June 21, 2016, http://business.gwu.edu/wp-content/uploads/2016/06/CREUA_Foot-Traffic-Ahead_2016.06.14.pdf.

"SANS-SOUCI."

Figure 2.1. "Sans Souci" in New Rochelle, New York, symbolized the idyllic vision of suburbs in the early twentieth century. (Image from *Modern New Rochelle and the National City Bank,* 1909)

2

From the Rise of Suburbs to the Great Reset

David Dixon

The story of American suburban development starts logically enough: America's earliest suburbs, spawned in the 1850s, made it possible for the wealthy to work by day in crowded, noisy commercial centers like Philadelphia, New York, and Boston, yet board a train to escape to new, semirural suburbs like Radnor, New Rochelle (see Figure 2.1), or Brookline. Equally important, these "garden suburbs" promised a return to the sense of community in the idealized small towns and English villages to which many affluent Americans aspired. Lively "downtowns" developed around suburban train stations and became the focus of small-town community life from Wellesley (outside Boston) to Evanston (outside Chicago).

As cars entered mainstream American life in the 1910s and 1920s, car-focused suburban schemes began to appear—often inspired by utopian ideals, such as those of England's Garden City movement, and drawn up on the assumption that suburbs would remain discrete, identifiable communities. The accessibility that the automobile promised meant that suburban communities could develop with no commercial district. The Depression and World War II suspended most suburban development, but during the era of rapid suburban growth that followed the war, the concept of a free-form suburb took root and flourished. The idea of a suburban downtown largely disappeared for more than 50 years. In these decades suburbs took on many of the qualities we recognize today. Prompted by prosperity, universal auto ownership, and racial fears, a rapidly expanding middle class pursued a new "American Dream" of mass-produced single-family houses on quarter-acre lots that offered an escape from work and the city. Suburban subdivisions brought assembly-line efficiency and market concentration (and limitations) to the housing market; in

Figure 2.2. In 1950 *Time* magazine estimated that Levitt and Sons was responsible for more than 10% of all housing produced in the United States.

1950 *Time* magazine estimated that Levitt and Sons was responsible for more than 10% of all housing produced in the United States (see Figure 2.2).[1]

From the 1960s through the 1980s Main Street merchants and the major downtown office tenants and retailers followed America's middle class to the suburbs. In response, developers began to broaden the palette of post–World War II suburban development beyond subdivisions and strip retail development to include new development forms that reproduced the traditional roles of Main Street and downtown. Strip retail centers appeared first, drawing shoppers from Main Street with convenient parking and the allure of "modernity." However, the 1950 opening of Southgate Center in suburban Detroit, the first enclosed shopping center, heralded a new trend. The mall itself soon included a movie theater and an office building. Malls like Old Villa Italia mall in Lakewood, outside of Denver (see Figure 2.3a, b), further undermined downtowns by drawing the

Figure 2.3a, b. The Belmar redevelopment replaced the once-thriving Old Villa Italia mall in Lakewood, outside of Denver. Opened in 2004, Belmar has served as a model for many walkable and higher-density suburban centers. Envisioned as roughly one million square feet of retail and office space, it has also attracted more than one million square feet of housing. (Villa Italia photo courtesy of the Lakewood Heritage Center, City of Lakewood)

Figure 2.4. Rosslyn in northern Virginia emerged as an early "edge city" in the 1970s and 1980s—and for many a safer alternative to downtown Washington, DC, just across the Potomac. (Brian Gratwicke under CC BY 2.0)

department stores that had long anchored Main Street. Suburban office parks began to proliferate, luring higher-income white collar jobs out of city centers and shifting the real estate tax burden increasingly to lower-income urban residents.

Ultimately a more significant development "product"— what journalist Joel Garreau labeled edge cities—accelerated the movement of the US economy from city to suburb. These higher-density but completely auto-oriented suburban centers, often built by a single developer, introduced office towers that outcompeted downtown as the center of economic activity in places like St. Louis (Clayton), Atlanta (Buckhead—outside downtown but still within the city limits), Tampa (West Shore), Columbus (Dublin—see Chapter 11), and Washington, DC (Rosslyn, Tysons Corner—see Chapter 12)[2,3] (see Figure 2.4). This exodus of employers from downtown to suburb also reinforced "white flight" from central residential neighborhoods, a development worth noting not just for historical accuracy but to underscore the change in circumstances today, in which demonstrating social and racial diversity has become a prerequisite for attracting knowledge workers.

Figure 2.5. Easton Town Center outside of Columbus is a highly successful lifestyle center, with retail lining re-created Main Streets and a town square.

Beginning in the 1980s and 1990s developers embraced still newer suburban development products that consciously mimicked qualities of traditional Main Streets and downtowns. Redevelopment transformed older malls into "lifestyle centers" that in effect turned malls inside out to face pseudo–Main Streets, often enclosing vast surface parking lots, and added cinemas and similar leisure attractions. Frequently cited examples include Mizner Park (Boca Raton, Florida), which replaced a dying mall, and Easton Town Center (suburban Columbus, Ohio), which today boasts roughly 2 million square feet of largely retail development (see Figure 2.5). At a still more ambitious level, major developers began to build de novo suburban downtowns—for example, Reston Town Center, outside of Washington, DC, and Belmar, outside of Denver.

Regional malls, edge cities, lifestyle centers, and de novo downtowns each broadened the forms of suburban development. They represented latter-day models of the suburban ethos that had predominated since World War II—new forms of commercial development shaped around economic and demographic homogeneity. They also represented

Figure 2.6. In 2015, New Rochelle, now a mature suburb of New York City, approved plans to redevelop the heart of its downtown as a high-density, contemporary urban center. (Courtesy of RXR Realty, master developer of downtown New Rochelle)

bold responses to changing office and retail markets, demonstrated ways to adapt to dramatic market changes, and recognized a yearning for a sense of intimate community that had inspired the first generation of American suburbs.

In fact the suburban boom that followed World War II drew not on nostalgia for community-rich small towns, but on a very different set of aspirations. The American Dream celebrated the individual, not community. Responding to the newfound freedom that near-universal auto ownership offered, it celebrated entry into the middle class and escape from the stresses of working-class urban life—no longer noise and smell so much as race and class. In the process, it replaced the traditional place-based (walkable) community that characterized urban Main Streets—the lifeblood for the "third places" (sociologist Ray Oldenburg's term for cafés, sidewalks, public parks[4]) that offer spontaneous opportunities for diverse interactions—with auto-oriented accesibility that ultimately proved to be isolating interaction with neighbors and unplanned activities. Ads for new subdivisions in the 1950s featured images of fathers happily mowing lawns, mothers showing off shiny new kitchens, and kids proudly standing with their parents in front of a two-car garage. These ads used language like "so up to date, so smart" and "live better in a home of your own"—and, of course, boasted about low prices made possible by mass-production efficiencies. They contained virtually no references to nostalgia for a sense of community found in earlier garden suburbs or small towns.

While some suburban communities are reinventing older downtowns as twenty-first-century mixed-use centers (e.g., the former garden suburb of New Rochelle; see Figure 2.6), most, predominantly single-use, auto-dependent suburbs, are ill prepared for a perfect storm of changing demographics, the rise of the knowledge economy, and rapidly shifting values.

The Great Reset: Demographics Are Destiny

The Great Reset, economist Richard Florida's term for the Great Recession of 2007–09, highlighted the impact of longer-term, structural changes laid bare by the recession that have come to dominate current thinking about urban and suburban growth and change.

The recession exposed a growing mismatch between North America's changing demographics, growing knowledge economy, shifting personal values, and spread of poverty from cities to suburbs on one side and the sprawl model that had defined suburban growth since World War II on the other. These trends emerged in the early 1990s, matured in the 2000s, and have since become the predominant forces shaping North American communities. Today suburbs have too much auto-dependent, single-family housing, for which

Figure 2.7. Fairfax County, which includes Lake Anne, one of five "villages" in Reston, is one of the most affluent counties in the United States and is widely admired for its schools and "family-friendly" services. (Jason Beske)

Figure 2.8. A food bank in Fairfax County, where poverty spiked 55% between 2008 and 2016, and the fastest-growing demographic group is people over 65. (Kona Gallagher under CC BY-SA 2.0)

demand is declining, and too little walkable, multifamily housing, for which demand is rising. Compounding this dynamic is the fact that North America's increasingly important knowledge economy is following its educated workforce to urban environments, whereas poverty is moving to suburbia.

An April 2016 *Washington Post* article captures the impact of these changes on one of America's most successful suburbs (see Figure 2.7): "For decades, Fairfax County has been a national model for suburban living [see Figure 2.7], a place of good governance and elite schools that educate children from some of the country's richest neighborhoods. But Virginia's largest municipality is fraying around the edges. A population that is growing older, poorer, and more diverse is sharpening the need for basic services in what is still the nation's second-wealthiest county, even as a sluggish local economy maintains a chokehold on the revenue stream."[5]

According to the *Post*, the number of people living in poverty in the county "spiked 55%" between 2008 and 2016.[6] Meanwhile, since 2000, more than one-third of the county's growth has consisted of people over 65 (see Figure 2.8) and 95% has consisted of people of color. Roughly two-thirds white in 2000, projections suggest Fairfax's population will have become roughly two-thirds nonwhite by 2030.

New Norm

There is a new norm for the general US population: society is growing younger and older—and raising fewer children. Year after year, decade after decade up to the early 2000s US population growth resembled a bell curve with a dramatic bulge of people between the ages of 35 and 65—prime years for living a life centered on kids, cars, and a house in the suburbs. But this pattern has reversed quickly and dramatically. Between 2010 and 2030, people younger than 35 and older than 65 will account for more than three-quarters of US population growth. During this period singles and couples will represent 75% or more of net new households (see Figure 2.9).

For suburbs, the baby boom of the mid-twentieth century has produced the senior boom of the early twenty-first century. Between 2010 and 2020 the number of people 65 and older living in suburbs will have increased by roughly 50%, making this group more than one-quarter of the total suburban population. Over the following 20 years, the fastest-growing suburban population segment will be people over 70.[7]

And while the share of US households with kids stood at 48% in1975, it had dropped to 37% by 2015 and is projected to fall to 25%, by 2025.[8] At the same time, the profile of family households has changed fundamentally; fewer than 10% were headed by a single parent in 1975, but that subset had grown to almost 50% by 2015 and is heading higher. Single-parent households are far more likely to prefer urban environments.[9] By 2025 two-parent households with children will represent only about 10% of all US households.

New Normal: A Society Growing Younger and Older

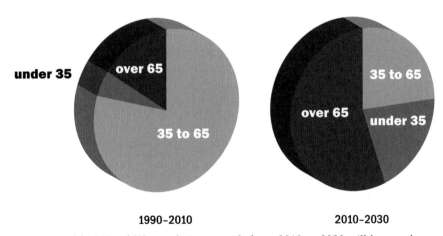

1990–2010   2010–2030

Figure 2.9. Roughly 75% of US population growth from 2010 to 2030 will be people younger than 35 and older than 65 and consist of singles and couples rather than families with kids. (Stantec graphic, based on data from Trulia.com)

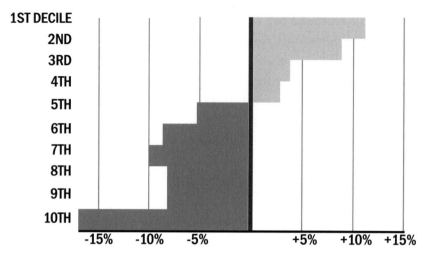

Figure 2.10. Urban cores are steadily becoming more affluent. Households with incomes in the bottom 60% are leaving because of rising housing costs, not a sudden desire to move somewhere else. (Stantec graphic, based on data for 2000–2014 from Trulia.com)

It's the Economy, Stupid

Writing for *Vox* in 2016, Matthew Yglesias noted that, on balance, people aged 25 to 49 (which includes millennials but also captures some of generation X) who have four or more years of higher education have been moving into "dense urban cores" since 2000, whereas those with less education had been moving out.[10] At the same time, looking across all ages, Yglesias noted that, "The top 20 percent of the population has become a lot more likely to live in a high-density urban neighborhood, and the next 20 percent is somewhat more likely. But the bottom 60 percent—and especially the bottom 10 percent—have become far less urbanized" (see Figure 2.10). These data do not suggest that lower-income households don't seek walkable lifestyles; instead they point to the rising costs of urban living.

Knowledge Jobs Follow Knowledge Workers

In addition to reshaping housing markets, younger, highly educated workers increasingly represent the key to growth in knowledge industries, which drive North American economic growth in most regions (see Figure 2.11). Demand for these workers outstrips supply at a time when growing numbers of aging knowledge workers are leaving the workforce. According to McKinsey & Company, in 2012 the United States already faced

Figure 2.11. Google's move into Bakery Square, in Pittsburgh's East End, reflects the importance tech companies place on following the knowledge workforce into reviving urban neighborhoods as well as booming downtowns. (Courtesy Walnut Capital)

a shortage of roughly 15 million knowledge workers[11] and the combination of an aging workforce and plateauing of students enrolled in higher education will exacerbate this shortage for two decades or more.

As a direct result, the real estate firm CBRE reported in 2016 that the top factor in selecting a new location for office users is "talent availability."[12] The knowledge economy that has taken over leadership in job creation and business investment is decamping to cities as employers calculate that the costs of high employee turnover outweigh higher rents and parking costs. According to McKinsey & Company knowledge workers (not just technology geeks but doctors, engineers, lawyers, managers, sales representatives) will account for most of the net US job growth over the last decade and today represent roughly 40% of all US jobs.[13]

Nor will telecommuting solve the problem. Companies point to the greater innovation and productivity that result from spontaneous, face-to-face communication.[14] Similarly, the more companies value innovation, the more they seek to cluster in higher-density,

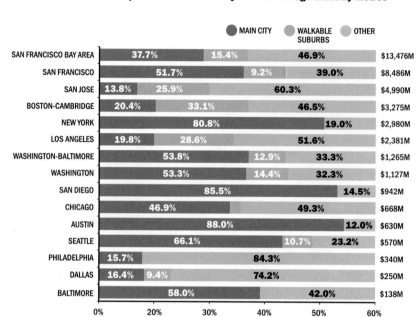

Figure 2.12. Venture capital is flowing to walkable urban places in suburbs in addition to urban cores. (Stantec graphic, based on 2015 data from CBRE Global Investors.com)

compact, walkable districts to promote interaction and shared discovery across industries. General Electric drew national attention in 2016 when it announced plans to move its headquarters from suburban Fairfield, Connecticut—an iconic midcentury suburb—to downtown Boston to be part of the innovation ecosystem there.

Small businesses and startups that generate a disproportionate share of better-paying new jobs and investment have led this trend. In June 2016, Richard Florida reported that "more than half of all startup neighborhoods are urban, with 57 percent of startup companies and 54 percent of venture-capital investments located in urban ZIP codes . . . [these] neighborhoods have considerably greater shares of commuters who walk, bike, or take transit to work."[15]

For several metros—notably San Francisco/Silicon Valley, Boston, Los Angeles, Dallas, Seattle, and Chicago—5% to as much as 33% of this investment is going to "walkable suburbs"[16] (see Figure 2.12). Suburban places ranging from the Research Triangle in Raleigh/Durham, North Carolina, to redeveloping Tysons Corner, Virginia (see Chapter 7), and communities such as Carmel, Indiana, and Dublin, Ohio (see Chapter 11), are creating walkable environments that compete for educated workers and venture capital—and demonstrating that the strategy works.

The Disappearing Middle

Rising demand from mid-twentieth-century households with children required an additional ingredient to support a suburban boom—a growing middle class (see Figure 2.13). Today the middle class is shrinking. Joshua Wright, who covers labor markets for *Forbes* magazine, explains how a knowledge economy has spurred this decline. In late 2013 he reported that 70 to 80% of all new US jobs created since 2000 had qualified either as "high-wage" or "low-wage" jobs.[17] Nor does this trend show any sign of reversing. In fact, 75% of all occupations projected to lose jobs support middle-class lifestyles. Wright noted that growth in knowledge industries also generates growth in "lower-paying service industries—more jobs for the baristas, cashiers, and retail clerks"—but shrinks the middle-class portion of the economic pie (see Figure 2.14). Even a much-discussed renaissance of US

Shrinking Middle Class Identification

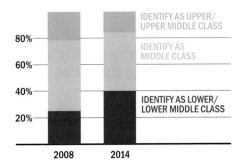

Figure 2.13. The share of Americans who identify as middle class has shrunk. (Stantec graphic based on data from billmoyers.com)

Share of Total Income earned by Middle-Class Households

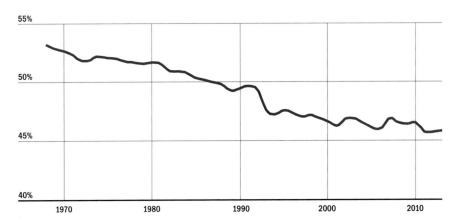

Figure 2.14. The middle 60% of households are earning a shrinking share of US income. (Stantec graphic based on data from U.S. Census Bureau)

manufacturing has tended to produce two categories of jobs—for highly educated, high-wage engineers and tech-savvy workers and for low-wage, nonunionized line workers.

The fastest growth in incomes has come at the higher end of the spectrum, whose economic power has ballooned. Between 1980 and 2017, real-dollar earnings growth for 90% of all Americans has risen roughly 15%. In contrast, real-dollar earnings for the top 10% of earners have shot up roughly 60%.[18] Meanwhile, as the knowledge economy has migrated into cities, lower-skill service jobs have increasingly moved to suburbs—and lower-income workers have followed.

Poverty Is Moving to the Suburbs

As the middle class shrinks, people living in poverty are moving to suburbs. As already noted, Fairfax County joins a surprisingly large group of suburbs across the United States whose perception as places of economic comfort masks a changing reality (see Figure 2.15). Data show that the number of people living in poverty in suburbs has

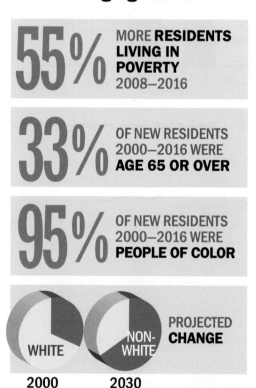

Figure 2.15. Poverty is growing much faster in suburbs than in cities. (Stantec graphic based on data from *The Washington Post*)

risen twice as fast as it has in cities since the 1970s, and this number jumped 64% between 2000 and 2010.[19] By 2013 more people in poverty lived in suburbs than in cities. Elizabeth Kneebone and Alan Berube capture the significance of this trend in *Confronting Suburban Poverty in America* (Brookings Institution, 2016): "For the first time, suburbs became home to not only the fastest-growing poor population in the country but also the largest."[20]

An analysis of suburban poverty data for America's 100 largest metros by Scott W. Allard and Sarah Charnes Paisner shows that poverty surged three times faster in suburban areas than in urban cores between 1990 and 2014. These 100 metros represent an excellent marker of how the United States and North America are growing and changing: they contain roughly two-thirds of the US population, a larger share of the US economy, and a still larger share of economic growth. By 2014 the suburban poor in these metros outnumbered those in the core by roughly 25%.[21] And while advocates have long championed the suburbs as an escape from the concentrated poverty and attendant crime, since the mid-2000s the concentration of poverty in suburbs has risen roughly twice as fast as in cities.[22] One result, reported by the Brookings Institution in 2011 is that, "In 90 of the 100 largest metro areas, the gap between city and suburban property crime rates narrowed from 1990 to 2008."[23]

Equal Opportunity Challenge

Dramatically rising suburban poverty has not been confined to specific types of suburbs, regions, or areas with especially strong or weak economies. According to Brookings's *Confronting Suburban Poverty in America*, "In prior decades, suburban poverty grew primarily in next-door 'inner suburbs' experiencing economic decline, particularly in struggling regions of the Midwest and Northeast. In contrast, poverty rose during the 2000s in fast-growing suburbs of booming regions like Phoenix as well as economically stagnant regions like Chicago. It could also be found in slow-growing and shrinking suburbs south of strong market cities like Seattle, and east and west of weak market cities like Cleveland."[24]

Much of the media attention has focused on growing poverty in mature, generally closer-in suburbs with an older housing stock. Indeed, the impacts on mature suburbs have been significant—Allard and Paisner's analysis of the 100 largest metros reported people living in poverty represented all the net population growth in these suburbs between 1990 and 2014 (see Figure 2.16). Yet faster-growing, newer, and generally farther-out suburbs are also experiencing a rapid increase in poverty, drawn by lower housing costs farther from the urban core.[25] The number of people living in poverty in these new suburbs grew by 135%, four times faster than poverty grew in urban cores and more than twice as fast as in mature suburbs (see Figure 2.17).

Figure 2.16. Between 1990 and 2014 all the net growth in mature suburbs (developed before 1970) in America's 100 largest metros consisted of people living in poverty, resulting in a new suburban sight—vacant and abandoned houses. (Richard Elzey under CC BY 2.0)

Figure 2.17. Between 1990 and 2014 the number of people living in poverty in newer suburbs (post-1970) more than doubled, increasing the volume of suburban foreclosures, particularly during the housing crash that began in 2007.

Regime Change: Shifting Perceptions of "Urban" and "Suburban"

Robert Campbell, the Pulitzer Prize–winning architecture critic of the *Boston Globe*, was one of the first observers to note a dramatic shift in perceptions of cities (see Figure 2.18). In the early 1990s Campbell noted the changing connotations that "urban" carried in popular culture. Pointing to headlines from the 1980s in which "urban" was used to describe particularly horrific crime, excessive crowding, and grim neighborhoods, he pointed to the new reality that in the early 1990s "urban" had taken on new associations like "cool," "edgy," and, increasingly, "upscale," and that most successful new network TV comedies of the period had urban, rather than suburban, settings.

The demographic and economic trends described earlier would have had less impact if they hadn't coincided with dramatic reversals in popular conceptions of cities and suburbs. Cities have come to be seen as healthier places to live; "urban," rather than "suburban," means more sustainable; and car ownership appears, for many, to limit rather than expand personal independence.

Figure 2.18. A derogatory term for much of the period after 1960, the word "urban" evoked images like this adult cinema in Boston, shown in the 1970s. Today "urban" suggests amenity and expensive housing. An upscale restaurant now occupies this historic theater building; its peep-show neighbors have given way to high-end apartments and condominiums, including a Ritz-Carlton Hotel. (City of Boston Archives under CC BY 2.0)

Urban Is Healthy

In 2004 *The New Yorker* published a much-discussed article (expanded into a book published in 2009[26]) that challenged traditional views on the connection between health and place. What got "Green Manhattan" noticed was writer David Owen's argument that Manhattan was a healthier place to live than its suburbs—because its residents walked. That assertion flew in the face of conventional wisdom. The belief that suburbs promoted health was a key argument for the first garden suburbs and was probably correct at the time. However, the perception has outlasted evolving urban reality.

Owen's article may not have exploded that perception by itself, but it reflected an emerging understanding, reinforced by subsequent studies linking the greater walkability of urban environments with better public health outcomes[27] than in typical suburban neighborhoods. University of Utah researchers found that men who lived in walkable neighborhoods weighed 10 pounds less than men in low-density neighborhoods. Another study found that auto fatalities—the leading cause of accidental deaths in the United States—rise roughly 400% along a continuum of density that extends from a city's center to its outer edges.[28] A European study reports a direct correlation between higher densities and fewer sick days at work.[29] More ominously, in 2015 the American Heart Association reported that between 1960 and 2015 the share of "physically active" jobs shrank from half to 20% of all US jobs.[30] Today Owen's article would surprise few readers. Walkable urban environments are considered healthier places to live.

Walkable Is Green

Owen's *New Yorker* article also exploded another popular myth—that suburbs were better for the environment than cities—going so far as to assert that Manhattanites had a smaller carbon footprint than residents of rural Vermont (and by a considerable margin). University of California at Berkeley researchers project that, primarily due to increased driving, "The average carbon footprint of households living in the center of large, population-dense urban cities is about 50 percent below [the US] average, while households in distant suburbs are up to twice the [US] average."[31]

When housing economists Laurie Volk and Todd Zimmerman (see Chapter 3) describe housing priorities today as reflected in market demand, sustainability ranks near the top; big yards and easy highway access no longer do. Developers compete to make sustainability claims, increasingly making their case by pursuing LEED (Leadership in Energy and Environmental Design) gold- or even platinum-level certifications.[32]

Auto Dependence Is Expensive

Auto dependence and associated low-density development also impose increasingly recognized burdens on individuals and their communities. Making the case that lower transportation costs were a factor favoring urban housing markets, Christopher B. Lein-berger (see Chapter 1) reported in 2010 that, "Households in drivable suburban neighbor-hoods devote on average 24 percent of their income to transportation; those in walkable neighborhoods spend about 12 percent . . . nationally, that amounts to $700 billion a year."[33] If anything, this gap has increased in subsequent years.[34]

Even before awareness of the economic costs of auto dependence took hold widely, North Americans had begun expressing concern about the costs of auto dependence. The Urban Land Institute's *America in 2015* study reported that "63% of Millennials prefer living in a 'car-optional' neighborhood."[35] For many decades roadway construction kept pace with increases in total miles driven in many regions. However, in the 1990s adding lanes became increasingly difficult due to environmental and cost constraints. The result? A spike in congestion, with measures of hours lost to congestion shooting up as traffic continued to increase. Analyzing the 2015 Brookings Institution report, *The Growing Dis-tance between People and Jobs in Metropolitan America,* City Observatory reported that, "In the 50 largest metro areas, sprawl costs commuters [an additional] 3.9 billion hours per year—or the equivalent of almost 100 million work weeks.[36]

How Walkable Urban Centers Help Suburbs Adapt to Change

The adage "drive 'til you qualify" has a hollow ring today, as people contemplate the complex trade-offs posed by the health, environmental, and economic costs of auto dependence—along with their own preference for walkable, mixed-use places that pro-mote a sense of community. Bringing the benefits of urban density to suburbs increasingly looks like a pragmatic response to the ills of suburbia. As one leader in Sandy Springs, an

Figure 2.19. In Sandy Springs, a suburb of Atlanta, residents developed a shared vision for City Springs, a new mixed-use downtown centered around a performing arts center and a town green. (City of Sandy Springs)

affluent Atlanta suburb known for its staunch defense of traditional suburban qualities, proclaimed at a meeting to discuss a new downtown, "Today, this is the right thing to do" (see Figure 2.19).

Shifting Markets

Virginia's Fairfax County is revising its planning and development policies to adapt to changing circumstances. A fundamental challenge the county shares with most suburbs is the growing imbalance between the supply and demand for detached single-family houses. As the number of aging Americans begins to far outnumber new households with children, Chris Nelson calculates that the United States already had more single-family suburban housing in 2010 than it would need to meet projected demand in 2030. Not surprisingly, Fairfax County is planning for a future in which 85% of all new housing built by 2035 will be multifamily.[37]

Reporting on a study by Nelson for *The Atlantic*'s CityLab website, Emily Badger likens the bulge in baby boomers moving through the demographic cycle to the proverbial very large (and hard-to-digest) mammal that, having been swallowed, is making its way through a python: "In the 20 years between 1990 and 2010, [baby boomers] were at their peak family size and peak income. And suddenly, there was massive demand in America from the same kinds of people for the same kinds of housing: big, large-lot single-family homes (often in suburbia). In those two decades . . . 77 percent of demand for new housing construction in America was driven by this trend."[38] Nelson translates this metaphor into numbers: "If there's 1.5 to 2 million homes coming on the market every year at the end of this decade from senior households' selling off, who's behind them to buy? My guess is not enough [buyers]." Nelson quantifies the imbalance—suggesting an annual surplus of 200,000 houses by 2020 that rises to 500,000 by 2030, a significant impact, given that the total of all houses sold in the US between 2010 and 2016 averaged around 5.5 million annually (see Figure 2.20).

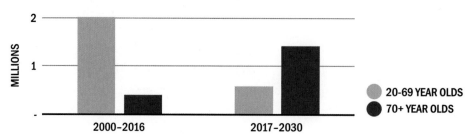

Figure 2.20. Aging suburban populations raise the specter of too many older sellers chasing too few younger buyers when they decide to sell their homes. (Stantec graphic, based on data from ZeroHedge.com)

Fairfax County sees opportunities in change. It is adapting its policies to guide growth to higher-density, higher-value, mixed-use urban centers like Tysons (see Chapter 7)—responding to good news in Nelson's study that indicates that the large majority of aging boomers won't seek to abandon suburbs for cities or rural communities (see Figure 2.21). Instead, they prefer places that combine the perceived safety, relative affordability, and welcome familiarity of suburbs with the walkability, amenities, and convenience of urban lifestyles.[39] A Freddie Mac survey of 6,000 baby boomer homeowners over age 55 backs up this perspective and suggests that more than 70% of older homeowners want to rent once they sell their house—and that this shift from owning to renting could result in five million boomers moving from owned to rented housing by 2020.[40] These boomers may depress suburban real estate tax bases by selling millions of houses over a relatively short period, but they also represent a potent market for higher-density, higher-value redevelopment of outmoded, low-density strip retail and office parks.

Ellen Dunham-Jones, leader of the urban design program at Georgia Tech and co-author with June Williamson of the influential *Retrofitting Suburbia*, sheds more light on senior housing preferences, reporting that more than two-thirds of aging baby boomers say they would prefer to live within walking distance of transit—generally defined as

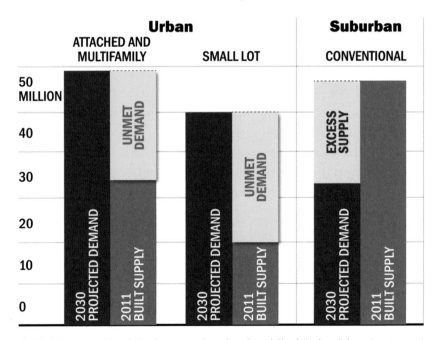

Figure 2.21. Demographic shifts have produced a shortfall of "urban" housing types in cities and suburbs alike.

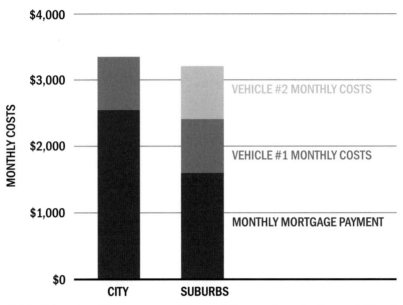

Figure 2.22. Urban densities support walking, public transit, and other mobility choices that significantly reduce household transportation costs. (Stantec graphic, based on data from Money After Graduation.com)

within a quarter mile.[41] Putting Nelson, Freddie Mac, and Dunham-Jones's observations together suggests a sizable market foundation for higher-density, mixed-use urban centers, particularly in light of the relative scarcity of high-quality suburban rental housing in walkable settings. This market should reach several hundred thousand units per year by the early 2020s. Christopher B. Leinberger (see Chapter 1) notes growing support in suburban communities for walkable centers because they prop up property values. CEOs for Cities research backs Leinberger's observation, concluding that higher WalkScores (a measure of the relative number of destinations within walkable distance of each other) correlate with higher housing prices (see Figure 2.22).[42]

Fiscal Challenges

Affluent Fairfax County faces fiscal challenges as it positions itself to address the impacts of growing poverty, an aging population, and increasing racial and ethnic diversity. The County's $3 billion annual budget faces a $300 million shortfall. Driven in large part by the costs of meeting the needs of a much more economically, racially, and ethnically diverse student body, County funding for schools shot up from $1.4 billion in 2005 to $2 billion in 2015 (see Figure 2.23).[43]

How Smart Growth Boosts the Municipal Bottom Line

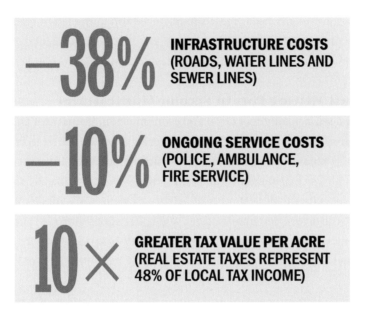

−38% INFRASTRUCTURE COSTS (ROADS, WATER LINES AND SEWER LINES)

−10% ONGOING SERVICE COSTS (POLICE, AMBULANCE, FIRE SERVICE)

10× GREATER TAX VALUE PER ACRE (REAL ESTATE TAXES REPRESENT 48% OF LOCAL TAX INCOME)

Figure 2.23. Walkable urban centers create significant fiscal benefits for suburbs. (Stantec graphic, based on data from Building Better Budgets by Smart Growth America)

For decades suburbs balanced relatively high fiscal costs of serving low-density, spread-out communities with lower service costs associated with their more affluent, younger populations. Today aging and poor populations are tipping that balance—in the wrong direction. Seventy percent of people who reach age 65 (or roughly 20% of the total suburban population by 2020) will experience the kinds of disabilities that generate demand for wellness and social services.[44] People living in poverty require a broad range of job training, wellness, family support, and similar services. Both groups are heavily dependent on suburban public transit, which generally is not up to the task. A study by the Rockefeller Foundation found that for lower-income suburbs across the United States, limited bus services means transit provides access to only 4% of the jobs within a 45-minute drive.[45]

For suburbs facing growing fiscal strains, walkable urban places can produce significant fiscal benefits. Joe Minicozzi, principal and founder of Urban 3 consultants, has done pioneering work in helping communities evaluate the fiscal trade-offs in shifting from traditional auto-oriented, low-density development to higher-density, walkable development models. He studied 36 communities across the United States and found that replacing a Walmart or retail strip with a three- to six-story, mixed-use development increased taxes per acre by a factor of roughly 8 to 25 or more.[46] These fiscal benefits far outweigh any added infrastructure and service costs. Minicozzi notes that, "More and more suburbs cannot afford the land use and development patterns today that they approved forty years ago. To pay for the services, transportation, and education systems that their 21st-century constituents need, these suburbs need to tap the latent value buried under outmoded malls and office parks by turning them into lively, walkable urban places that are worth ten to twenty-times as much in today's real estate economy."[47]

Moving Past Melting Pots to Become Multicultural

As they trade a self-perception of racial and economic homogeneity for an appreciation of newfound diversity, Fairfax County's leaders express growing interest in creating places in which different kinds of people don't just live side by side, but also come together, interact, and build a sense of shared community. Higher-density, walkable, mixed-use urban centers can generate the critical mass of activity to support sociologist Ray Oldenburg's third places—the diverse restaurants, cafés, and coffee shops; libraries; cinemas and other entertainment venues; stores; cultural venues; a city hall; social service agencies,[48] and other activities—that invite people to cross lines of race, ethnicity, income, and other distinctions.

Reese Fayde, former president of Living Cities, a consortium of some of America's largest foundations working to invest more than $1 billion in revitalizing US cities, talks about the specific role that density plays in transforming diversity into community:

"One of the greatest challenges we had was making diversity work. Community came naturally when you looked like each other or were related to many of your neighbors—but those days are gone in cities and suburbs. One advantage cities have today . . . and suburbs can build the same advantage . . . is what I call 'the fog of density'—urban places where no one stands out and everyone is on a sort of equal footing because there are lots of people of different ages, races, ethnicities, lifestyles—you name it—living, working, playing, shopping . . . no one 'owns' these places. They can be everyone's community."[49]

"Disruptive" Change in Mobility

Computers, cell phones, and social media launched disruptive changes in how we live, work, and play. Over the next decade autonomous mobility will launch another round of disruption, with profound—but on balance distinctly positive—implications for walkable urban places in cities and suburbs alike. Although individually owned autonomous vehicles (AVs) will likely promote sprawl as commuters read, work, or nap unencumbered by driving, the real story will be the rapid growth of shared autonomous vehicles (SAVs). Over the next five years SAVs will become familiar sights in compact, dense urban places that support a critical mass of people and trips. More important, they will outcompete private cars based on cost, convenience, and environmental benefits.

Sharing, Not Growing
WORLDWIDE FORECAST

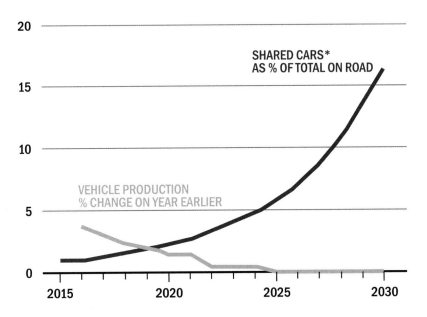

* INCLUDING TAXIS, EXCLUDING RENTAL CARS

Figure 2.24. By the mid-2020s, shared autonomous vehicles will represent all of the growth in global auto production. (Stantec graphic, based on data from Morgan Stanley)

In turn, SAVs will reduce development costs by removing much of the demand for parking (as much as 25% in initial stages, as SAVs magnify the impact of ride-sharing services, and up to 80% by the late 2030s), increase development (and fiscal) values by offering convenient connections to transit and other destinations, and enhance livability by making mobility more convenient. Perhaps most compelling, Rod Schebesch, leader of Stantec Consulting's autonomous vehicles research program, notes, "Looking across North America, switching from owning one car to using SAVs would save the average household roughly $5,000 every year—and this is before taking advantage of the fact that SAVs drop you off and you don't have to pay for parking."[50]

SAVs will play the same synergistic role for North America's twenty-first-century demographics and knowledge economy that universal automobile ownership played for baby boomers and a growing industrial economy more than a half century ago. SAVs will reinforce a pro-urban lifestyle and market preferences and provide a catalyst for expanded compact, walkable development in cities and suburbs alike. A 2017 advisory bulletin by Morgan Stanley to its investors, "Car of the Future Is Shared, Autonomous, Electric," emphasized how close and dominant this mobility revolution will be. Among its projections, Morgan Stanley advised clients that by 2025 electric SAVs would dominate growth in global auto production (see Figure 2.24).

A Cautionary Note

Roughly 60% of US suburbanites live in communities where the median household income equals or surpasses $66,000 per year, meaning household incomes exceed the nationwide median by 20% or more. These suburbs are not only more likely to be able to afford the initial infrastructure investments (e.g., a new street grid) often required to launch a new urban center and attract private investment, but they are also more likely to be in regions with real estate markets that can support development of higher-density, mixed-use, walkable urban places. These suburbs can capitalize on surging real estate markets for high-quality multifamily housing (Dublin, outside of Columbus, see Chapter 11); draw on a strong knowledge economy (Bellevue—see Chapter 13), or pursue transit-oriented development (Tysons, outside of Washington, DC, see Chapter 7) to create higher-density, mixed-use urban places. These urban places in turn attract higher-income, educated residents who pump energy and dollars into their communities. Real estate recessions are inevitable, but the underlying demographic and economic logic of creating new urban environments in suburbs will remain compelling well into the 2030s.

Roughly 25% of suburbanites live in communities with median household incomes close to the nationwide US median of around $56,000 per year. These suburbs may have fewer resources to invest in initial infrastructure and at the same time may need to offer tax or other incentives to attract private investment. However, many of them may be able to tap unmet regional demand to help create vibrant new walkable urban places.

The remaining 15% of suburban residents live in communities where household incomes lag the nationwide US median. They face much greater challenges. Without significant public investment in new transit or a regionally significant educational or medical facility or similar draw, these suburbs risk losing aging residents downsizing from single-family houses and with no prospect of relocating to an urban environment in the same community. Miami Township, outside of Dayton (see Chapter 8), demonstrates that strong local leadership can help such communities figure out ways to benefit from demographic and economic trends and negotiate the transition from sprawl to new urban Main Streets, but they will face a tougher path than their more affluent peers.

Notes

1.   State Museum of Pennsylvania, *Levittown: Building the American Dream*, accessed July 12, 2016, statemuseumpa.org/levittown/one/b.html.

2   Joel Garreau, *Edge Cities: Life on the New Frontier* (New York: Anchor Books, 1991).

3.   Eric Jaffe, "The Urban Future of the American Suburb," *The Atlantic*, November 2014, accessed August 28, 2017, https://www.theatlantic.com/magazine/archive/2014/11/the-urban-future-of-the-american-suburb/380797/.

4. Ray Oldenburg, *The Great Good Place: Cafes, Coffee Shops, Community Centers, Beauty Parlors, General Stores, Bars, Hangouts, and How They Get You through the Day* (New York: Paragon House, 1989).

5. Antonio Olivo, "This Model of Wealthy Suburban Living Is Starting to Fray," *Washington Post*, April 2, 2016, accessed August 18, 2017, https://www.washingtonpost.com/local/ virginia-news/this-model-of-wealthy-suburban-living-is-starting-to-fray/2016/04/02/ e9ad0ace-f107-11e5-a61f-e9c95c06edca_story.html?utm_term=.fb56d4e03710.

6. Ibid.

7. Stephen M. Golant, "Aging in the American Suburbs: A Changing Population," accessed June 24, 2016, http://todaysgeriatricmedicine.com/news/ex_06309_01.shtml.

8. CBRE Global Investors, *U.S. Urbanization Trends: Investment Implications for Commercial Real Estate,* January 2015, accessed February 22, 2017, http://www.cbreglobalinvestors .com/research/publications/Documents/Special%20Reports/US%20Urbanization%20 Trends_JAN%202015.pdf.

9. Laurie Volk, conversation with the authors, October 23, 2016.

10. Matthew Yglesias, "America's Urban Renaissance Is Only for the Rich," *Vox*, March 30, 2016, accessed August 8, 2017, https://www.vox.com/2016/3/30/11331938/class-urban -revival-kolko.

11. Joe Cortright, "Are the 'Burbs Really Back?" City Observatory, June 12, 2016, accessed August 6, 2017, http://cityobservatory.org/are-the-burbs-really-back/.

12. CBRE Research, "2015/2016 Americas Occupier Survey," March 2016, accessed, August 6, 2017, https://www.cbre.com/research-and-reports/occupier-survey-2015-16.

13. Ibid.

14. Arthur Acolin, Richard Voith, and Susan Wachter, "City and Suburbs—Has There Been a Regime Change?" Penn Institute for Urban Research, June 2016, accessed August 8, 2017, http://www.penniur.upenn.edu/uploads/media/City_and_Suburbs_%E2% 80%93_Has_There_Been_a_Regime_Change_web.pdf.

15. Richard Florida, "Startups and Venture Capital Are Going Urban," CityLab, June 7, 2016, accessed August 6, 2017, https://www.citylab.com/life/2016/06/startups-and-venture -capital-are-going-urban/485978/.

16. CBRE Global Investors, "U.S. Urbanization Trends: Investment Implications for Commercial Real Estate," January 2015.

17. Joshua Wright, "The Cities Creating the Most High-Paid Jobs and Why They're Good for Low-Wage Workers, Too," November 13, 2013, accessed February 23, 2017, http: //www.forbes.com/sites/emsi/2013/11/14/the-cities-creating-the-most-high-paid -jobs-and-why-theyre-good-for-low-wage-workers-too/.

18. Economic Policy Institute, "Top 10 Charts on Income Inequality and Wages," January 5, 2015, accessed August 6, 2017, http://billmoyers.com/2015/01/05/top-10-charts -2014/.

19. Elizabeth Kneebone and Alan Berube, *Confronting Suburban Poverty in America* (Washington, DC: Brookings Institution Press, 2016).

20. Christine Serlin, "Poverty in the Suburbs a Growing Problem: Brookings' Elizabeth Kneebone Highlights Causes and Challenges of This Shifting Trend," *Affordable Housing Finance*, May 17, 2016, accessed August 6, 2017, http://www.housingfinance.com/news /poverty-in-the-suburbs-a-growing-problem_o.

21. Scott W. Allard and Sarah Charnes Paisner, "The Rise of Suburban Poverty," Oxford Handbooks Online, September 2016, accessed February 2017, http://www.oxfordhand books.com/view/10.1093/oxfordhb/9780199935307.001.0001/oxfordhb-97801999 35307-e-96.

22. Elizabeth Kneebone and Steven Raphael, "City and Suburban Crime Trends in Metropolitan America," Brookings Institution, May 2011, accessed August 6, 2017, https://www .brookings.edu/research/city-and-suburban-crime-trends-in-metropolitan-america/.

23. Elizabeth Kneebone and Natalie Holmes, "US Concentrated Poverty in the Wake of the Great Recession," Brookings Institution, March 31, 2016, accessed August 6, 2017, https: //www.brookings.edu/research/u-s-concentrated-poverty-in-the-wake-of-the-great -recession/.

24. Elizabeth Kneebone and Alan Burube, *Confronting Suburban Poverty in America*, Brookings Institution, 2013, Frequently Asked Questions, accessed August 6, 2017, http://confrontingsuburbanpoverty.org/about/faqs/.

25. Joe Cortright, "Are the 'Burbs Really Back?" City Observatory, June 12, 2016, accessed August 6, 2017, http://cityobservatory.org/are-the-burbs-really-back/.

26. David Owen, *Green Metropolis: Why Living Smaller, Living Closer, and Driving Less Are the Keys to Sustainability* (New York: Riverhead Books, 2009).

27. Richard Florida, "Walkability Is Good for You: A Slew of New Research Links Walkable Neighborhoods with Safer, Healthier, More Democratic Places," December 11, 2014, accessed August 6, 2017, https://www.citylab.com/design/2014/12/growing-evidence -shows-walkability-is-good-for-you-and-for-cities/383612/.

28. David E. Clark and Brad M. Cushing, "Rural and Urban Traffic Fatalities, Vehicle Miles, and Population Density," *Accident Analysis & Prevention* 36, no. 6 (2004): 967–72.

29. Hallberg, Örjan, "Public Health versus Population Density," *European Journal of Cancer Prevention* 23, no. 6 (2014): 566–67.

30. American Heart Association, "The Price of Inactivity," October 26, 2015, http://www .heart.org/HEARTORG/HealthyLiving/PhysicalActivity/FitnessBasics/The-Price-of -Inactivity_UCM_307974_Article.jsp#.WLM8Em_yvIU.

31. "Suburban Sprawl Cancels Carbon-Footprint Savings of Dense Urban Cores," *Berkeley News*, January 6, 2014, accessed August 6, 2017, http://news.berkeley.edu/2014/01/06 /suburban-sprawl-cancels-carbon-footprint-savings-of-dense-urban-cores/.

32. Conversation with the authors, February 26, 2017.

33. Christopher B. Leinberger and Patrick C. Doherty, "The Next Real Estate Boom," accessed August 6, 2017, https://www.brookings.edu/articles/the-next-real-estate-boom/.

34. Rachel Quednau, "The Cost of Commuting vs. Living Close," My Sidewalk: Helping local leaders and city experts build better communities, March 15, 2016, accessed August 6, 2017, https://blog.mysidewalk.com/the-cost-of-commuting-vs-living-close- e28bf28c7df9.

35. Urban Land Institute, *America in 2015: A Community Survey* (Washington, DC: Urban Land Institute, 2015), 25.

36. Daniel Hertz, "Introducing the Sprawl Tax," City Observatory, June 2, 2016, accessed August 6, 2017, http://cityobservatory.org/introducing-the-sprawl-tax/.

37. Demographic Reports 2016, County of Fairfax, Virginia, accessed August 6, 2017, http: //www.fairfaxcounty.gov/demogrph/demrpts/report/fullrpt.pdf.

38. Emily Badger, "The Great Senior Sell-Off Could Start the Next Housing Crisis," City-Lab, March 5, 2013, accessed March 1, 2017, http://www.citylab.com/housing/2013/03/aging-baby-boomers-and-next-housing-crisis/4863/.

39. Mark Heckman, "From the Suburbs to the City: Trends in Senior Housing," blog post, August 7, 2014, accessed February 28, 2017, Marks-Thomas.com, http://marks-thomas.com/2014/08/suburbs-city-trends-senior-housing/.

40. "Get Ready for a Baby Boomer Sell-Off," Realtor.Mag (National Association of Realtors), June 28, 2016, accessed March 1, 2017, http://realtormag.realtor.org/daily-news/2016/06/29/get-ready-for-baby-boomer-sell.

41. Ellen Dunham-Jones and June Williamson, *Retrofitting Suburbia, Updated Edition: Urban Design Solutions for Redesigning Suburbs* (Hoboken, NJ: John Wiley & Sons, 2011).

42. Joe Cortright, *Walking the Walk: How Walkability Raises Home Values in U.S. Cities* (Washington, DC: Impresa, Inc., for CEOs for Cities, August 2009), accessed August 6, 2017, http://community-wealth.org/content/walking-walk-how-walkability-raises-home-values-us-cities.

43. Antonio Olivo, "This Model of Wealthy Suburban Living Is Starting to Fray," *Washington Post*, April 2, 2016, accessed August 6, 2017, https://www.washingtonpost.com/local/virginia-news/this-model-of-wealthy-suburban-living-is-starting-to-fray/2016/04/02/e9ad0ace-f107-11e5-a61f-e9c95c06edca_story.html?utm_term=.80738f850b7b.

44. Joint Center for Housing Studies of Harvard University, "U.S. Unprepared to Meet the Housing Needs of Its Aging Population," September 2, 2014, accessed August 6, 2017, http://www.jchs.harvard.edu/us-unprepared-meet-housing-needs-its-aging-population.

45. Rockefeller Foundation, "Suburban Poverty in the United States," May 2013, accessed August 6, 2017, https://www.rockefellerfoundation.org/report/suburban-poverty-in-the-united-states/.

46. Joe Minicozzi, "The Smart Math of Mixed-Use Development: Are Cities across the Country Acting Negligently in Ignoring the Property Tax Implications of Different Development Types?" Planetizen, January 23, 2012, accessed August 6, 2017, https://www.planetizen.com/node/53922.

47. Joe Minicozzi, principal and founder of Urban 3, conversation with David Dixon, February 16, 2017.

48. Leo W. Jeffres, Cheryl C. Bracken, Guowei Jian, and Mary F. Casey, "The Impact of Third Places on Community Quality of Life." *Applied Research in the Quality of Life* 4, no. 4 (2009): 333–45, doi: 10.1007/s11482-009-9084-8. ISSN 1871-2584.

49. Reese Fayde, Reese Fayde and Associates, conversation with David Dixon, February 17, 2017.

50. Conversation with Rod Schebesch, vice president, Stantec Consulting, February 28, 2017.

PART II SUBURBAN MARKETS

Part II brings a new perspective from real estate analysts who study the dramatic changes taking place in housing, office, and retail markets and advise developers and governments—in cities and suburbs alike—how to respond. The authors draw on deep experience in identifying emerging markets that even recent history can't fully gauge, but that instead require a data-based examination of changing demographics and values. They also demonstrate how their findings support public/private partnerships that unlock opportunities to create new walkable urban places.

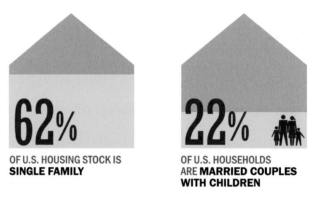

More Houses Built Than Families to Live in Them

62% OF U.S. HOUSING STOCK IS **SINGLE FAMILY**

22% OF U.S. HOUSEHOLDS ARE **MARRIED COUPLES WITH CHILDREN**

Figure 3.1. The United States has an oversupply of single-family detached houses. Most were designed for a married couple with children, which today represents a minority of all US households. (Stantec graphic, based on data from the American Community Survey, 2015)

3

Housing

Laurie Volk, Todd Zimmerman, and Christopher Volk-Zimmerman[1]

In many locations, properly positioned new housing that responds to changing housing markets can represent the foundation for mixed-use, walkable suburban centers. In 1920, most Americans lived in mixed-use, walkable urban neighborhoods, and both the suburb and the automobile were already well established in the nation's culture and economy. Who could have foreseen that by the 1970s the typical new suburban neighborhood would be an isolated auto-dependent subdivision? And who in 1970 could have predicted, roughly four decades later, the rise of a new generation of mixed-use, walkable urban neighborhoods in cities and suburbs alike? Conventional demographic and life-stage analysis, based on historical norms, would forecast a boom in suburban and exurban neighborhoods as members of the millennial generation, the largest in the nation's history, marry and begin families. But our research and experience suggest that historical norms are once again proving to be poor predictors of future settlement patterns. The assertion that the current urban preference is a mere pause in the dispersal of households, jobs, and shopping into the farther reaches of our metropolitan areas—the nation's historical thinning out—ignores structural changes in every aspect of American life. Over the next several decades, demographic, technological, and, perhaps most importantly, changing values and lifestyles could combine to create a transformation of American settlement patterns equal in impact to the metro-area thinning out it would partly reverse. It is conceivable that, before too long, many auto-dependent suburbs will be struggling to remain economically viable, or even socially relevant.

Today, based on our firm's target-market household cluster analysis,[2] nearly a quarter of the approximately 121 million US households (2015), or about 29 million, live in suburban areas.[3] Although the definition of "suburbs," and thus the share of the US population that lives in suburbs, varies by source, all sources reviewed for this book indicate that the largest share of households and individuals lives in suburbs. These are communities that meet the classic definition of a suburb as "a residential district lying just beyond the boundaries or limits of a city, typically within commuting distance of the city center," and have a clear relationship to an urban center—metropolitan city, second city, or satellite city. They range from the relatively close-in, townlike suburbs, often linked to an urban core via transit, to newer suburbs in locations that include corridors of office and retail. Excluded, however, are not only city neighborhoods, towns, and rural areas, but also the hard-to-measure patchwork of exurban subdivisions at the outer limits of thinned-out metropolitan areas.

When American neighborhoods are divided into five levels of urban intensity, suburban areas contain a plurality of American households. The other four settlement types, in declining order of population density, are as follows:

- **Large cities**—that form the core of an expansive region (metropolitan cities), home to 22 million households (18%)
- **Smaller cities**—at the core of geographically smaller regions or stand-alone smaller cities (second cities/satellite cities), also 22 million households (18%)
- **Rural towns and villages**—23 million households (19%)
- **Farmland and hamlets**—24 million households (20%)

As the dominant American settlement pattern of the past half century, suburbs are still home to the largest concentration of families. Because many couples have remained in place long after their children have grown and started households, the suburbs have also become the largest concentration of empty-nest households. As would be expected today, cities (large and small) account for more than half of the nation's younger households, compared with less than a quarter in the suburbs, 10% in towns, and 12% in rural and exurban areas.

Many, if not most, of the original transit-served suburban neighborhoods—most of which now sit inside city limits—are walkable and often include a mix of uses, even when the original transit (such as the streetcar) is no longer there. Their small commercial nodes are still within walking distance of housing, and the network of streets disperses traffic and makes walking and biking safer. These original suburbs, which were viewed as lower-cost options for most of the last half of the twentieth century, when set in contrast to post–World War II settlements, are now seen as quite urban in character and are more in line with evolving housing market preferences. The suburbs where property values could be most threatened by generational changes are those that have arisen since the

1970s. These, unfortunately, often have a physical form and ownership pattern that present the most challenges to redevelopment. In fact, suburbs now have more people living in poverty than the nation's big cities.[4]

Even in a scenario where change is more moderate, American suburbs could still end up sharply divided between winners and losers, with the key metrics being density, diversity, and transportation choice. Winners would be those suburban neighborhoods where meaningful and useful destinations, such as shopping, recreation, and even employment, are within an agreeable walk, an easy bike ride, or a convenient and pleasant transit trip. Losers would be those areas unable to adapt to these new standards, either because their physical form or ownership pattern resists infill and retrofit development, or because they lack resources or political will to drive such a transformation.

"Reurbanization" of the Housing Market

The most visible and dramatic transformation of settlement patterns is already well under way—the revitalization and densification of the nation's downtowns and in-town neighborhoods. Although temporarily interrupted by the Great Recession,[5] the reurbanization of America's cities, large and small, has been the major housing trend of the twenty-first century. Reurbanization will also have a positive impact on urban centers in small town centers and the establishment of suburban centers at every scale. From the market perspective, reurbanization will expand housing options, regardless of a household's preferred location along the rural-to-urban "transect" (continuum from urban core to rural fringe).

The United States does have an abundance of single-family detached houses; they constitute nearly 62% of all dwellings[6] (see Figure 3.1). Most of those houses were designed for a family grouping that now represents only a minority of US households: a married couple with children. Married couples with children now make up less than 22% of US households, and the traditional, one-worker family with children—once the predominant household type—now accounts for less than 8% of US households.[7]

Today nearly 60% of US households consist of just one or two people.[8] The demographic characteristics of these households have driven reurbanization. The United States is in the midst of an unprecedented generational convergence. The two largest generations in US history are the 75 million baby boomers born between 1946 and 1964, and their children, the millennials born between 1977 and 1996, who surpassed the boomers in population in 2010 and now number more than 87 million. [9]

Both generations made a strong break with earlier generations by delaying marriage and childbirth, but the millennials are defying convention even more than the boomers did. Delayed first marriage has become pronounced. In 2014 the average man was significantly older on his first wedding day than his 1960 counterpart—29.3 as opposed to 22.8

years old. Similarly, the average woman was 27 years old when she married as compared with 20.3 in 1960.[10]

Perhaps the most startling change, at least to their parents' generation, is that for many millennials, children often come before marriage. More than half of children born to women under 30 are now born outside of marriage—many of those to cohabiting couples.[11] Perhaps the most significant child-related fact, though, is the relative lack of children in millennial households. The country's fertility rate has reached an all-time low, driven largely by record low percentages of births to women under 30.[12]

Historically, fertility rates have generally moved in tandem with the nation's economy; however, the low fertility rate of millennials may not simply be a result of the Great Recession. Economist Richard Easterlin has hypothesized that fertility during a generation's child-bearing years directly reflects economic circumstances and job prospects.[13] This would suggest that millennial couples, measuring their "relative status" to that of their childhood, will delay having children until acceptable jobs are relatively plentiful.

Despite dozens of surveys predicting otherwise, millennials have yet to embrace home ownership at anything like the rate of predecessor generations. In 2015, first-time buyers made up just 32% of all buyers of housing, well below the typical share of 40%.[14] A lack of first-time buyers disrupts the entire ownership-housing chain, reducing both the market for potential move-up buyers and the market for the potentially massive baby boomer sell-off.

Would-be housing buyers most frequently cite the challenge of amassing a down payment. One problem for young households, with no solution in sight, is the unprecedented cumulative level of student debt, estimated at over $1.3 trillion carried by 40 million Americans (see Figure 3.2). Graduates who earned baccalaureate degrees with student debt—69% of all 2014 graduates—owe approximately $29,000 each.[15] Three-quarters of millennials name student debt as a barrier to buying a residence, and nearly half say debt has made them postpone having children.[16]

Naturally, income is the most significant metric for potential housing buyers. Many millennials entered the job market when the Great Recession had severely constrained employment opportunities. The recovery brought only slow growth, with most employment gains limited to low-paying jobs. At the same time, the American economic compact that built the middle class over a half century has been shattered. A white-collar worker can no longer join a corporation and expect that hard work will secure lifetime employment, advancement, and a comfortable pension. As union membership has shrunk, fewer blue-collar workers can rely on unions to help sustain employment conditions and wage growth. Little wonder, then, that many millennials, over 10 million,[17] now earn or augment incomes through the "gig economy," where work is short-term, peer-to-peer, and on-demand—often made possible by digital platforms. As noted previously, the Easterlin

$1.3 trillion
TOTAL U.S. STUDENT DEBT

Figure 3.2. ▲ Student debt is one reason millennials have less interest in taking on mortgages than previous generations. (Stantec graphic, based on data from Forbes.com)

Figure 3.3. ▶ Many millennials require less living space for possessions, but they have a strong interest in places that offer easy access to community. (KRC Research [2015]/Zipcar Annual Millennial Survey, *"Millennial" Is a State of Mind*)

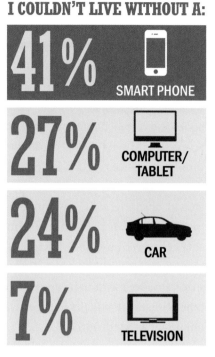

I COULDN'T LIVE WITHOUT A:

41% SMART PHONE

27% COMPUTER/TABLET

24% CAR

7% TELEVISION

hypothesis would suggest that it could be some time before millennials feel comfortable with the prospect of starting a family and buying a house.

Then there is millennials' attitude toward automobiles. It has become part of millennial lore that they value their smartphone more than the car they've failed to purchase, despite the obvious flaw of comparing a $200, 5-ounce device and a $34,000, 2.5-ton machine. So prevalent is the comparison that Zipcar includes it in an annual survey of millennials. The most recent study found that 41% of millennials said giving up their smartphone would have a much greater negative impact on their life than giving up their computer/tablet (27%), car (24%), or television (7%) (see Figure 3.3).[18]

Just as Zipcar would like to emphasize the value of its business model to the nation's largest generation, the auto industry and industries dependent on driving like to debunk the idea of millennial agnosticism about autos. Articles frequently point out that millennials actually now buy more cars (3.7 million in 2015) than members of generation X (3.3 million). Some reports suggest that these data show millennials are "more likely" than gen X to be car buyers when, in fact, according to the data, millennials are 36% less likely to purchase a car. The missed data point is the radically different sizes of the two generations; the millennial generation is 74% larger than gen X.[19] This shows a failure, as Joe Cortright of City Observatory pointed out, to execute simple long division. Millennials'

lack of interest in owning a car may signal a significant cultural shift away from ownership toward greater reliance on renting and sharing.

Compared with predecessor generations, Millennials are generally more comfortable
with smaller living spaces. Technology has relieved them of much of the storage requirements their parents had. Many if not most millennials feel no desire to accumulate possessions. Indeed, many of the things that were a necessity for their parents—such as
books and recorded music in its various formats—are redundant to millennials, who have
access to any song ever recorded, every book ever written, and any movie ever made,
through a device that fits in the palm of the hand. Even their televisions—if they have
them—require much less real estate (or no floor space when they're hung on a wall). Millennial offspring are rarely interested in, and the market is already oversupplied with,
their boomer parents' furniture, china, silver, books, and nearly every other type of dur-
able consumer product. Millennials, and particularly young knowledge workers, spend
more time in the public realm—in some instances "alone together" at a café, bar, or work-
space, involved with their devices but pleased to be sitting across a communal table from
other millennials equally engaged with their own devices. Furniture space is not nearly as
important as bandwidth.

Projecting Housing Markets for Urban Places in Suburbia:
Five Examples

In more than a quarter century of determining the market potential of hundreds of mixed-
use, walkable neighborhoods of every type, we have yet to encounter a location—urban,
suburban, or exurban—that lacked any market potential. The potential market for suburban redevelopment can vary widely, depending on a suburb's proximity to a significant urban center, regional market conditions, and other factors. However, the following case studies reflect the housing market potential for a broad range of new urban
centers in suburbs. (Because these specific case studies are proprietary, the actual projects
are not identified; the images shown represent projects chosen to meet similar market
characteristics.)

Example One: Retrofitting a Suburban Office Campus

Over the second half of the last century, the dispersal of employment throughout metropolitan areas and the creation of self-contained office campuses—often for specific corporate users—occurred as workplaces followed workers moving to the suburbs. Like master-
planned residential communities, office campuses have little flexibility. Example one,
located in New England, is a mixed-use walkable center built to serve not only a cluster
of suburban corporate campuses, but also as a catalyst for the potential transformation of
those campuses into flexible mixed-use neighborhoods (see figure 3.4).

Figure 3.4. Retrofitting a suburban office campus—Legacy in Plano, Texas. (Eric Fredericks under CC BY-SA 2.0) Because the market studies in this chapter include proprietary data, the images for each of the five examples similar approaches to development.

Example Two: Creating a Walkable Center in a Newer Suburb
The introduction of a walkable center into a low-density suburb is intended to make it more competitive and to shore up values in a time of a growing market preference for urban living. Example two is in an existing auto-dependent suburb of a major city in the Southeast (see Figure 3.5).

Example Three: Expanding a Traditional Suburban Center
Even suburbs where a small historic downtown is already present benefit from a mix of housing choices in the context of a walkable core. Example three is the proposed enhancement of the existing downtown and introduction of a variety of housing types and mix of uses in an affluent suburb of a rapidly growing midwestern city with a predominance of expensive single-family houses and Fortune 500 companies in parklike settings (see Figure 3.6).

Figure 3.5. ▲   Creating a walkable center in a newer suburb—similar to City Springs, in Sandy Springs, Georgia. (Lord Aeck Sargent)

Figure 3.6. ▶   An example of expanding a traditional suburban center: Federal Real Estate Investment Trust integrated a higher-density urban development, with retail and restaurants, offices, housing, and a cinema, into the heart of Bethesda, Maryland, outside Washington, DC. (Federal Realty Investment Trust)

Example Four: Retrofitting a "Dead Mall"

Over the past several decades, suburban malls and shopping centers have become candidates for redevelopment as mixed-use, walkable town centers. They usually have an advantageous location and often single ownership. The most widely recognized suburban retrofit opportunity is the dead mall. Example four is the proposed retrofit of a mid-twentieth-century regional mall, located in the Mountain West, into a walkable, mixed-use center for an affluent suburb of a major city (see Figure 3.7).

Example Five: Introducing an Urban Center to a Large Planned Community

Suburbs in the West tend to be newer and often represent the master-planned community formats popular since the 1970s. They have perfected the integration of the automobile, but their success in buffering uses one from another has sacrificed walkability. Example five is the proposed development of a district of walkable neighborhoods anchored by a

Figure 3.7. Retrofitting a dead mall—Belmar in Lakewood, Colorado. (Chris Whitis)

mixed-use center on the last significant developable land in a rapidly developing, auto-oriented suburb less than an hour from a major city on the West Coast (see Figure 3.8).

Building a Housing Market from Diverse Sources

Relying on a history of comparable projects to forecast the nature and extent of housing demand for the five examples is highly misleading because the projects respond to rapidly emerging and changing market demand. Understanding the housing market for each of these examples requires a "deep dive" into demographics, examining and integrating data from a variety of US Census and other sources.

Where Are the Potential Residents Coming From?

Table 3.1 shows the geographic distribution of the potential market (the "draw area") for each of these examples. Taxpayer-migration data provide the framework for determining each draw area, which typically contains a mix of urban intensities.

In example one, more than three-quarters of the potential market currently live in suburban or exurban locations; the remainder would be moving from small cities. In example two, nearly half the potential market comes from other suburbs and 46% from the urban neighborhoods of large and small cities. Similarly, in example three, more than half of the market would come from other metropolitan suburbs and the rest from urban

Figure 3.8. Introducing a walkable urban center into a large planned community—Reston, Virginia. (La Citta Vita under CC BY-SA 2.0)

Table 3.1. Current location of potential market (future residents)

Examples	One	Two	Three	Four	Five
Metropolitan cities (%)	0	13	21	45	42
Small cities/satellite cities (%)	22	33	23	18	12
Metropolitan suburbs (%)	42	48	56	37	39
Town and county/exurbs (%)	36	6	0	0	7

neighborhoods. In example four, 63% of potential buyers currently live in urban neighborhoods, and the remainder come from other metropolitan suburbs. There is no measurable market potential from town and rural areas. Similarly, in example five, a plurality of 42% of the draw comes from the urban center at the heart of the metro area, and nearly 40% comes from other metropolitan suburbs.

What "Life Stages" Do Potential Residents Represent?

Table 3.2 shows the life stages of the potential market for each example. "Life stage" denotes which stage of life the household falls into, from initial formation (typically when a young person moves out of his or her parents' household into his or her own dwelling unit), through family formation (typically, marriage and children), empty nesting (after the last adult child has left the household), and finally retirement (typically, no longer employed full time). There are three main life stages:

- **Younger singles and couples**—largely one- and two-person households with the head of household typically aged between 20 and 35, comprising mainly the millennial generation, who were born between 1977 and 1996
- **Families**—comprising both "traditional" structures (married couples with one or more children) and "nontraditional" structures (from a single parent with one or more children to an adult caring for younger siblings to a grandparent with custody of grandchildren to an unrelated, same-sex couple with children), primarily generation X, born between 1965 and 1976
- **Empty nesters and retirees**—largely one- and two-person households with the head of household typically 50 or older, primarily encompassing the baby boom generation, born between 1946 and 1964, as well as earlier generations.

Table 3.2. Life stages of potential market

Examples	One	Two	Three	Four	Five
Younger singles and couples (%)	63	68	84	57	42
Families (%)	14	14	7	17	46
Empty nesters and retirees (%)	23	18	9	26	12

Younger singles and couples are the majority of the potential market in four of the five examples, ranging from 84% of the market to 57%; in example five, this group is only four percentage points behind households in the families life stage. Empty nesters and retirees are the second-largest group in four of the examples, ranging from just 9% of the market to 26%; again, example five is different, with this stage constituting the smallest group. With the exception of example five, families account for less than 20% of the potential market. In example five, where families represent a 46% plurality of the potential market, family-oriented detached housing situated in nonwalkable subdivisions is by far the most prevalent housing type in this and surrounding suburbs. This clearly demonstrates the appeal to the family market of housing in walkable mixed-use neighborhoods.

Do the New Residents Prefer to Buy or Own?

Table 3.3 shows the tenure preferences of the potential market within each example. Housing tenure is almost always a critical consideration. It is important to provide options for both owners and renters, but in most cases the early introduction of rental housing is the most rapid way to establish or reestablish a successful, walkable suburban center.

Many communities, particularly affluent suburban municipalities, have a deeply rooted prejudice against rental housing, seeing renters as lower-income, more transient, and less invested in the community. However, these characteristics are not necessarily negative. Renters may be all of these things generally, yet these characteristics can actually assure the success of an emerging suburban center. All renters risk is a 12-month lease rather than a 30-year mortgage. Young renters—and the huge millennial generation still comprises mainly renters—can be the pioneers that establish suburban centers for less risk-tolerant buyers.

Rentals don't draw only younger households, however. Many older households are shifting from owning to renting, and not just those that trade a single-family house for senior housing because of declining health. Some empty nesters, often quite affluent

Table 3.3. Tenure preferences of potential market

Examples	One	Two	Three	Four	Five
Renters (%)	28	35	43	19	42
Buyers (%)	72	65	57	81	58

Table 3.4. Housing type preferences of potential ownership market

Examples	One	Two	Three	Four	Five
Condominium (%)	23	18	39	31	14
Townhouse (%)	13	27	16	25	21
Urban detached house (%)	64	55	45	44	65

households, simply prefer the flexibility of renting, where one monthly payment covers everything; the appeal of renting for older households is particularly pronounced in high-tax locations.

The market preference for rental housing ranges from 19 to 43%. Younger households make up 60% of potential renters in example five, 75% in example four, almost 80% in example one, more than 90% in example two, and 92% in example three. Although more affluent younger households also represent a segment of the ownership market, family and empty-nester/retiree households are significantly more likely to purchase new units within suburban redevelopments that include a mix of uses in a walkable setting (see Table 3.4).

What Types of Housing Do Potential Residents Want?

There are clear differences between the preferences of renters and those of buyers. Renters overwhelmingly prefer multifamily buildings. Renters by choice, both young and older, particularly appreciate the flexibility and true maintenance-free living afforded by professionally managed multifamily housing. Renters out of necessity—generally young people just starting out and low- and moderate-income households—have limited housing options, ranging from older apartment properties to marginally maintained attached and detached houses.

Owners are much more likely to prefer single-family or attached houses and seek more space than renters do when they buy condominiums. However, both renters and buyers share a clear preference for walkable neighborhoods, preferably with a mix of uses.

How Much Housing Will the Market Support?

Table 3.5 shows that, by capturing only 10 to 15% of the annual potential market, each of the examples could absorb sufficient numbers of units to create critical mass and support the development of a mix of uses.

Table 3.5. Five-year absorption forecasts

Example	One	Two	Three	Four	Five
Units Absorbed	1,500+	1,000+	1,000+	850+	2,500+

A Caveat about Autonomous Mobility

Individually owned autonomous vehicles (AVs) and shared autonomous vehicles (SAVs) will disrupt real estate markets. By 2030 the United States could see reduced demand for 61.4 billion square feet of real estate currently devoted to parking for 205 million cars. By 2040 much of this space will no longer be needed.[20] As noted in Chapter 2, Morgan Stanley and many others suggest a boom in SAVs will improve the convenience of urban life and accelerate demand for urban places. At the same time, sprawl apologists see autonomous vehicles reducing the pain of a lengthy commute, making cheap houses in remote exurbs viable once more as a Big Data–sponsored autonomous vehicle chauffeurs the relaxed new exurbanite to a sprawling "estate" where even the lawn maintenance is handled by an autonomous mower. Both trends could well play out, and they represent parallel realities that further distinguish not city from suburb but walkable from auto-dependent places.

Notes

1. Editors' note: Zimmerman/Volk has developed a unique, demographics-based methodology for projecting emerging and changing housing markets. The firm has successfully identified, analyzed, and quantified housing markets for new urban, mixed-use centers in both cities and suburbs.

2. Confirmation bias. "There are three kinds of lies: lies, damned lies, and statistics," runs the oft-quoted quip Mark Twain attributed to Benjamin Disraeli. From the third, most pernicious, form of falsehood much mischief arises. Studies drawing dubious conclusions from statistics have provided fodder for articles, Internet "click bait," vapid television news features, and countless silly graphics-supported speeches by politicians in venues ranging from local municipalities to C-SPAN. Studies—particularly those commissioned by entities with a specific advocacy position—often have bias built into the questions. Even more common is confirmation bias, which is the citation of selected findings that support a previously held position or opinion.

    Everyone has a confirmation bias. The trick is to guard against bias, particularly when presented with statistical evidence. One must examine the context, sample size, sample composition, error rates, and the myriad other elements that can compromise either a study or the interpretation of its findings. Take the hypothetical example of a reported 75% increase in millennial condominium purchases in suburban downtown X—a finding that might well be presented in a book like this. However, if the 75% represents merely an increase from 9 to 12 buyers out of a total of 200 sales, although the statistic is technically accurate, when presented as a percentage rather than actual numbers and outside the context of total sales, it falls firmly into the third category of lies.

3. Zimmerman/Volk Associates, Inc., proprietary target market analysis.

4. Elizabeth Kneebone and Alan Berube, *Confronting Suburban Poverty in America* (Washington, DC: Brookings Institution Press, 2013).

5. Officially December 2007 through June 2009.

6. US Census Bureau, "Selected Housing Characteristics: 2010 to 2014 American Community Survey 5-Year Estimates," accessed August 6, 2017, https://factfinder.census.gov /faces/tableservices/jsf/pages/productview.xhtml?src=bkmk.

7. US Bureau of Labor Statistics, "Families with Own Children: Employment Status of Parents by Age of Youngest Child and Family Type, 2013–2014 Annual Averages," 2015, accessed August 6, 2017, https://www.bls.gov/news.release/famee.t04.htm.

8. US Census Bureau, "Households by Type and Tenure of Householder for Selected Characteristics: 2016," accessed August 6, 2017, https://www.census.gov/data/tables/2016 /demo/families/cps-2016.html.

9. US Census Bureau, "Annual Estimates of the Resident Population by Sex, Single Year of Age, Race, and Hispanic Origin for the United States: April 1, 2010 to July 1, 2014," accessed August 6, 2017, https://factfinder.census.gov/faces/tableservices/jsf/pages/product view.xhtml?src=bkmk.

10. US Census Bureau, "Current Population Survey, March and Annual Social and Economic Supplements, 2015 and Earlier," accessed August 6, 2017, https://www2.census .gov/programs-surveys/cps/techdocs/cpsmar15.pdf.

11. J. A. Martin, B. E. Hamilton, M. J. K. Osterman, S. C. Curtin, and T. J. Mathews, "Births: Final Data for 2014," *National Vital Statistics Reports* 64 no. 12 (2015).

12. J. A. Martin, B. E. Hamilton, M. J. K. Osterman, S. C. Curtin, and T. J. Mathews, "Births: Final Data for 2013," *National Vital Statistics Reports* 12 no. 4 (2015).

13. R. A. Easterlin, "An Economic Framework for Fertility Analysis," *Studies in Family Planning* 6 no. 3 (1975): 54–63.

14. National Association of Realtors, "2015 NAR Profile of Home Buyers and Sellers," accessed August 6, 2017, https://www.nar.realtor/sites/default/files/reports/2015/2015 -home-buyer-and-seller-generational-trends-2015-03-11.pdf.

15. US Federal Reserve System. "Consumer Credit: January 2016," press release, http://www .federalreserve.gov/releases/g19/HIST/cc_hist_memo_levels.html.

16. American Student Assistance, "Life Delayed: The Impact of Student Debt on the Daily Lives of Young Americans," 2013, accessed August 6, 2017, http://aicum.org/wp-content /uploads/2013/08/ASA.pdf.

17. D. Farrell and F. Greig, *Paychecks, Paydays and the Online Platform Economy* (Washington, DC: JPMorgan Chase Institute, 2016).

18. KRC Research, *Zipcar Annual Millennial Survey: "Millennial" Is a State of Mind* (Boston: Zipcar, 2015).

19. US Census Bureau, "Annual Estimates of the Resident Population by Sex, Single Year of Age, Race, and Hispanic Origin for the United States: April 1, 2010 to July 1, 2014."

20. M. Bertoncello and D. Wee, "Ten Ways Autonomous Driving Could Redefine the Automotive World," released June 2016, accessed August 22, 2017, http://www.mckinsey.com/industries/automotive-and-assembly/our-insights/ten-ways-autonomous-driving-could-redefine-the-automotive-world.

Labor Force Participation Rate, 1947-2017, And Projected to 2022

* PROJECTION
SHADED REGIONS REPRESENT RECESSIONS AS DESIGNATED BY THE NATIONAL BUREAU OF ECONOMIC RESEARCH. TURNING POINTS ARE QUARTERLY.

Figure 4.1a ▲ and Figure 4.1b ▼

A wave of baby-boomer retirements has slowed workforce growth and contributed to a significant shortage of knowledge workers. Projections show the shortage growing into the 2030s and possibly beyond. (US Bureau of Labor Statistics)

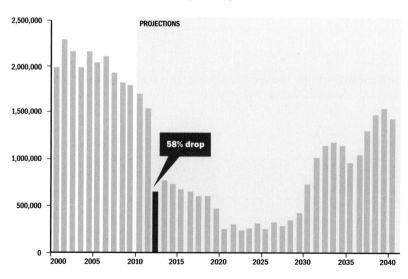

4

Office

Sarah Woodworth

Demographic, social, and technological changes in the United States alter the way businesses operate. These changes influence the location and type of office spaces that businesses demand. Communities have an opportunity to plan for these changes and, in so doing, broaden their economic base by becoming more attractive locations for business. Businesses drive employment; generate demand for housing, goods, and services; and contribute to the tax base.

Worker productivity correlates highly with how satisfied workers are with the environment in which they work. This is particularly true within the technology, advertising, media, and information (TAMI) industries where millennials make up a substantial portion of the workforce.

The work "environment" is not limited to the office space itself, but encompasses all the people, services, and amenities that create a place, enable communication, and contribute to quality of life. The combination of private and public environments creates value for a community and for a company.

Demographic and Technological Dynamics Facing
Today's Businesses

According to the US Bureau of Labor Statistics,[1] during the 1970s and 1980s the labor market was fueled by women entering the labor force, increasing college attainment, and baby boomers. The labor force participation rate for women peaked in 1999, college attainment has plateaued, and the baby boom generation is aging. Since 2000, the labor force participation rate has been on the decline (see Figure 4.1a, b).[2]

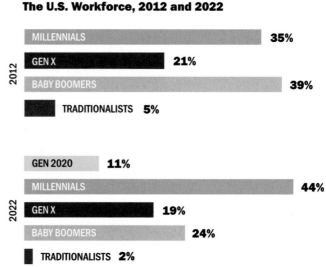

The U.S. Workforce, 2012 and 2022

Figure 4.2. By 2022 millennials will represent the largest segment of the US workforce—and their preferences for more urban work settings will play a growing role in determining where employers seek to locate. (Stantec graphic, based on data from US Census and Cushman & Wakefield)

As a result, by 2024, the Bureau of Labor Statistics projects that labor force participation will be significantly lower than it has been for decades (see Figure 4.2).[3] Employment is projected to grow by 1% per year and the labor force at half that rate. The implications? Employers will have to compete harder for employees and find ways to increase employee productivity.

To do this, office employers are adapting to the needs and lifestyles of their employees and/or outsourcing work. For many businesses, employees span multiple generations, including the traditionalists, the baby boomers, generation X, and generation Y—all of which have their own needs and preferences. Older workers think flexible time and office convenience is important. Younger workers demand that the office and its location satisfy their preferences, like transit access, walkability, and nearby amenities.

In addition to demographic changes, there has been a change in the types of industries demanding office space. According to research conducted by TIAA-CREF,[4] historically 75% of office demand was driven by the FIRE (finance, insurance, and real estate) together with professional and business service industries. Since the Great Recession, however the TAMI industries have accounted for a majority of office demand. Businesses in this cluster rely on young knowledge workers and, as such, select locations that satisfy this workforce's preferences.

The young knowledge worker is mobile, well educated, predominantly female, and more likely to be from an ethnically or racially diverse background. The stakes are high regarding these millennials. For a company, they represent future leadership. For a community, they represent the future citizens

The millennials' competencies and values are different from those of prior generations. This cohort is digitally savvy and expects employers to have seamless technological integration between devices and locations. Millennials value social diversity and environmental stewardship. According to research conducted by CEOs for Cities, they are much more likely than prior generations to land in a larger metropolitan area and live in the urban center or a close-in neighborhood. The research indicates that millennials are more likely to choose a location that suits their lifestyle and then find a job—rather than the other way around.[5]

While demographics and the economy are changing the profile of the office worker, the Internet and telecommunications technology have changed the way the office worker works. Telecommunications has untethered the employee from the desk: approximately 60% of employees conduct some work outside of the office. Mobile working has blurred the lines between working and private life.

Initially, so much work-location flexibility gave rise to concern that the value of office space would diminish precipitously. Instead, recent research indicates that the opposite is true. Sociometric Solutions, a Massachusetts Institute of Technology spin-off, uses employee behavioral data to provide insight into those factors that increase business productivity. While no surprise to Silicon Valley, the research concludes that there is a significant correlation between face-to-face interactions and productivity and innovation. Thus, while technology allows for employee autonomy, office employers must encourage face-to-face interaction among the workforce to maximize productivity and innovation.

To do this, employers are working hard to make the physical office a place that attracts workers. Spaces are designed around how people work, with plenty of space allocated to enabling interactions. Whereas interaction space used to represent 20% of office space, it now accounts for 60 to 80% of the space. In a 2015 white paper entitled "Amenities: A Hot Commodity," Colliers International notes that building owners and tenants today need to set aside 10 to 12% of their buildings for amenities like gyms, showers, weather-protected bike storage, and other features, versus the 3% of space such amenities claimed in the past.[6] A 2013 Cushman & Wakefield research report states that global average work space per worker stood at 225 square feet in 2010. Just over half of corporate real estate managers who answered a survey on office space predicted that this number would shrink to 100 square feet by 2018.

As office design has shifted to maximizing employee productivity, office location plays an important role in employee recruitment and retention. With the boundary between living, working, and playing dissolving, the assets of a community could not be more important. Generally, today's workforce values goods and services within walking distance of the office, transit access, and a high level of amenity. While there has been considerable press about how these dynamics are revitalizing 24-hour central business districts, suburban communities are also reaping the benefits of the renewed emphasis on quality-of-life factors.

The Suburban Opportunity

In spite of changing demographics and renewed interest in downtowns, the reality is that more than 75% of the office space in the United States is in suburbs.[7] Suburban office space is located in traditional town and village centers, along commercial corridors, in new town centers, and in older office parks. Between 2005 and 2013, among the top 48 US metropolitan area office markets, suburbs leased more office space (both absolutely and relatively) than central business districts. The characteristics of successful suburban office locations have changed, however, from single-use office parks to vibrant centers.

In recent research sponsored by NAIOP (a leading North American commercial real estate organization),[8] real estate brokers indicate that tenants rarely search for office space in *both* a metropolitan area's central business district and its suburbs. The tenants know which environment best suits their business needs and select a location based on that understanding. So the question is not downtown Washington versus suburban Washington, but one suburban Washington location versus another suburban Washington location.

The NAIOP research, conducted by Emil Malizia, used survey results to understand business-location preferences among metropolitan area central business districts (metro CBDs), suburban vibrant centers, and single-use suburban areas. The study defines a suburban vibrant center as a place that is compact, connected, walkable, relatively dense, mixed use, primarily employment oriented, and served by transit. A suburban vibrant center could be a downtown, a village center, or a new mixed-use project. Good examples of a vibrant center include Reston Town Center in the Washington metro market, Blue Back Square in the Hartford metro market, downtown Pasadena in the Los Angeles market, and Waltham in the Boston metro market.

As would be expected, given the trends outlined earlier, the research concludes that suburban office tenants preferred suburban vibrant centers to single-use suburban office locations. Of those surveyed, 83% preferred a mixed-use center to a single-use office park. The study concludes that "companies seeking suburban locations appear to favor amenity-rich places that include other commercial, residential and civic facilities."[9]

The NAIOP research also evaluated office market performance in metro CBDs, suburban vibrant centers, and typical single-use office locations. The study assessed performance by a variety of measures, including average asking rents, vacancy rates, and relative absorption rates for the 2005–2013 period. The suburban vibrant center outperformed the single-use office location in terms of rent (vibrant center average rent per square foot is $3.39 higher), vacancy (vibrant center average vacancy rate is 4.5 percentage points lower), and office absorption. The suburban vibrant center outperformed the single-use office location on almost all measures.

The NAIOP research also compared the performance of the metro CBD with the suburban vibrant center. The research indicates that "suburban vibrant centers performance is the same as or better than CBD performance."[10] These findings suggest that the trend toward mixed-use settings is not simply an opportunity for big, 24-hour cities; suburban mixed-use centers can capitalize on it as well.

Suburban vibrant centers have some advantages over the CBD office space. They tend to have a lower cost of occupancy and are more convenient to the driving workforce than a CBD. In larger metropolitan areas these centers often have transit. Suburban vibrant centers offer the benefits of mixed use without big-city issues like safety concerns, congestion, and high parking costs.

How to Be a Successful Suburban Center for Office Space

As the dynamics of the workforce and the workplace change, suburban communities must adapt to remain competitive locations for office space. The key factors for success are understanding the office tenant's objectives, encouraging a mix of office types, encouraging and sustaining a balanced mix of land uses, and developing robust infrastructure.

Understanding the Office Tenant's Objectives

According to a Cushman & Wakefield publication, *Supply-Side Risk in the New Age of Work*,[11] today's office tenants see their space as a tool for reaching five key goals: productivity, flexibility, cost control, employee recruitment, and sustainability. The community around an office can help businesses realize these goals.

Productivity

Leasing accounts for the largest expense after salaries in many organizations. A 2013 survey by Gensler, an architecture and design firm, found that more than 95% of companies surveyed believe that the design of the workplace has a direct impact on worker productivity.[12]

Although some buildings may be so architecturally "cool" that tenants tolerate inefficiencies, most suburban centers have office buildings that are simply old and outdated. To compete, property managers must renovate traditional buildings to better align with today's business needs. Building managers upgrade systems to support state-of-the-art technology, provide better air circulation, increase digital/power access, and upgrade lighting. Spaces are being reconfigured to allow for more flexibility of use. In suburban settings, property managers are investing in lifestyle amenities like walking trails, shuttles, cafés, and on-site daycare. To further the community's own economic development, municipalities need to support landlords in these renovation/revitalization efforts.

Part of the productivity equation is digital connectivity. Tenants seek locations and buildings that satisfy their broadband needs. Internet capacity and service availability vary among buildings and locations. The quality of Internet infrastructure has become so important that the New York Economic Development Corporation has contracted with WiredScore to rank-certify New York City buildings in terms of broadband availability. It is important for communities to create a robust and competitive telecommunications environment.

Flexibility

Tenants don't just focus on how space and the location will meet their current needs, but also on how adaptable space and location are should their needs change. Communities that encourage a range of office products offer tenants future options. Development regulations should be crafted to allow for office product diversity, including low-rise tech space and coworking space. In an effort to maintain a balanced office supply, Annapolis, Maryland, has defied redevelopment pressure and preserved an area of the downtown for light industrial use.

Cost Control

Related to productivity, businesses must control costs to be successful. While most of the cost-control issue lies in the private market, there are steps a community can take to help businesses manage costs. Encouraging a sustainable land use mix is one. There is no need for the tenant to provide a fitness center or café if these exist elsewhere in the neighborhood. Transit, rider-subsidy programs, and/or convenient low-cost public parking are assets communities can provide to support office tenants and landlords.

Employee Recruitment

More than ever, companies must market the lifestyle their location offers to prospective employees. A mix of land uses within walking distance, well-maintained parks, transit, walking and biking infrastructure, Internet connectivity, and a mix of housing types are all amenities the community can work to provide.

Sustainability

Many companies are making the transition to "greener offices" to achieve triple bottom line benefits. These benefits include environmental stewardship, worker satisfaction, and economic benefits. Locating the office in a mixed-use setting supports physical activity, as employees can walk or bike to shop, reside, or recreate. Green design minimizes harmful effects on human health and the environment. Eco-friendly construction practices, design that allows for plenty of natural light, and energy-efficient building systems are important to many businesses. These attributes make economic sense and result in a healthy, more productive work environment.

Encouraging a Mix of Office Types

Different types of businesses demand different types of space.

Traditional Office Space

Traditional office space has a central lobby, an elevator and stair core, shared bathrooms on each floor, and office space. Traditional office space is typically leased for a three- to five-year term. While the landlord often grants an allowance, the tenant pays to fit out the space. More and more traditional office buildings—which have long satisfied the needs of the FIRE and professional and business services industries—are being renovated to better align with contemporary working norms.

"Cool Space"

Cool space is office space in older buildings that is either architecturally distinct or located in a cool neighborhood. Cool space is unique and authentic. Cool space tenants are willing to pay a premium to occupy distinctive space that reflects the company's culture (see Figure 4.3). While some have suggested that the cool space movement simply reflects an interest in less-expensive space, there are plenty of examples of tenants paying top dollar for such space. Cool space is attractive to the TAMI industries.

Flex Tech Space

Flex tech space typically has high ceilings, lots of natural light, and private bathrooms and kitchen areas for the business. Essentially flex industrial space, this type of office space is

Figure 4.3. In most regions, demand for traditional office space remains stagnant, while demand for "cool space" to house startups, creative firms, technology, and other knowledge-based businesses is growing. (Raysonho under CC0 1.0)

highly flexible. Flex tech space allows tenants to expand and contract horizontally, which is much more efficient in terms of both cost and operations. New flex tech space is typically "green" and less expensive to operate than traditional office space. Except in the largest cities, tech space is typically in low- to midrise buildings.

Because these buildings are essentially shells, they are relatively inexpensive to develop, yet they can command rents comparable to traditional office buildings. For tech space, a much higher percentage of the rent covers space customization costs rather than building costs. These "branding" investments directly affect the tenant's business and are thus considered well worth the money.

On-Demand Office Space or Executive Suites

On-demand office space is more affordable and flexible than traditional office space. Tenants can lease on-demand space on a daily, monthly, or annual basis and expand and contract their space depending on their needs. The landlord provides the tenant with a fully furnished office space, high-speed Internet, a private mailbox and phone line, and shared services, such as a receptionist and/or secretarial services, conference rooms, and printing. Because the services are shared within the building, the cost of operating a business is typically lower than that of a conventional office. On-demand office space offers the tenant a professional image and flexibility with no up-front capital for tenant fit-out and lease flexibility.

Coworking Space

Coworking spaces are places people go to work in a space they share with other people doing work. The difference between coworking space and on-demand space is the emphasis on "community." Coworking facilities encourage interaction among members. When asked in a 2011 survey by *DeskMag* what coworkers loved about their coworking space, an overwhelming majority cited a friendly atmosphere and other coworkers that made coworking settings enjoyable (see Figure 4.4).[13]

Coworking spaces typically offer amenities such as desks, printers, Internet, meeting rooms, lounging areas, and kitchens with snacks. People pay by the hour, day, week, or month to become a "member." Typically, the space offers a variety of packages to allow for flexibility and affordability. Coworking space tends to represent the most affordable office lease option available.

Managers of coworking spaces target certain markets to facilitate community-building. The services and amenities offered in the space respond to the needs and values of the target markets, as does the location of the space. In the *DeskMag* survey, over 80% of coworkers rated food options nearby, such as snack bars and restaurants, as highly important.[14] Having a food store nearby also rated highly.

Figure 4.4. Coworking spaces serve as a good barometer of what knowledge workers value. In a 2011 survey by DeskMag, more than 80% of coworkers rated nearby food and restaurant choices as highly important. (Senseitells under CC BY 3.0)

Encouraging and Sustaining a Balanced Mix of Land Uses

Office workers and office tenants seek locations where work and lifestyle benefits create a harmonious mix (see Figure 4.5). Left only to market forces, the land use mix in a given location can easily skew toward uses that generate the highest investment return. Without a full complement of land uses, places become less livable and less attractive from a community-building perspective. Businesses and their employees demand community.

In Kendall Square (Cambridge, Massachusetts), one of the country's most prominent innovation districts, the city introduced new regulations and incentives to encourage residential and retail development to complement the highly lucrative lab space that had clustered in the district but made it a notoriously dull place, particularly at night. These initiatives are designed to make Kendall Square more livable and walkable. Although developers initially opposed them because housing and retail produced less rent than research space, major property owners and developers ultimately came to support these initiatives because they saw them as essential to maintaining Kendall Square's competitiveness in retaining and attracting knowledge workers.

Across the country, single-use office parks are being revitalized to offer the live, work, and play environment people and their companies demand. In Marlborough, a suburb of Boston, Atlantic Management, Inc., purchased a 110-acre Hewlett Packard office campus with the intention of creating a place where people can live, work, and play. Atlantic

Figure 4.5. Developer Crawford Hoying brought back "offices above the store" at its walkable new Bridge Park development in Dublin, Ohio, a suburb of Columbus. To appeal to start-ups and creative businesses, some buildings include one floor of office space sandwiched between ground-floor retail and upper-floor housing. (Crawford Hoying)

is refurbishing two office buildings, building apartments and a hotel, and plans to add 50,000 square feet of retail and restaurant space. Key to the success of this project was the city's approval of an overlay district that allows for mixed-use development.

Develop a Robust Infrastructure

Connectivity is important to a business's ability to function and recruit talent. For some businesses, a downtown location makes sense; for others, proximity to the airport or an easily driven commute for target employees is important. Locations that offer a variety of transportation choices like driving, biking, walking, and transit are typically more attractive to today's workforce and, as such, the businesses that employ them.

There is plenty of evidence that proximity to rail offers an advantage to offices. A JLL study of the suburban New Jersey office market[15] reveals that rail-served submarkets outperformed nonconnected suburban markets in both rental and occupancy rates.

Conclusion

Demographic, social, and technological changes are forcing the office market to adjust to new workplace demands. Businesses rely on their office space and office location to help recruit and retain talented employees. Employees are increasingly interested in balancing the live, work, and play dynamics of their lives. As such, the location of the office and its associated lifestyle amenities are becoming increasingly important job criteria for prospective employees. Suburbs can compete successfully as office locations, particularly when they offer vibrant mixed-use settings suitable for working, living, and recreating.

Notes

1. US Bureau of Labor Statistics, "Labor Force Projections to 2022: The Labor Force Participation Rate Continues to Fall," *Monthly Labor Review* (December 2013), accessed February 6, 2017, https://www.bls.gov/opub/mlr/2013/article/labor-force-projections -to-2022-the-labor-force-participation-rate-continues-to-fall.htm.

2. US Bureau of Labor Statistics, "Labor Force Statistics from the Current Population Survey," accessed April 23, 2017, https://data.bls.gov//timeseries/LNS11300000.

3. US Bureau of Labor Statistics, "Labor Force Projections to 2024: The Labor Is Growing, but Slowly," *Monthly Labor Review* (December 2015), accessed April 23, 2017, https:// www.bls.gov/opub/mlr/2015/article/labor-force-projections-to-2024.htm.

4. "Shopping for Suburban Office Investments," *TIAA-CREFF Asset Management* (September 2015), accessed October 5, 2017, https://www.tiaa.org/public/pdf/Shopping_for _Suburban_Office_Inv_+White+Paper.pdf.

5. CEOs for Cities, "The Young and the Restless in a Knowledge Economy," (December 2005), accessed August 8, 2017, http://planning.sanjoseca.gov/planning/gp_update/ meetings/6-23-08/The%20Young%20and%20the%20Restless.pdf. Economist Joe Cortright, author of the 2005 study for CEOs for Cities, issued an update in 2014 through his City Observatory website. It reached conclusions very similar to those in the original study, accessed August 10, 2017, http://cityobservatory.org/ynr/.

6. Colliers International, *Amenities: A Hot Commodity* (Colliers International, Summer 2015), accessed February 6, 2016, http://www.colliers.com/media/files/united%20 states/white papers/office amenities 2015.pdf.

7. Randyl Drummer, "Once Left for Dead, Suburban Office Making a Comeback," November 12, 2013, accessed August 29, 2017, http://www.costar.com/News/Article/ Once-Left-for-Dead-Suburban-Office-Making-a-Comeback/154320.

8. Emil Malizia, *Preferred Office Locations: Comparing Location Preferences and Performance of Office Space in CBDs, Suburban Vibrant Centers and Suburban Areas* (Herndon, VA: NAIOP Research Foundation, October 2014), 3.

9. Ibid., 3.

10. Ibid., 7.

11. Cushman & Wakefield/NorthMarq, "Supply-Side Risk in the New Age of Work," October 1, 2013, accessed August 8, 2017, https://compasspoints.cushwakenm .com/2013/10/01/supply-side-risk-in-the-new-age-of-work/.

12. Gensler, "What Factors Drive Workplace Performance? The 2013 U.S. Workplace Survey," accessed August 8, 2017, https://www.gensler.com/research-insight/research/ the-2013-us-workplace-survey-1.

13. Cecilia Amador, "Deskmag's Global Coworking Survey First Results," November 16, 2015, accessed August 8, 2017, https://allwork.space/2015/11/deskmags-global-co working-survey-first-results/.

14. Ibid.

15. JLL, *Transit Hub Perspective*, Spring 2016, no. 2, accessed February 6, 2017, http:// www.us.jll.com/united-states/en-us/Research/US-New-Jersey-Transit-Hub-Perspective -Spring2016-JLL.pdf.

Figure 5.1. Architect Victor Gruen, who pioneered the form at places like Southdale in Edina, Minnesota, saw shopping malls as twentieth-century downtowns, equally at home in city centers and suburban highway interchanges. (Bobak Ha'Eri under CC BY 3.0)

5

Retail

Michael J. Berne

The traditional downtown appears more popular now than it has been since at least the 1950s, not only in central cities—where an urban renaissance has helped to improve the prospects of the historic commercial core and, increasingly, neighborhood business districts—but also, a bit less expectedly, in the suburbs, where residents and workers crave a similar sort of environment and experience—albeit on a more modest scale.

Why and how did this happen? To illuminate the forces that drive this phenomenon, this chapter traces and analyzes the evolution of the American retail landscape and consumer culture since the 1950s, beginning its discussion of the suburban context with a review of the urban one from which today's renewed interest in downtowns presumably springs.

The Dominant, Then Declining Downtown

From the mid-1800s to the mid-1900s, the center of retail gravity for every city was downtown. At the hub of an extensive streetcar network, it was a city's premier (if not only) shopping and entertainment destination. Everybody went there, and it was part of the city's collective understanding of itself, with stores that most everyone shopped in and traditions that most everyone participated in.[1]

Downtown's role and relevance as a retail location, however, was eclipsed in the postwar era by the rise of the shopping center. Of the shopping-center formats that dominated retailing from the 1950s to the 1980s, the regional mall most directly competed with the traditional downtown, whose retail function it was deliberately designed to mimic, while eliminating the attendant dangers and inconveniences: it offered a similar mix of goods and services but in a pedestrian-only, climate-controlled, highly amenitized environment free of the noise, grime, congestion, and chaos that plagued the central business district.

In the hands of visionary architects like Victor Gruen, the regional mall aspired to capture more of downtown's role, serving as the community gathering place that suburbs otherwise lacked and many suburbanites desperately sought. And whether as the intended result of such socially minded design or simply as the desired outcome of efforts to extend "dwell time" and maximize retail sales, it evolved into the beating heart—or in contemporary parlance, the "third place"[2]—of postwar America (see Figure 5.1).

Because these centers represented a relatively new and unproven investment, lenders—risk-averse insurance companies and pension funds—required developers to lease as much as 85% of the retail space to creditworthy national chains, and most tenant mixes were designed with a mass-market consumer (white, middle-class, 25- to 50-year-old female) in mind.

The Derivative Downtown

By the 1970s, retail developers had started to search for new models that could work in settings where land costs were escalating. One innovation was the vertical mixed-use project, in which a regional mall would sit on the lower levels of a larger development that might also include offices, hotels, and housing. Pioneered at the suburban Houston Galleria (1970 and 1976) (see Figure 5.2), it was transported to the tightly developed, high-value core in the form of Chicago's 74-story Water Tower Place (1976).

Downtown emerged as the new frontier for regional malls in the 1980s, as the industry matured and competition for the best suburban sites intensified. Developers believed that such projects would attract suburban shoppers, and some were in fact surprisingly successful at luring highly coveted, "first-to-market" brands. Cleveland's Avenue at Tower City Center (1990), for example, opened its doors with luxury names like Barneys New York, Fendi, Gucci, and Versace.

Vertical urban malls in affluent, built-out catchments (where potential competitors faced high barriers to entry) remained solid performers. In some cases, though, urban malls were tagged as failures not on the basis of objective metrics, but rather, as a result of the observer's own ethnic and class biases. Indeed, centers catering primarily to racially diverse, working-class shoppers could be among the highest grossing in the country.[3]

The Distinctive Downtown: Part I

The mass-market tastes that had dominated retailing in the postwar era showed the first signs of splintering into smaller niche submarkets in the turbulent 1960s and 1970s, with the reemergence of the specialty store. When it opened on a San Francisco street corner

Figure 5.2. Ice skating at the Houston Galleria. In the 1970s the Galleria, Chicago's Water Tower Place, and other developments sought to use malls to revive cities—in most cases without success. (Postoak at English Wikipedia under CC BY-SA 3.0)

Figure 5.3. Kansas City's Power & Light District, a contemporary take on festival marketplaces, uses many of the same elements—food, a sensory-rich environment, entertainment, and opportunities to meet people—that help urban places succeed in suburbs. (Visit KC)

in 1969, The Gap—referring to the generation gap—aimed to reach bell-bottomed, long-haired baby boomers who were rejecting the suburban conformism of their parents.

In time, new kinds of shopping centers were devised to appeal to specific slivers of the consumer marketplace. The format known as the festival marketplace, which first exploded into the public consciousness with Boston's wildly popular Faneuil Hall Marketplace (1976),[4] offered an entirely new model for enticing suburbanites to return to the neglected urban core, one that did *not* attempt to replicate or re-create the regional mall (see Figure 5.3).

These marketplaces led with food, festivity, and sensuality. They offered an alternative form of leisure-driven consumerism (versus "shop 'til you drop") that could potentially overcome forces seemingly dooming the central city, including outdated buildings, limited parking, and a perception of danger.

Versions of the format that followed in other cities proved less successful, and even the ones that endured were overrun with workers and tourists, evolving into food courts and trinket shops and, ultimately, repelling urban sophisticates. However, as the first sign of life in areas that had been left for dead and as a foreshadowing of the attributes that would drive today's urban renaissance, the format represented a turning point.

At the same time as this new model was proliferating, so-called yuppies were leading a "back-to-the-cities" movement. These urban newcomers would ultimately become ambassadors for the new lifestyle, and as members of the cultural elite, their tastes would later start to spread more broadly.

The Dormitory Downtown, the Delicious Downtown, and the Distinctive Downtown: Part II

If the 1970s was the decade in which Americans first started to refamiliarize themselves with the cities, the 1990s was the one in which the growing popularity of the urban lifestyle reached the proverbial "tipping point."

Changing demographics and reduced crime receive much of the credit, but another grossly undervalued factor in reviving the urban brand was *popular culture* itself. Take, for example, TV sitcoms: in the 1980s, the most popular ones typically centered on nuclear families living in single-family homes located in anonymous suburbs (e.g., *Family Ties*, *Growing Pains*),[5] but the biggest hits of the 1990s usually focused on unmarried singles residing in apartments and enjoying city life (e.g., *Seinfeld* and *Friends*)—often in that most urban of cities, New York City.

The city in these shows served not only as setting but also as aspiration. The haircut known as "The Rachel" might have become a cultural touchstone of the 1990s, but it was Jennifer Aniston's spacious loft apartment and café-centered lifestyle in *Friends* that had longer-lasting implications for urban America, likely inspiring countless suburban middle-class teenagers to seek out their own version of *Central Perk* once they left for or graduated from college.

Indeed, the 1990s saw the rise of "third place" theory, namely, the notion, popularized by sociologist Ray Oldenberg,[6] that every subculture needs and has some sort of hangout, separate from home and work, where its members gather, socialize, and feel a sense of belonging. Coinciding with the rapid spread of Starbucks Coffee across many US and Canadian cities, this phenomenon was at the time understood largely as a defining feature of the urban (not suburban) lifestyle. For the first time in decades, cities were defining community, and on their own terms.

Another driving force behind the urban renaissance was the rise of so-called foodie culture, which gathered steam in the later 1990s and early 2000s as a growing number of Americans came to fetishize food as the new art form and to elevate chefs to celebrity status. This phenomenon dovetailed with reemergent cities in that food and fun—as the festival-marketplace format had demonstrated—rank among the only retail categories for which consumers are willing to travel outside their comfort zones.

The unique ability of dining and nightlife to inject renewed vitality into previously moribund urban areas would offer an intriguing counterpoint to the oft-repeated industry assertion that "retail follows rooftops." Indeed, as the pioneers essential to putting the "there, there," which in turn lured new residents to struggling inner-city settings, the script had to be flipped.

With their historic fabric and lived-in feel, cities were also well positioned to take advantage of changing tastes and sensibilities related to the built environment. For a growing number of Americans, a gleaming, chain-filled regional mall (and similar suburban retail forms that followed) increasingly came across as too polished, stylized, and corporatized. Beginning with the festival marketplaces of the late 1970s and 1980s, they would start to crave something with more detail and texture, even some rough edges—in other words, the anti-mall.[7]

This preference is grounded in a deeper longing for spaces and businesses that operate on a smaller and more relatable scale. Indeed, the current demand for the artisanal and handcrafted can be read as a desire for retrenchment from the sheer bigness that has come to dominate so many US industries and as a backlash against highly efficient yet impersonal corporations that feel far beyond the reach of any one consumer.

That this anti-mall/anti-chain sensibility should first take hold in urban areas is to some extent a reflection of the demographics driving their resurgence. Most shopping centers and retailers seek the most efficient means of getting consumers to part with their money. Yet for baby boomers raised on the ideals of the 1960s ("yupsters") and millennials grounding their buying habits in a heightened social consciousness ("neo-hipsters"),[8] such naked pursuit and blatant manipulation rub the wrong way.

These various attributes—fondness for the historic and lived-in, celebration of the small-scale artisan, wariness of slick marketing and smooth surfaces—coalesce into what such urbanites like to call authenticity. That term is problematic on several levels, but the retail formats that it has spawned have proven hugely popular and served to reintroduce the positive aspects of the urban experience to those who had forgotten or never known them.

Indeed, while one would expect to find such destinations in New York City and San Francisco, they have also emerged as the latest "it" projects and districts in less likely metros such as San Antonio (Pearl Brewery) and Oklahoma City (Midtown), suggesting that, once a certain population threshold has been reached, the latent market for "authenticity" becomes large enough to support something along these lines.

These destinations channel the ethos of the earlier festival-marketplace while updating it with a younger, neo-hipster flair and a higher level (or more overt form) of social consciousness. But do they necessarily translate to the suburbs?

The Changing Suburbs

The renaissance of urban areas follows from multiple trends that have been growing and converging since the 1970s. Less predictably, however, a similar sort of evolution is occurring in suburbs as well, where communities have begun to crave a somewhat more urbanized feel and purpose for their "Main Streets."

As the current market share of craft brewing shows, a desire for smaller-scale enterprise has clearly spread beyond the central core. At the same time, however, these residents are also responding to other dynamics that, while not specific to the suburban lifestyle, certainly have a greater impact on it.

The regional mall had reached a crossroads, for example. At the dawn of the 1980s, the maturing industry confronted limits to its geographic spread for the first time. This was also the decade when competitive pressures on the department store, which had been building since the 1960s, came to a head with a series of ill-fated leveraged buyouts that relied on unsustainable levels of corporate debt and subjected many storied names to bankruptcy and consolidation.

The growing number of working women also meant that shopping was in the process of becoming less a form of leisure and more a purpose-driven activity, something else that simply needed to get done. The regional mall, expressly designed for the former, was particularly ill suited to provide for the latter and therefore quite vulnerable as consumer culture turned decisively toward quick "in-and-out" convenience in the 1990s.

Separately, American consumers had been developing a taste for value-oriented big- and medium-box stores since the 1960s, with the initial growth of the discount department store (e.g., Wal-Mart, Kmart, Target); followed in the 1970s by the emergence of the off-price channel (e.g., Marshalls, T.J.Maxx); then, in the 1980s, the expansion of the warehouse-club format (e.g., Price Club, Costco Wholesale) and the introduction of the "category killer"[9] (e.g., Toys"R"Us, Home Depot).

The 1990s, though, witnessed something new: the agglomeration of all of these different kinds of retailers in one place.[10] The spread of the power center throughout the 1990s hastened the decline of the regional mall. And inasmuch as the latter had effectively been serving as the third place for many suburban communities, its weakening position—combined with the former's strict utilitarianism—created something of a sociocultural vacuum that more urbanized downtowns were theoretically capable of filling.

This did not happen immediately, however. Developers first introduced the so-called lifestyle center in the late 1990s.[11] An unanchored strip lined with the sorts of up-market, comparison-goods brands that had historically occupied in-line spaces of upscale regional malls, it, too, catered to the purpose-driven suburban lifestyle that prioritized in-and-out convenience, with attributes like visible store entrances and in-front parking.

Yet while developers often marketed the lifestyle center as an amenitized and walkable Main Street experience, it fell short as a new third place for the suburbs, with the added

Figure 5.4. Americana at Brand, in suburban Los Angeles, demonstrates the trend toward developing mixed-use, walkable town centers in suburban settings. (Chris Yarzab under CC BY 2.0)

bits of greenery and attempts at architectural embellishment barely able to disguise the underlying strip-mall skeleton of set-back storefronts facing a large surface parking lot.

The next iteration of the lifestyle center, the town center, offered something a bit closer. It featured the same sorts of large national brands, but centered on a built-from-scratch, two-sided Main Street. It also added nonretail uses, like office space, residential units, and civic/community facilities.

Designed to look and feel historic, the town-center format—as exists, for example, at City Place (West Palm Beach, Florida), The Americana at Brand (Glendale, California), and Perkins Rowe (Baton Rouge, Louisiana)—represented an attempt to co-opt the atmospherics and nostalgia of Main Street while still accommodating the prototypes of large chains as well as the proven philosophy behind shopping center development (see Figure 5.4).

While such "faux" or "Disneyfied" Main Street environments meet with skepticism if not outright derision from many city dwellers, their popularity suggests that, for large numbers of suburban consumers, they are *close enough* to the real thing, offering a sort of "sanitized urbanity."

The most recent force upending suburban retailing is e-commerce. With its powerful combination of convenience and value, the online channel first took aim at utilitarian formats like power centers. But with Amazon quickly rising to become the nation's top seller of apparel in 2017, many regional malls have also found themselves vulnerable, with lifestyle and town centers perhaps soon to follow.

However, emerging walkable urban places are positioned to deal with the latest competitive threat. The spread of the shopping center had long ago forced people to search for and ultimately start to adapt to a new paradigm, one fueled by categories—dining and entertainment, for instance—that can only be patronized in person. Such draws have, in turn, helped create a "there, there," which has attracted new residents, workers, and visitors.

Today's suburbs are also far more *psychographically* diverse. Take, for example, many of those urban pioneers from the 1990s and 2000s who later suburbanized in order to raise families and brought their cosmopolitan sensibilities with them, resulting in what might be called the Brooklyn-ification of the beltway.

The Resurgent Suburban Downtown

In light of the formidable competition posed by the shopping-center formats, is there any room in suburban communities for large-scale, walkable urban places, with their multiplicity of property owners and stakeholders? If so, does the model look much like the one that has been emerging in the cities? Or is it a hybrid, reflecting some urban values, sensibilities, and preferences yet specific to its suburban milieu in other respects (see Figure 5.5)?

Although anomalies can be found across North America, suburban downtowns with vibrant and compelling retail mixes typically display most of these attributes: urban-ist, broader trade area, destination-driven, enough nearby parking, niche positioning, destination and niche-driven retail mix, and nonconventional anchors.

Urban-ist

While urbanites might highly value the detail, texture, and patina of the built environment, their suburban counterparts tend to give it comparatively less weight. For the latter, the only essential feature is that the setting be *open-air* (versus enclosed),[12] and that the primary commercial corridor be *double-loaded*, with retail on both sides, and *zero-setback*, with storefronts meeting the sidewalk.

Many newer downtowns west of the Rockies, for example, contain few buildings built before 1950 (if any at all), yet they retain the basic skeleton of a traditional Main Street. And while the aforementioned town-center format unapologetically embraces derivative architecture, its supposed lack of "authenticity" is almost never fatal.

Indeed, today's suburban downtowns tend to keep to a sort of "sanitized urbanism," free of the grime, vagrancy, and criminality that still often color perceptions of city life. Unlike younger neo-hipsters, many Americans aged 40 and older—including even baby

Diversity

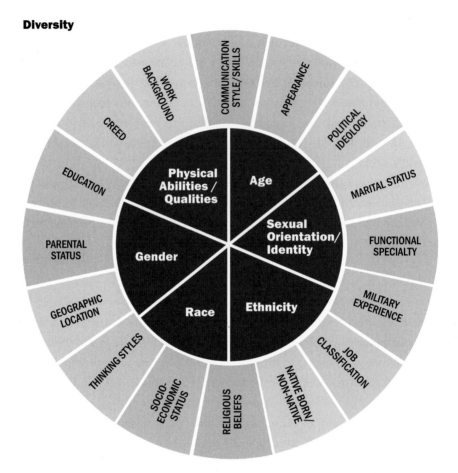

Figure 5.5. Walkable urban places need to draw on increasingly diverse consumer markets—representing a growing range of lifestyles, incomes, ages, and values. (Stantec graphic, adapted from Marilyn Loden's diversity wheel model)

boomers who live in the central core—have very little tolerance for such inconveniences and dangers, and will reflexively start to avoid settings that show initial signs of them.

Broader Trade Area

Vertical mixed-use development, with housing and/or offices on the upper levels, is generally viewed as a critical component for suburban downtowns. However, the additional consumer demand generated by new residential and commercial projects within the core itself tends to be overvalued, falling well short of the amount needed to effect meaningful change in the retail dynamic and mix.

Indeed, while new mixed-use projects in the heart of the suburban downtown might draw the most attention (and new ones should be encouraged), the bulk of the consumer demand often still lies in—and the assortment of retailers remains largely driven by—the residents living in "close-in" neighborhoods and, in some cases, destination-oriented traffic generated from even farther afield. In fact, this broader trade area might even encompass adjacent municipalities or parts thereof.

Destination-Driven

Businesses selling basic commodities—drug stores, dry cleaners, or pet supplies, for instance—require either a sufficient number of "captive" consumers within walking distance, or, in lieu of that, availability of nearby (within the block), easy in-and-out parking to accommodate those who must drive.

For example, a small, 10,000-square-foot greengrocer without adjacent parking would need either a minimum of 4,000 people living within a quarter-mile—or a hefty subsidy from its landlord—in order to survive. Most suburban downtowns do not even approach that threshold, nor can they offer the spacious in-front lots provided by the larger supermarkets and other convenience-oriented anchors along arterial thoroughfares.

Except in cases where property owners are motivated to work with these businesses or local residents are willing to consider upzoning, suburban downtowns will find themselves challenged to attract and retain purveyors of such goods and services. They are more likely to succeed with *destination-oriented* retail for which consumers will be willing to drive longer distances and tolerate some level of parking-related inconvenience.

Enough Nearby Parking

Parking is almost always a hot-button issue in the suburbs, even when, from the perspective of an urbanite, it seems plentiful and painless. The amount of grumbling on the subject makes more sense, however, in light of the large, in-front and free parking lots provided at most shopping centers, which create a set of expectations that downtowns simply cannot meet.

That said, there are some important nuances to consider. For example, a destination-oriented retail mix does not depend to the same extent on convenient or free parking. Rather, it merely requires an *adequate supply of spaces within walking distance*—especially as millennials, who are generally less sensitive on the matter, start to age into suburbia.

Furthermore, supply is rarely the problem in suburban downtowns. Indeed, if effectively managed, market-driven approaches—which charge varying rates as based on demand—can improve outcomes, particularly the frequency of on-street turnover and the utilization of peripheral spaces, without the need to build costly garages.

Niche Positioning

For most people living in the suburbs or the exurbs, downtown retail has *not been* essential to their lifestyles for some time. Once the only, the primary, or the default option for consumers from across the entire metro, today's downtowns must now assume the burden of proving why they even belong in the conversation at all.

The suburban downtowns that have managed to retain or regain their relevance tend to be ones that have differentiated themselves by identifying and exploiting a particular niche in the broader competitive ecology that has yet to be filled or that is not served well. In so doing, they have given at least *some* consumers a reason to pay attention.

Today's suburban downtown, then, reinserts and keeps itself in the conversation not by striving to be "all things to all people," but rather, *something* to *some* people. (This implies, of course, that in its recast identity, it might be *nothing* to *many* people, including those who lived through its glory days—*and* who might still have influence in civic and political affairs).

Examples of niches that downtowns have successfully cultivated in recent decades include the students, faculty, and visitors associated with Yale University in New Haven, Connecticut; yupsters and neo-hipsters in the Atlanta suburb of Decatur, Georgia; and first- and second-generation Korean Americans on Broad Avenue (also known as Koreatown) in the New York City suburb of Palisades Park, New Jersey.[13]

In some of these cases, the niche submarket is heavily concentrated in and around the suburban downtown, but it does not necessarily have to be. By definition, a niche-oriented retail mix cannot be found everywhere. It can therefore draw from further afield, beyond more conventionally tenanted competitors. In theory, then, this broader reach can overcome the limited presence of the target customer in close-in neighborhoods.

One last point on niches: they can even help to fortify traditional downtowns against the e-commerce threat. By catering to the specific needs, preferences, and sensibilities of a given submarket, such a retail mix can impart a sense of belonging, creating a powerful lure capable even of overcoming the online channel's enticements of convenience and value. Consider, as an example, the revival of independent book and music stores in recent years, amidst the devastation caused by the online channel in those categories.

Destination and Niche-Driven Retail Mix

With their proven ability to catalyze a renewed sense of energy and momentum in long-neglected districts, the categories of food, beverage, and entertainment have often been the ones that jump-start the revival of suburban downtowns. Mirroring industry-wide leasing trends, they account for most of the new businesses in such settings, and an ever-growing percentage of the overall tenant mixes.

The role of comparison-goods shopping, on the other hand, is much reduced, often limited to a small number of longtime merchants with loyal followings or paid-off mortgages. There is still a place, however, for concepts with a narrow yet very sharp focus on the niche submarkets that gravitate to their respective downtowns. Examples include vintage clothiers, skate shops, western-wear purveyors, or community-minded bookstores.

Indeed, even certain kinds of convenience-oriented businesses—ones that cater specifically to niche tastes and preferences (as opposed to selling interchangeable commodities)—can be sustained if the submarkets they target lack any or many alternatives elsewhere across the metro. This might be the case with, say, an ethnic food market or a hipster barber shop.

Finally, except for affluent yet built-out markets with limited retail inventory, suburban downtowns usually do not attract much interest from large national brands. More often, the retail mix combines smaller regional or local "chain-lets" with one-off or entrepreneurial businesses, then *maybe* a few select nationals that want to cater to or associate themselves with a particular niche submarket. That said, the disdain for or wariness of large national brands that one often encounters in resurgent urban areas is generally less pronounced among suburban and exurban consumers, for whom broader sociocultural issues and concerns tend to figure less prominently in buying decisions. Indeed, most town-center projects are dominated by ubiquitous chains.

Nonconventional Anchors

Without the department store to generate large numbers of potential shoppers, the suburban downtown has had to look elsewhere for possible anchors. And while the multiplex can still serve this purpose in the evenings, the magnets of today are more often ones that do *not* take the form of individual businesses. They might, for example, consist of an assemblage of sit-down restaurants—a "restaurant row" of sorts. Or retail might not even be the anchor at all. For some downtowns, the setting itself—on a waterfront, for instance—draws the pedestrian traffic, which then feeds the businesses. "Placemaking" initiatives can also serve this purpose, if on a sufficiently large scale.

It is critical to keep in mind that, unlike department stores, nonretail anchors are not necessarily attracting pedestrians who are going to shop. This puts a premium on their placement, so as to encourage patterns of circulation that maximize impulse buying, and also calls for the kinds of tenants that are most likely to appeal to such foot traffic.

In sum, this discussion at least provides a template that can work, a new niche-driven paradigm to replace the mass-market orientation and positioning that have not been appropriate for decades. For the first time in a long while, there is a path forward.

Notes

1.   With the notable exception of African Americans, who were often limited by the realities of segregation.

2.   According to a 1973 *U.S. News & World Report* article, Americans of all ages spent more time in shopping centers than anywhere but home and work (or school)—as quoted in *America's Marketplace: The History of Shopping Centers*, a 2002 book from the International Council of Shopping Centers written by Nancy Cohen and published by Greenwich Publishing Group.

3. The author explored this phenomenon in a February 2002 article for *Urban Land* magazine entitled "Working Class Malls." The article cited properties like Queens Center, which has long ranked among the 10 highest-grossing malls in the United States on a sales-per-square-foot basis, even though its customer base, like the borough in which it sits, is overwhelmingly nonwhite and moderate income.

4. While San Francisco's Ghirardelli Square actually opened much earlier, in 1964, and has been credited as one of the country's first instances of adaptive reuse, Faneuil Hall Marketplace catalyzed the larger festival marketplace trend, with its instant success spurring widespread interest from other cities, resulting in such projects as Baltimore's Harborplace, New York City's South Street Seaport, Washington, DC's Union Station, and many others. The format can also be said to encompass other revitalization schemes that were not explicitly associated with the format yet followed a similar formula, like Denver's Larimer Square and Seattle's Pike Place Market.

5. Although the nuclear family in the decade's most popular sitcom, *The Cosby Show*, lived in brownstone Brooklyn, the urban setting was otherwise largely ignored.

6. Oldenburg introduced his theory in his 1989 book, *A Great Good Place: Cafes, Coffee Shops, Bookstores, Bars, Hair Salons, and Other Hangouts at the Heart of a Community*, published by Da Capo Press.

7. One of the most astute observers of these trends was based, ironically enough, in heavily suburbanized Orange County, California: Sadeen Sadeghi was a former surf-wear executive who, in the early 1990s, transformed an old night-googles factory on a nondescript arterial road in the shadow of the famed South Coast Plaza into The Lab Anti-Mall.

8. Yupsters and neo-hipsters are two of the psychographic segments that feature in MJB Consulting's proprietary lifestyle-segmentation scheme. A tool of analysis that has grown in popularity amidst the continued splintering of the mass market, psychographics assesses both the quantitative data on a given trade area, such as its median household incomes and home values, and qualitative characteristics, such as its prevailing lifestyles, sensibilities, and aspirations, in order to arrive at a more complete and meaningful understanding of its consumer profile.

9. The "category killer" specializes in a particular category of goods and, with deep selection and discounted prices, is able to dominate (or "kill") its competitors.

10. The project credited as the first power center, 280 Metro Center (San Francisco Bay Area), actually opened in 1986, but the format did not spread across the US retail landscape until the 1990s.

11. The first lifestyle center, The Shops at Saddle Creek, opened in 1987 in suburban Memphis, though the format did not proliferate until the late 1990s.

12. In many regions of the United States, where the weather can prove challenging at certain times of the year, the embrace of open-air retailing might seem counterintuitive. Indeed, climate control has been an important part of the regional-mall formula since it was introduced in the 1950s. Interestingly, however, local climate seems to have little impact on willingness to patronize Main Street settings. Although hot and humid conditions in the Sun Belt can prove challenging in the summer, that's not generally a critical season for retailers. Meanwhile, those who live in colder (even snowy) regions paradoxically seem to relish their time outdoors in the winter, and they might be even more eager to take advantage of milder weather when it does return.

13.   When the regional mall first started to spread in the 1950s, the suburbs consisted almost exclusively of white, middle-class, nuclear families who lived in newly built, single-family homes and exhibited remarkably similar tastes and preferences as consumers. Many of these communities, however, have become far more ethnically and socioeconomically diverse in recent decades.

   In contrast to the *Leave It to Beaver* era of the 1950s, there are today the Korean Americans of Palisades Park, as well as the middle-class African Americans of Prince George's County (outside Washington), the first-generation immigrants of Gwinnett County (Atlanta), and the blue-collar "Reagan Democrats" of Macomb County (Detroit)—to name just a few.

Figure III.1. North American case study communities. The places shown on this map appear in Part III. (Ma Shuyun, Xumengqi, and Anushree Nallapaneni)

PART III CASE STUDIES FOR WALKABLE URBAN PLACES

Part III shifts from the forces shaping suburbia and its real estate markets to case studies that describe how suburban communities have already begun creating the next generation of walkable urban places. The case studies tell a story of suburban transformation, full of obstacles and challenges, from a policy, process, and design perspective. The choice to pursue a higher-density, walkable urban agenda cut against the grain of deeply held values for these communities. Yet each moved ahead, spurred by a mix of reasons that included economic competitiveness, environmental responsibility, market pressures, and—to a very real extent—the desire to create a vital new heart.

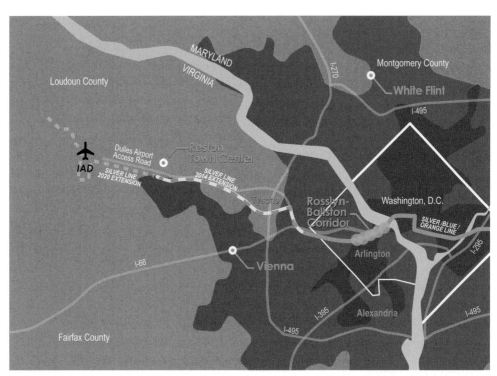

Figure 6.1. Thanks largely to the work of smart growth advocates, the Washington Metro Area contains the second highest concentration of walkable urban places in the US. (Ma Shuyun, Xumengqi, and Anushree Nallapaneni)

6

Blueprint for a Better Region: Washington, DC

Stewart Schwartz

The Washington, DC, region, home to the US capital and divided among two states and the District of Columbia, is a challenging multijurisdictional environment. Perhaps that's why the region never managed to embark on a grand public dialogue on the order of the well-known Envision Utah in Salt Lake City; Portland, Oregon's Metro 2040; or Sacramento's Blueprint.

Nevertheless, it has been engaged in a multiyear dialogue, resulting in profound shifts in land use policy and new investments in transit. These changes prepared the region to take advantage of the demographic and market shifts that have driven demand for walkable urban places, and will enhance its future economic competitiveness, even in the face of reduced government spending.

The experience of the Washington region (see Figure 6.1) illustrates the dynamic between regional dialogue and the local action essential for transforming the city and suburbs. It illustrates the central role that nonprofit advocacy groups can play in shaping change, the importance of local elected leadership, and the power of partnerships. It shows that although regional intergovernmental bodies may lack real power, they offer a venue for sharing knowledge and crafting a regional vision. Finally, it shows the value of strong partnerships among nonprofit advocacy groups and developers, architects, planners, and transportation consultants, who have collectively made the case for walkable urbanism to the general public and elected officials.

This is the story of how the Washington region adopted a sustainable regional vision built around transforming the suburbs with urban, transit-oriented centers—the dramatic results and the challenges going forward.

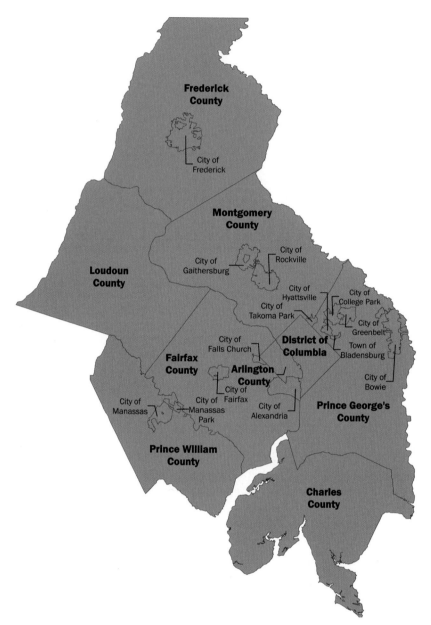

Figure 6.2. The Metropolitan Washington Council of Governments comprises the District of Columbia, eight counties, the City of Alexandria, 12 smaller cities, and one town. (Metropolitan Washington Council of Governments)

Context

The regional Council of Governments (COG) comprises 23 local governments along with state representatives (see Figure 6.2). Decision making can become complicated with differing interests among DC, Maryland, and Virginia, and the federal government; between local governments and their states; and between inner and outer suburbs.

COG hosts the Transportation Planning Board, which is responsible for the regional financial Constrained Long-Range Plan, and the Metropolitan Washington Air Quality Committee responsible for compliance with the Clean Air Act. COG also hosts committees on housing and land use, among others, but area elected officials have resisted granting COG any authority to direct land use at the local level. Separately, the Washington Metropolitan Area Transit Authority (WMATA), established by a long-standing legal compact between the federal government and states, governs Metrorail and Metrobus.

Beginning with the New Deal and World War II, the region has experienced periods of significant growth. Tens of thousands of garden apartments to house federal civilian and military workers were built in first-ring suburbs on what was often still farmland. Growth boomed again with the War on Poverty and the Vietnam War, the defense buildup of the 1980s, and again during the long wars in Afghanistan and Iraq in the 2000s, and it has continued as knowledge industries have grown.

As was typical, most of DC's suburbs are characterized by separated land uses, low densities, looping roads, and culs-de-sac. This has overburdened the region's arterial roads, which carry the vast majority of the traffic. However, the DC region's new suburban experiment had a head start because of the region's economic strength, the 117-mile Metro system, early local models of walkable urbanism, the role of nonprofits and strong local leaders, and nonprofit partnerships with a strong cadre of urban developers and consultants.

First out of the gate was Arlington County, Virginia (see Chapter 12), which, in the early 1970s, launched one of the country's earliest smart growth planning initiatives in anticipation of METRO service (see Figure 6.3). Yet, although Arlington (and soon Montgomery County in Maryland) launched an early transit-oriented-development (TOD) boom that produced significant community and fiscal benefits and became a national model, all did not progress smoothly.

For years "Arlington" could barely be used in public discussions about growth in Fairfax, where community members expressed concern about density. Thus Fairfax, along with other suburban jurisdictions, was slow to take advantage of its Metro station areas, and rapid traditional suburban growth continued up to the early 2000s. However, in recent years, the positive results of Arlington's TOD have inspired a new era of TOD in Fairfax and other suburbs. The region's ultimate embrace of urban development has created significant development opportunities in the city and inner suburbs and along Metro routes throughout the region—making the region uniquely competitive in attracting knowledge workers and investment and drawing millennials and empty nesters to TODS in the city and suburbs alike.

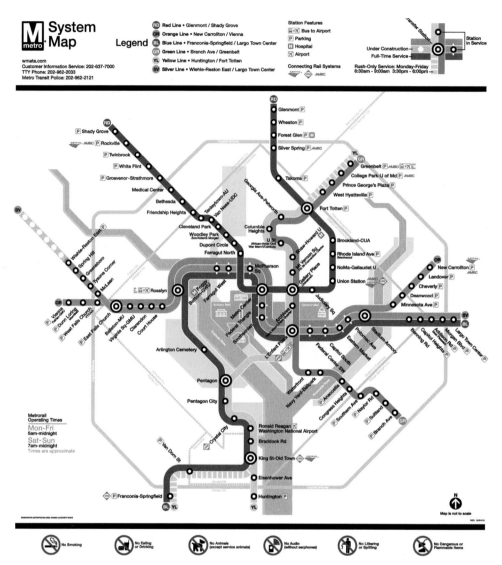

Figure 6.3. The Washington Metropolitan region's 117-mile Metrorail system includes 91 stations. The second phase of the Silver Line to Dulles Airport will add six more stations. (Washington Metropolitan Area Transit Authority)

Process: A Long Debate Leads to a Consensus Regional Vision

The extended debate about where and how the region should grow began in earnest in 1988 with debate about whether to build outer beltways—first conceived of in the Eisenhower era. Environmental advocates led the challenge because of impacts on natural resources, diversion of investment from the city and older suburbs, and the sprawling development that the beltways would induce—just as Washington's first beltway fueled explosive growth of second-ring suburbs. Subsequently a showdown with the Disney Corporation over its proposed history theme park just west of Manassas National Battlefield in 1994, followed by more debates about an outer beltway in the late 1990s, pitted developers and business groups against local residents and conservation groups that promoted alternative approaches to regional growth.

Perhaps the starting point for efforts to offer an alternative to outer beltways and suburban sprawl was the publication in 1992 of *A New Approach: Integrating Transportation and Development in the National Capital Region* by the Washington Regional Network for Livable Communities (WRN). A joint effort by volunteer planners and nonprofit conservation leaders, WRN's report offered a vision for a revitalized city, for rural land conservation, for mixed-use development, and for greater investment in transit, walking, and bicycling.

The report helped to frame the discussion by the COG when it began a transportation visioning process required under the 1991 federal transportation law, the Intermodal Surface Transportation Efficiency Act (ISTEA, pronounced "ice-tea"). Business leaders, conservationists, and progressive planners engaged in intense debate over the next six years, and conservation advocates issued two more reports in 1996: *Network of Livable Communities,* which demonstrated that a network of transit-oriented communities and pricing policies would result in less congestion, and *A Better Way to Grow,* illustrating new urbanist design alternatives in three contexts: rural, suburban, and urban. In 1997, the COG Transportation Planning Board finally approved its "Getting There" vision, which incorporated many of the concepts offered by the conservationists and progressive planners. That same year conservation groups formed the Coalition for Smarter Growth (CSG), which has since played an important role in changing the region's approach to growth, both in regional discussions at the COG and in advocating for smart growth at the local level.

Unhappy with the regional process, a group of Northern Virginia business leaders issued its own set of transportation reports that advocated the outer beltway and a network of other major highways. The back-and-forth continued and included a referendum for a regional sales tax for transportation in Northern Virginia. The CSG and partner groups challenged the referendum for its failure to tie the funding to better land use planning, for failing to allocate an adequate share to transit, and for inclusion of segments of the outer beltway. The arguments ultimately convinced voters. Spending a fraction of that spent by the business community, the conservation groups won the debate when the public rejected the sales tax by a significant margin.

The defeat of the sales tax earned the CSG political clout that enabled great progress over the next decade and brought recognition of the importance of addressing land use to address the region's transportation challenges. During this time, the group issued its "Blueprint for a Better Region," demonstrating the role of poor land use in traffic congestion and the benefits of city revitalization and transit-oriented development. Shown hundreds of times, the photographic narrative proved extremely effective with the public and elected officials.

In the early 2000s, CSG participated in the formation of the Washington Smart Growth Alliance (WSGA) with the Greater Washington Board of Trade, the Urban Land Institute, Metropolitan Builders Council, Chesapeake Bay Foundation, and Enterprise Community Partners. WSGA cosponsored and planned with the Urban Land Institute's DC Council the 2005 Reality Check conference. The conference gathered 300 elected officials, business leaders, and civic activists to discuss where and how the region should grow. The conference represented a turning point, endorsing a smart growth vision to transform the region's suburbs.

"Acting locally" remained critical throughout this period. Perhaps the most significant milestone was a hard campaign for a major mixed-use development at the Vienna Metro station in suburban Fairfax County. Vehemently opposed by neighbors, the conservation organizations generated support through educational forums, email alerts, letters to the editor, and even phone banking to turn out members to support the project, which the Fairfax Board of Supervisors ultimately approved.

Following Reality Check and the Vienna Metro fight, Fairfax County embarked on perhaps the most significant new suburban experiment yet seen—the redesign of Tysons Corner. CSG sparked the replanning, hosted early educational forums with national experts, participated in the planning, and kept its members engaged throughout. Five years of analysis and discussion resulted in the publication of the Tysons plan in 2010, followed by a formal comprehensive plan update and numerous implementation steps described in the Tysons Case Study (see Chapter 7).

Over the past 12 years, CSG has reviewed, endorsed, and campaigned for nearly 100 plans and projects, comprising millions of square feet of development and tens of thousands of housing units. The group has also played a leading role in efforts to implement inclusionary zoning to ensure that a share of units in new development projects are affordable to those making less than the area median income (AMI), with a particular focus on those at or below 60% of the AMI.

Meanwhile, across the river in suburban Montgomery County, Maryland, a group of local developers served as catalysts in the replanning of the White Flint Metro station area, dominated by strip shopping centers and one of the region's largest malls, now on the decline. Forming the White Flint Partnership, the landowners and developers hired progressive urban and transportation planners and offered concepts for a network of streets and an urban-transit boulevard, supporting mixed-use development. They hosted educational forums that included Christopher B. Leinberger, a developer, academic, and leading advocate of the benefits of walkable urbanism, and former governor Parris Glendening, an early champion of state smart growth policies. The county ultimately approved a plan for White Flint nearly as ambitious as that for Tysons.

Back at COG, the 2005 Reality Check sparked an official regional effort called the Greater Washington 2050 Coalition, involving a large multijurisdictional and multisector task force, public polling, public engagement, and analysis. Representatives of foundations, affordable housing advocates, smart growth groups, local governments, universities, business and developers, and planning professionals were all at the table. The group's consensus vision, *Region Forward*, adopted TOD as a framework for sustainable and equitable regional growth. All 23 jurisdictional members of COG formally endorsed the *Region Forward Vision* as part of a regional compact.

Challenges

Although the region has seen a boom in TOD, it faces many challenges. The political complexity of the region, a deep-seated east–west economic divide, problems with Metro, housing affordability, federal government downsizing, civic association push-back on infill development, and a persistent lobbying effort for the outer beltway to fuel outer-suburban growth, all threaten the region's shift to more sustainable TOD.

The region's political complexity has always created challenges for reaching consensus. Maryland has been strongly Democratic for years, but it recently elected a Republican governor, while retaining a Democrat-dominated legislature. Virginia has been turning "purple," with a growing Democratic base in the DC suburbs helping to elect a Democratic governor and two Democratic senators, while Republicans dominate in the state legislature. Outer-ring suburbs have long been more supportive of new highways and traditional suburban development, whereas older inner suburbs see TOD as central to their economic futures.

Developers who invested in land in rural areas have favored highway expansion and opposed changing the direction of regional growth. Their recent lobbying has focused on segments of an outer beltway, including upriver Potomac bridges between Virginia and Maryland (Loudoun and Montgomery Counties) and a highway through the historic landscape of Manassas National Battlefield. Some transportation planners and engineers in state and local agencies hamper the shift of public investment from highways to transit, local street networks, and other infrastructure necessary to support TOD. Elected officials, faced with constituents upset about traffic congestion, have also been reluctant to make a more definitive shift in transportation spending from highways to transit.

Meanwhile the region continues to experience an east–west economic divide, and analysis of the regional long-range transportation plan shows the divide could get worse.

Metro is aging and faces serious management and reliability problems, which has led to declines in ridership and could dampen demand for TOD. The rapid revitalization of the city and transit-accessible neighborhoods, meanwhile, has contributed to a crisis in housing affordability.

The pace of TOD has prompted a push-back from civic associations in urbanizing communities, citing concerns about density, traffic, property values, and crowded schools. Despite planners' efforts to demonstrate that well-designed TOD reduces driving and traffic and increases tax base, many civic associations are not assuaged.

Finally, government downsizing and high office vacancy levels—reaching 21% or more in the suburbs—have prompted a crisis of confidence. The risk is that local leaders may push for "anything goes" to promote economic development, rather than focus on continuing to create the vibrant urban places most effective in attracting next-generation workforce and investment.

Plan: Region Going Forward

Region Forward and dozens of local TOD plans represent a comprehensive new approach to development in the region. Regional and local plans share common attributes, including walkable street networks, connections to existing and planned transit, higher-density developments with buildings built to the sidewalks, green building standards, modern stormwater management, and requirements for the inclusion of affordable housing.

The development of *Region Forward* included "Big Moves," the product of a full-day scenario workshop by the Greater Washington 2050 Coalition to brainstorm how the region could respond to global and national trends that would likely influence the region's future. The process revealed 10 common growth and development strategies: pursue TOD, leverage emerging sustainable technologies, emphasize green economic development, develop Greater Washington as a knowledge hub, strengthen regionalism, use financial innovations, ensure availability of moderate- and low-cost housing, focus on quality of life, improve public education, and promote health.

Scenario planning, public surveys, and extensive discussions resulted in the *Region Forward* report.[1] The plan sets goals for nine areas: land use, transportation, environment, climate and energy, economy, housing, health and human services, education, and public safety, and at its core, transit-oriented land use and a less car-dependent future.

Seeking to track progress in meeting the goals, the CSG commissioned a Baseline Progress Report to provide the initial measurement of regional performance related to 28 targets found in *Region Forward*. With land use at the center of the *Region Forward* plan, planners identified, defined, and mapped the region's Activity Centers, which are intended to accommodate the majority of future growth. They include existing urban centers, priority growth areas, traditional towns, and transit hubs. Together, Activity Centers are intended

Figure 6.4. Founded in 1749, Alexandria has preserved a pedestrian-friendly street network that offers a good model for urbanizing suburban communities. (Norman Maddeaux under CC-BY NC ND 2.0)

to play a central role in achieving *Region Forward*'s prosperity, sustainability, accessibility, and livability goals (see Figure 6.4).

According to the COG, although they take many different forms throughout the region, Activity Centers share some common characteristics: communities that offer a range of housing, transportation options, jobs, services, and amenities. Most importantly, they provide access to opportunity for residents, workers, and businesses. Activity Centers will more efficiently accommodate the significant growth projected for the region. Centers with a mix of uses, amenities, and good pedestrian infrastructure have been shown to attract more people and growth, perform better economically, and prove more resilient during recessions than neighborhoods lacking walkability and a mix of uses.

To assist local governments in the planning and development of Activity Centers, CSG commissioned the *Place + Opportunity* report. Examining a cross section of the region's 141 Activity Centers (see Figure 6.5), the consulting team conducted detailed analysis of each center's market, urban form, and socioeconomic characteristics to identify six common Activity Center place types and four opportunity types. For each place and opportunity type, the report provides a set of development goals, strategies, and tools for enhancing economic development, urban form, and access to opportunity in Activity Centers.

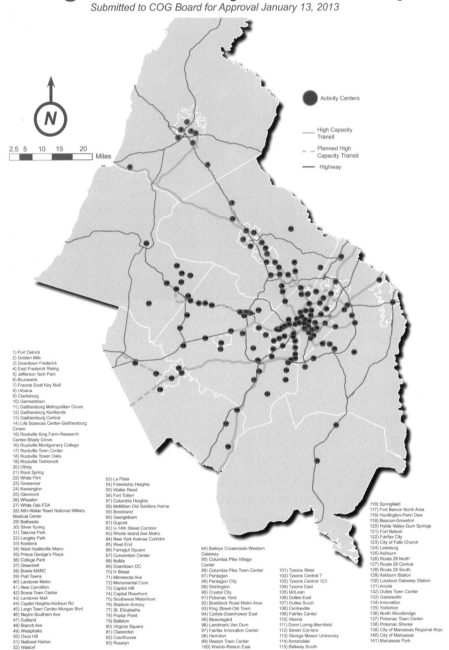

Figure 6.5. Activity Centers are current or planned concentrations of higher-density, walkable, mixed-use development. Most are, or will be, connected to high-capacity transit. (Metropolitan Washington Council of Governments)

Naturally, under existing legal structures, the plans, zoning, and policies for each Activity Center must be developed by each local jurisdiction. Since the early 2000s dozens of local plans have been developed to support TOD in the city and suburbs. In addition to the aforementioned redevelopment, many urban plans have been developed in the suburbs throughout the Washington region.

A Sampling of Implementation Strategies

Place + Opportunity identified 15 types of strategies for creating mixed-use, mixed-income, walkable, and transit-oriented Activity Centers.[2] These include mixed-use zoning; development incentives; focusing on accessibility for pedestrians, bicyclists, and transit users; affordable housing preservation; and branding and marketing.

COG has also established a Transportation and Land Use Connections (TLC) program, which provides small grants for studies and implementation projects for TOD across the region.[3]

In addition, a review of local planning reveals a range of local implementation strategies that include:

- **Design charrettes**—Popularized by the Congress for the New Urbanism, these are intensive education and planning efforts with community members who roll up their sleeves to help design or redesign an entire neighborhood or center.
- **Form-based zoning codes**—Rather than complex regulations that specify the use of individual parcels, these codes focus on building form and design, and seek to streamline approvals for projects built to the form-based code. A prominent example is Columbia Pike in Arlington.
- **Urban street design guidelines**—New urban street design guidelines negotiated between Fairfax County and the Virginia Department of Transportation feature narrower lanes, bike lanes, wider sidewalks, safer crossings, and, where needed, dedicated transit lanes. Developers, residents, and county officials have created similar guidelines for White Flint in Montgomery County. Efforts are under way to apply "complete streets" standards to urbanizing centers regionwide.
- **Special tax districts**—These districts, in which local landowners within transit-station areas agree to an additional assessment to fund a new street network, transit, and other infrastructure, have been used successfully for Metro's Silver Line extension to Tysons, Reston, and Dulles; for the Tysons and White Flint plans; and to fund construction of the NOMA and Potomac Yard Metro stations.
- **Inclusionary zoning**—Requirements that 10 to 15% of new housing units be affordable to those who make less than the AMI are in place in nearly every jurisdiction in the Washington region. The ordinances target households with incomes at

or below 80% AMI. Some also include "workforce units" affordable to households making between 80 and 120% AMI. Housing advocates are seeking to prioritize incomes at or below 60% AMI, where there is the greatest need. As compensation, developers gain density bonuses that allow for additional market-rate units.

- **Density bonuses for community benefits**—In addition to their use as an incentive to provide affordable housing, density bonuses above existing zoning provide incentives to developers to provide a range of community benefits, including public spaces, local street connections, more effective stormwater management, and the like.

- **Location of government facilities**—The location of government offices at Metro stations can be a catalyst for private development, especially in weaker real estate markets. The State of Maryland and Prince George's County have moved the state housing agency to one Metro station and plan to build a new regional medical center at another. A long-standing executive order requires the federal General Services Administration to locate government agencies in downtowns or within a half mile of transit stations.

- **Progressive parking standards**—A factor in any urban development is the high cost of structured above- and underground parking, which can range from $30,000 to $50,000 per space. Jurisdictions are working to lower required parking, allow for shared parking between uses, and separate the price of a parking space from the purchase price of a condo or the lease of an apartment.

Results

Today, the Washington region ranks second behind only New York City for walkable urban centers and has many more examples of walkable urban places in its suburbs than does the New York metro area, according to Chris Leinberger.[4] Eighty-six percent of new office development in the pipeline in the region is within a quarter mile of a Metro station, and 92% of office leases over 20,000 square feet are within a half mile of a Metro station.[5] Thousands of housing units have been developed within walking distance of Metro stations in the city and suburbs.[6]

The addition of millions of square feet of development—26 million square feet of retail and office space, 30,000 housing units, and 3,800 hotel rooms—in Arlington's Rosslyn-Ballston corridor over the past 40 years[7] has been achieved with just minor increases in traffic.[8] Fifty percent of Arlington's property tax base comes from its two Metro corridors, comprising just 11.7 percent of the county's land.[9] The development in the Rosslyn-Ballston corridor occupies about 2.4 square miles but would consume 14 square miles were it developed in a suburban pattern (see Figure 6.6).

Since Fairfax County approved the Tysons plan in 2010, developers have won rezoning approval for 13 projects (see Figure 6.7). Combined with 6 approved before 2010, they

Figure 6.6. An aerial view east toward Washington takes in transit-oriented development at Arlington County's Virginia Square, Clarendon, Courthouse, and Rosslyn Metro stations. (Arlington County)

Figure 6.7. The Silver Line under construction in Tysons. This first phase, now open, has spurred millions of square feet of development four stations in Tysons and one in Reston. (Virginia Department of Transportation, by Trevor Wrayton, under CC-BY NC ND 2.0)

Figure 6.8. "Pike and Rose"—a large mixed-use development within walking distance of the White Flint Metro Station in Virginia. (Federal Realty Investment Trust)

will increase office space from 28 million to over 41 million square feet, and residential space from 12 million to over 28 million square feet, or from 10,000 units to over 25,000 units.[10] In White Flint, the first phase of the Pike and Rose development comprising nearly 1 million square feet has opened to great success (see Figure 6.8).

Seventy percent of daily trips in the core jurisdictions of Washington, Arlington, and Alexandria are walk/bike (26%), transit (19%), and carpool, illustrating the benefits of compact development. Non–single-occupant vehicle trips make up 58% of trips in the middle suburbs and 52% of those in the outer suburbs.[11]

Residential property values and sales for urban, inner suburban, and transit-accessible locations held up following the 2008 real estate crash and have continued to perform better than outer suburban locations. The flip side is that housing affordability has become a significant challenge, especially for lower-income households. DC is earmarking $100 million for housing investments, and efforts are being made to strengthen inclusionary zoning policies and the use of public–private deals to preserve affordable housing and create new units.[12]

The region has evolved from an era when most developers and officials deemed sprawling development inevitable to one in which a network of mixed-use, transit-oriented centers and corridors is the adopted framework for growth. Despite a number of instances of local opposition to the pace and scale of suburban infill development, smart growth politicians won majorities in every locality in the fall 2015 elections. In recognition of the role of the CSG in shifting thinking about where and how the region should grow, in 2015 the *Washington Business Journal* named the organization to its Power 100 list of most influential regional business leaders for the third time in four years.[13]

Significance

The Washington region has advantages with the presence and economic power of the federal government and the high-capacity 117-mile Metro system, but it also shares the challenges of other regions with uneven economic growth and the difficulty in reaching agreement among multiple jurisdictions.

The region's experience shows that regional dialogue and planning with all sectors at the table can make a difference; that local implementation led by elected officials and effective planners is essential; and that in this context developers can be confident about where to invest.

Effective nonprofit advocacy over many years, supported by the foundation community, plays an important role in promoting and winning a new approach to suburban development. Partnerships between these nonprofits and progressive business and development leaders are particularly powerful. Finally, creating successful walkable urbanism with the full range of supportive transportation, parking, housing, and public amenities offers models from which other jurisdictions can borrow (see Figure 6.9).

Fairfax, once the largest dairy-producing county in Virginia, saw rapid conversion of farms to development between the 1950s and 1980s, including the creation of Tysons Corner, a suburban megacenter with two large malls and dozens of office buildings. The central character in Joel Garreau's *Edge City*, Tysons has become a central character again—in the new suburban experiment of the last decade.

The debate over where and how to grow in the region has been a long one. It illustrates the value of a strong nonprofit advocacy community with a vision to offer and staying power made possible by sustained foundation support. The arc of engagement has included reports, engagement in the public planning process, grassroots mobilization, communications through the media, and partnerships with other sectors, including smart growth–oriented developers. Advocates learned to "talk regionally, but act locally" to win support for smart growth, because change would not have been possible without

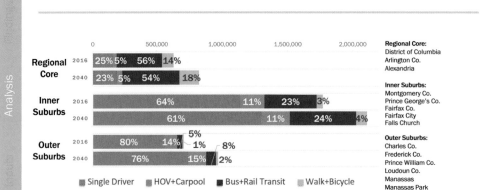

Figure 6.9. Walkable, transit-oriented neighborhoods contribute to remarkably high non-auto-mode shares in the three core jurisdictions of the Washington region. (Transportation Planning Board, Metropolitan Washington Council of Governments)

local elected leadership and land use and transportation planners who crafted the local plans and policies necessary to support smart growth.

Notes

1. Metropolitan Washington Council of Governments, *Region Forward: A Comprehensive Guide for Regional Planning and Measuring Progress in the 21st Century*, January 28, 2010, accessed April 24, 2017, https://www.mwcog.org/documents/2010/01/28/region-forward-vision/.

2. Metropolitan Washington Council of Governments, *Place + Opportunity: Strategies for Creating Great Communities and a Stronger Region*, January 8, 2014, accessed April 24, 2017, https://www.mwcog.org/documents/2014/01/08/place-opportunity-strategies-for-creating-great-communities-and-a-stronger-region-land-use/.

3. Metropolitan Washington Council of Governments, Transportation and Land Use Connections Program, accessed April 24, 2017, https://www.mwcog.org/transportation/planning-areas/land-use-coordination/tlc-program/.

4. Christopher B. Leinberger and Michael Rodriguez, *Foot Traffic Ahead: Ranking Walkable Urbanism in America's Largest Metros, 2016*, 16, June 14, 2016, accessed April 24, 2017,

http://business.gwu.edu/wp-content/uploads/2016/06/CREUA_Foot-Traffic-Ahead_2016.06.14.pdf.

5.   Jonathan O'Connell, "Pair of Suburban Office Buildings Drop $126M in Value Since 2007," *Washington Post,* March 27, 2015, accessed April 24, 2017, https://www.washingtonpost.com/news/digger/wp/2015/03/27/pair-of-suburban-office-buildings-drop-126m-in-value-since-2007/; and "Why and at What Stations Metro Expects Ridership to Grow," *Washington Post*, April 27, 2015, accessed April 24, 2017, https://www.washingtonpost.com/news/digger/wp/2015/04/27/why-and-at-what-stations-metro-expects-ridership-to-grow/.

6.   In his research on walkable urban places, Christopher B. Leinberger of George Washington University and his research team confirmed that 48% of new rental apartment spaces in the DC region were in walkable urban places, up from 19% in the early 2000s and 12% in the 1990s, "DC: The WalkUP Wake-Up Call: The Nation's Capital as a Model for Walkable Urban Places," February 22, 2016, accessed April 25, 2017, http://business.gwu.edu/wp-content/uploads/2016/02/CREUA_DC-Walkupd.pdf.

7.   Arlington County, "Rosslyn–Ballston Corridor," accessed April 24, 2017, https://projects.arlingtonva.us/planning/smart-growth/rosslyn-ballston-corridor/.

8.   Arlington County, "30 Years of Smart Growth: Arlington County's Experience with Transit-Oriented Development in the Rosslyn–Ballston Corridor," July 2008, slide 60-61, accessed April 24, 2017, http://www.fairfaxcounty.gov/dpz/projects/reston/arlingtonpresentation.pdf.

9.   Arlington County, "40 Years of Smart Growth: Arlington County's Experience with Transit-Oriented Development in the Rosslyn–Ballston Corridor," December 6, 2012, slide 64, accessed April 24, 2017, https://arlingtonva.s3.dualstack.us-east-1.amazonaws.com/wp-content/uploads/sites/31/2014/03/40_Years_Smart_Growth.pdf.

10. Fairfax County, "Transforming Tysons," accessed April 24, 2017, http://www.fairfaxcounty.gov/tysons/.

11. Metropolitan Washington Council of Governments, Transportation Planning Board, *Briefing on the Performance Analysis of the Draft 2016 CLRP Amendment* (PDF)/slide 30, October 19, 2016, 32, accessed April 24, 2017, https://www.mwcog.org/assets/1/28/10192016_-_Item_9_-_2016_CLRP_Performance_Analysis.pdf.

12. "Mayor Bowser Supports Historic Investments in Affordable Housing," October 7, 2017, accessed April 24, 2017, https://dhcd.dc.gov/release/mayor-bowser-celebrates-historic-investments-affordable-housing.

13. *Washington Business Journal*, "Power 100," slide 11, October 19, 2015, accessed April 24, 2017, http://www.bizjournals.com/washington/feature/power/2015/, Innovators list.

Figure 7.1a. Tysons, 1936. Once a corner store in a bucolic setting, Tysons would grow to become one of the largest office districts in the United States. (Fairfax County Economic Development Authority)

Figure 7.1b. Tysons, 1993. In 1993 (then called Tysons Corner), Tysons had grown to exemplify the "edge city," with strip shopping centers, two malls, and office towers surrounded by thousands of parking spaces. (Fairfax County Department of Planning and Zoning)

Figure 7.1c. Tysons, 2013. Tysons is undergoing one of the most ambitious suburban retrofits in the United States (and has dropped "Corner" from its name). The Metro Silver Line has begun to reshape the sprawling office and retail center and attract thousands of residential units around four new stations. (Dulles Corridor Metro Rail Project)

7

Tysons, Virginia

Linda E. Hollis and Sterling Wheeler

Tysons (also known as Tysons Corner) is located in suburban Fairfax County west of Washington, DC. The decision to extend Metro service to Dulles Airport, with four stations located at Tysons, resulted in a plan completed in 2010 to transform the area from a suburban to an urban place. Rail service on the extension began in July 2014, and the redevelopment of Tysons is ongoing.

Context

A mature area of low-density suburban development, Tysons is located in Fairfax County, Virginia, about halfway between the District of Columbia and Dulles International Airport. Tysons includes 2,100 acres and is located at the intersection of the Capital Beltway (Interstate 495), Virginia Routes 7 and 123, and the Dulles Airport Access Road (DAAR) and Toll Road (Virginia Route 267).

The crossroads of Routes 7 and 123 was first named Peach Orchard for the crops grown nearby and later named Tysons Corner after a local landowner. Until 1964 it was a rural area with a general store. In the 1960s the Beltway and the DAAR improved access to Tysons, and its first regional mall, Tysons Corner Center, opened (see Figure 7.1a, b, c).

Since that time, Tysons has transformed from a rural crossroads to an "edge city," as described by Joel Garreau in his 1991 book *Edge City: Life on the New Frontier*. It attracted a second regional mall and the county's largest concentration of hotel rooms. Tysons is also home to five Fortune 500 company headquarters and many prominent national firms. In 2014, Tysons contained more than 90,000 jobs, 19,000 residents, and almost 36 million square feet of nonresidential development. Of this total, 28 million was office space, 5 million was retail, and 3 million was hotel space.

Opportunities

The opening of the Capital Beltway and the DAAR in the 1960s greatly increased regional accessibility to Tysons. The County saw this as an opportunity for economic development and planned the area for regional retail, office parks, and multifamily development. Because Tysons was still a rural crossroads, initial plans did not include rail stations. By the late 1960s, Tysons had begun developing into what would become one of the country's largest and most successful suburban employment centers. By the late 1980s, despite success with the suburban model of development, the policy direction for Tysons was about to undergo a paradigm shift.

In 1990, Fairfax County's board of supervisors adopted "The Concept for Future Development," which designated Tysons as the county's "Urban Center" and called for a special study to help guide the area's evolution to an urban, pedestrian-oriented environment. Under the suburban model of low-density development, Tysons would approach full buildout in the 1990s. Urbanization offered an opportunity to increase overall development and assure greater long-term sustainability.

Between 1990 and 1994 the County's planning staff worked with a 24-member task force to develop the new plan for Tysons. A key feature of the plan, as adopted in 1994, was moving the planned Metro alignment out of the Dulles Airport Access Road and running it through Tysons. This new alignment, with three planned stations, would kickstart the transformation from a suburban to an urban model of development.

Over the next 10 years, officials at all levels of government worked through the federal process to make the new alignment possible. The Final Environmental Impact Statement (FEIS) for the realignment, issued in 2004, identified four transit stations in Tysons (see Figure 7.2).

After the FEIS won approval, the board of supervisors in 2005 established a task force to update the 1994 plan. The County directed a newly formed Tysons Land Use Task Force to assess land use and development issues around the four Metro stations, and review all other aspects of the 1994 plan. The 36 members of the task force represented a wide range of community interests and perspectives. Task force members were developers, residents, community activists, and advocates for the environment, affordable housing, bicycling, accessibility, and the arts. With an extensive team of consultants, the task force and planning staff formulated and analyzed alternative development concepts based on transit-oriented communities in the United States.

To facilitate its work, the task force formed six committees that met regularly and provided detailed recommendations for review by the full group. The committees addressed

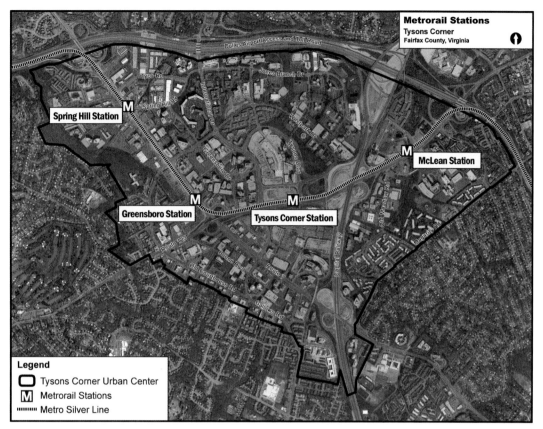

Figure 7.2. Located at the crossroads of major highways and arterial roads, Tysons is now bisected by Metro's Silver Line. Four Metro stations have brought a new focus on mixed-use, transit-oriented development to a district once dominated by the automobile. (Fairfax County Department of Planning and Zoning)

community outreach, communications, transportation, affordable and workforce housing, livability and walkability, and implementation. The land use task force presented its vision for transforming Tysons to the board of supervisors in 2008. The planning commission and its Tysons committee then met for almost two more years before submitting the plan amendment to the board of supervisors, who adopted the new Tysons Plan in 2010 (see Figure 7.3).

Challenges
Neither community nor landowner appointees to the 1990s Tysons Land Use Task Force liked the board of supervisors' 1990 decision to make Tysons the county's urban center. Landowner and developer interests saw the familiar suburban model as successful and

Figure 7.3a. Tysons, suburban grid. The existing suburban street system limits connectivity for automobiles and pedestrians throughout Tysons. (Fairfax County Department of Planning and Zoning)

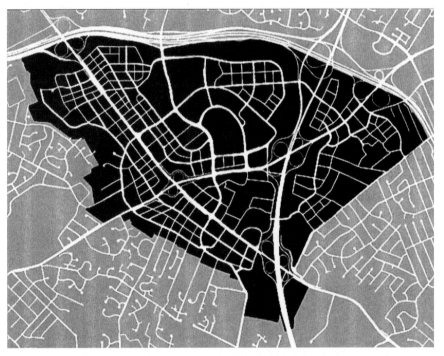

Figure 7.3b. Tysons, urban grid. The burgeoning urban grid for Tysons will enhance connectivity for all modes of transportation. (Fairfax County Department of Planning and Zoning)

didn't think urban-form development could be financed or marketed so far from down-town Washington; they considered the Rosslyn-Ballston corridor in nearby Arlington County, which had adopted urban-form development in the 1970s, a totally different market than Tysons. The residential community interest on the task force thought that urban development would increase traffic congestion and crime, both of which would undermine their quality of life. The County's planning staff worked with the task force over several years to reach consensus on conditions for urban redevelopment. By 1994, there was general acceptance of the proposed urbanity. However, the 1994 plan's urban-form development options were difficult to implement under the County's suburban regulatory regime, which required street designs to meet suburban standards and usually forced buildings to sit well back from the streets. The only way to address this dilemma was on a piecemeal basis with exceptions and modification provisions as well as a planned development district in the zoning ordinance. The suburban regulatory regime contin-ued to plague the Tysons transformation to an urban place until after the 2010 plan was adopted.

During creation of the 2010 plan, landowners in nearby residential communities opposed a significant increase in development from the amount allowed under the 1994 plan. Landowners and developers, on the other hand, wanted a dramatic increase in development potential throughout Tysons. They advocated intensities that doubled the maximums allowed around the Metro stations under the 1994 plan. The gulf between the two sides, as well as many other issues, turned the update into a lengthy process that took over five years to conclude.

Another significant challenge during the planning process for the new plan was uncer-tainty about Metro's extension to Dulles Airport. Six months after the formation of the task force, an organization called TysonsTunnel.org began advocating an underground route for the Silver Line. A tunnel, it argued, would provide superior connectivity, with escalators leading directly into buildings, and would create fewer physical and aesthetic obstructions than an aboveground route. The proposed aboveground route was to be on aerial structures in the medians of Virginia Route 7 and Route 123.

This configuration issue absorbed hours of discussion and led to an evaluation of the implications of the two approaches. In 2006, however, the governor of Virginia cut the debate short with his announcement that the state would move forward with an above-ground alignment, since the tunnel option was too costly. The cost estimate for Phase 1 of the Silver Line increased from $1.5 billion in 2004 to $2.7 billion by 2007. As a result, the inspector general for the US Department of Transportation reported that the project might not meet guidelines for federal funding. In August 2007, members of Congress from Northern Virginia and the governor met with federal transportation officials to save the project. A month later, following extensive negotiations over costs and funding, the governor declared that the project was within budget and would proceed. This again freed the task force to focus on developing recommendations for transforming Tysons.

Civic Engagement Process

The 24 members of the task force appointed in 1990 represented local businesses, developers, and civic associations. Viewed as reflecting all stakeholder interests, the task force held only a few community sessions and met with civic and business groups on request. Once the task force and staff had compiled their recommendations, the planning commission and board of supervisors held a public hearing, which became the primary means of community outreach.

Community engagement for the 2010 plan took on a much more central role. In 2005, the board of supervisors directed the new Tysons Land Use Task Force to undertake extensive outreach and charged it with taking into account the views of residents of surrounding communities, citizen groups, smart growth advocates, businesses, employees, environmentalists, landowners, and developers. The task force convened more than 60 times, in addition to the meetings of its subcommittees. It held another 45 outreach meetings and workshops, which attracted more than 2,000 stakeholders.

The process for the 2010 plan made extensive use of the Web to promote transparency in civic engagement. All documents, notices, presentations, and videos were posted on the Tysons website. The site encouraged members of the public to provide their input, as well. Public outreach helped to shape the recommendations and vision for transforming Tysons that the task force presented to the board of supervisors in September 2008.

The board referred the task force's areawide recommendations report to the planning commission and staff for development of a detailed comprehensive plan text. The board directed that, in addition to the task force recommendations, the plan text be guided by the population and employment forecasts for Tysons developed by George Mason University's Center for Regional Analysis, extensive transportation and public-facility impact studies, and a fiscal-impact analysis.

The planning commission established a Tysons committee that held its own meetings and public hearings designed to achieve consensus on the amount and phasing of redevelopment and the infrastructure needed to support it. The committee worked with planning commission staff and with the task force's draft review committee to formulate a plan amendment, which the board of supervisors adopted on June 22, 2010.

The lengthy civic-engagement process of the plan update translated into widespread acceptance of the plan. The transparency of the process helped to build trust and credibility, a key to reaching a consensus on the plan's many and complex issues. And the extensive analyses of transportation and other facilities helped assure the public that Fairfax County had the capacity to accommodate the growth envisioned at Tysons.

Highlights of the Plan

The 2010 plan calls for Tysons to grow from 19,000 residents and 93,000 jobs to 100,000 residents and 200,000 jobs by 2050. Other features include the following:

- A new "Transit Station Mixed-Use" land use category
- No fixed ceiling on development intensity within a quarter mile of Metro stations, with intensity determined through the rezoning process
- Twenty percent new-housing affordability for households with incomes between 50 and 120% of the area median income
- Nonresidential development contribution of $3 per square foot to an affordable housing trust fund
- Leadership in Energy and Environmental Design (LEED)-certified residential buildings and commercial buildings that reach the LEED silver standard
- A green network of parks, open space, and trails, with urban standards for parks and recreational facilities
- An urban grid of streets, designed for use by pedestrians and bicyclists as well as automobiles
- Circulator routes linking residential neighborhoods to the station areas, and other transit service linking Tysons to communities outside its borders
- Rigorous transportation demand-management measures
- A phase-in of parking maximums to replace suburban-oriented parking minimums

Implementation Strategies

The implementation chapter of the plan included strategies for addressing the provision of affordable housing, green buildings, and green infrastructure. Several of these strategies are detailed in this section.

To accommodate the plan's recommendations for mixed-use and higher-intensity development, the board amended the County's zoning ordinance, creating the Planned Tysons Corner Urban Center District (PTC). The PTC zoning district and the 2010 plan were concurrently adopted by the board (see Figure 7.4).

Improvements in Development Review

An important implementation strategy has been the establishment of an interdepartmental "core team" of staff responsible for development review at Tysons. Led by a branch chief from the Zoning Evaluation Division of the Department of Planning and Zoning, this team works collaboratively to identify and resolve issues with applicants in all Tysons rezoning applications. Another process redesign improvement has been an expedited review of site plans by the Department of Public Works and Environmental Services.

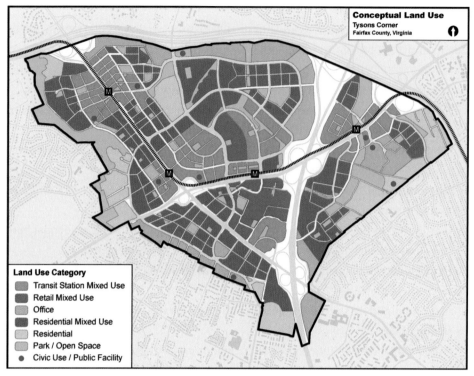

Figure 7.4. Tysons conceptual land use map. Land uses in Tysons now focus on accommodating mixed-use development near its four Metro stations. (Fairfax County Department of Planning and Zoning)

Remaking the Transportation System

Central to the transformation of Tysons from a suburban to an urban place will be implementation of a new transportation system that includes not only Metro and circulator bus service but also an urban grid of streets with facilities for bicyclists and pedestrians. In late 2012 the planning commission proposed, and the board endorsed, a transportation funding plan to cover the $3.1 billion in road and transit improvements to create this new system by the year 2050.

In early 2013 the supervisors established mechanisms to fund the various facilities. Redevelopment will pay for the grid of streets, with contribution rates tied to the area of new nonresidential space and residential unit totals. Tysons-wide road improvements will be funded half by redevelopment (funded as already described) and half by taxes assessed on all properties within a new Tysons Transportation Service District. The County will fund neighborhood and access improvements (including sidewalks, trails, and bicycle facilities), expanded local and regional bus routes, and circulator bus service.

The Tysons Multimodal Transportation Hub Analysis, completed in 2013, provides a plan for the area around each Metro station. The planning staff uses these plans—which include locations for car-share programs, bike-share programs, bike racks and lockers, taxi stands, kiss-and-ride lots, and commuter kiosks—to review applications for rezoning near the stations.

Urban Design Guidelines

The "Areawide Recommendations" section of the 2010 plan includes information on urban design. It covers the street grid and block pattern, streetscape design, and building and site design. After plan adoption, the planning staff worked with a panel of experts to develop more detailed urban design guidelines. The board endorsed these guidelines in January 2012, and the County uses them to work with the development community to ensure that proposed projects are consistent with the urban environment envisioned in the plan. The guidelines will undergo modification periodically to address emerging issues.

Tysons Partnership

The adopted plan recommends creation of an "implementation entity" to help carry out the urban vision for Tysons. In 2011, the board established the Tysons Partnership, which now has almost 100 affiliates, including businesses, associations, and government agencies.

The Partnership's initial activities have included planning annual events such as the Tour de Tysons bike race, a farmer's market, and art, music, and food festivals. Many of these events have taken place at Lerner Town Square at Tysons II Mall, adjacent to Tysons Corner Station. The privately owned 10-acre parcel is slated for future development but hosts community space as an interim use.

In 2014 the Partnership worked with County staff to develop a Tysons-wide wayfinding plan. It includes entry/identification signs, pedestrian-scale wayfinding signs, and streetlight banners. When Metrorail opened in July 2014, the board authorized the Partnership to become the operator of a new Tysons Transportation Management Association. In that role, the Partnership will work with its members to reduce the traffic they generate and coordinate alternatives to single-occupancy vehicle trips.

Placemaking: Public Facilities, Parks and Recreation, and Public Art

Placemaking measures will play a key role in transforming Tysons, as will the establishment of a network of parks, open spaces, and trails all designed to urban standards. In 2014, the Park Authority Board endorsed the *Tysons Park System Concept Plan*, which will be incorporated into the plan as an amendment. The plan calls for establishment of a

5-mile recreational trail loop and a linear park under and around the Metro guideway, an idea that emerged from a 2014 design charrette.

Current applications for rezoning include commitments for 41 acres of publicly accessible urban parks; several athletic fields; two fire stations; one elementary school site; the renovation and expansion of another elementary school; and provision of spaces for a community center, for recreational programming, and for an educational facility.

In July 2014 a privately owned and maintained public open space opened at the Tysons Corner Center. Over an acre in size, the plaza sits near both the mall entrance and the pedestrian bridge to Tysons Corner Station. It hosts events such as concerts and outdoor markets. The plaza includes *Early Bird*, a sculpture comprising 63 life-size birds, representing five local species, scattered around the plaza.

In August 2013, the Arts Council of Fairfax County won a $50,000 grant from the National Endowment for the Arts for a community-engagement program entitled *Imagine Art Here*. Under the program, artists install temporary public art for the enjoyment of residents, workers, and shoppers in Tysons.

Results

The scale and pace of growth in Tysons exemplify an urbanizing suburb in America. Given the right tools and community outreach strategies, Tysons is quickly becoming a more walkable, mixed-use, and amenity-rich *place*.

Land Use

To date, 19 rezoning applications with Metro-related intensities have received approval in Tysons. Six won approval prior to plan adoption in June 2010. The board approved the 13 post-plan applications under the PTC zoning district (described earlier under "Implementation Strategies"). When space under construction is added to these approved projects, total office space at Tysons will increase from 28 million to more than 41 million square feet, and residential space will more than double from 12 million to more than 28 million square feet—with aggregate residential units rising from 10,000 to more than 25,000. The residential population is expected to grow from approximately 19,000 to 45,000, and employment from 93,000 to around 137,000 (see Figure 7.6).

Three major multifamily buildings have been completed since 2010, bringing more than 1,050 new units of housing to Tysons. Two of these buildings are the first high-rise apartments at Tysons, at 19 and 26 stories. The Tysons Tower office building at the Tysons Corner Center was completed in July 2014. At 526,000 square feet and 22 stories, it is the first office building over 500,000 square feet delivered at Tysons since 2002. An urban-format Walmart opened at Tysons West Promenade in 2013, boasting public art, benches, and other urban amenities (see Figure 7.5).

Figure 7.5. Urban Walmart in Tysons. Retailers are beginning to develop urban format concepts with structured parking where parking lots and auto dealerships were once predominant. (Jason Beske)

Transportation

Multiple regional transportation improvements have been completed, are under construction, or have been funded and programmed:

- Phase 1 of the Silver Line Metro
- Expanded and modified Fairfax Connector and Metrobus service, concurrent with the start of Silver Line operations
- Three express bus service routes, which began operation in 2013, connecting Tysons to other regional destinations
- A total of 37 pedestrian and bicycle improvement projects, which are under way under the umbrella label Tysons Area Metrorail Station Access Improvement Projects

Significance or Transferability

Fairfax County has begun applying new policies and practices developed at Tysons to urban development elsewhere. Most recently, they were included in the plan amendment for the Reston Transit Corridor, which encourages more intense development along Phase 2 of the Silver Line extension to Dulles Airport.

Based on the County's work with the Virginia Department of Transportation on urban street standards at Tysons, similar standards are being applied to redevelopment in the

Reston Transit Corridor. Similarly, the Park Authority has applied the urban park standards developed for Tysons to the Reston Plan. Contributions for affordable and workforce housing are also expected from commercial redevelopment in the Reston Transit Corridor.

Applications for rezoning under the Reston Plan are being reviewed using the "core team" development review process established for Tysons. Core team review is also being used for other major projects in the county.

Transferability of the lessons learned at Tysons might be limited to local governments seeking to redevelop already successful areas, rather than redeveloping blighted or aging commercial districts. Among the remaining challenges at Tysons are long-term achievement of an urban street grid and other infrastructure, such as ballfields and other public spaces. Although the County has encouraged landowners to consolidate their applications for rezoning, many new applications do not reach a minimum of 10 acres, the scale envisioned in the plan.

Another issue is creating a unique character in each of the four transit-oriented developments at Tysons, such as an arts and entertainment community in the Tysons West District. While transformation of Tysons has begun, with Silver Line ridership exceeding expectations, and demand for surface parking less than anticipated, achieving a truly urban place will take many more years.

◀ **Figure 7.6.** The Ovation at Parkcrest. High-rise residential development is the new norm for Tysons. (Kettler /copyright: John Cole)

Figure 8.1. The case study communities of Dayton and Dublin. (Ma Shuyun, Xumengqi, and Anushree Nallapaneni)

8

From Dayton Mall
to Miami Crossing, Ohio

Chris Snyder

Miami Township in Montgomery County, Ohio, is a typical suburban community of nearly 30,000 people with a regional shopping mall and a fairly diverse array of offices along with some industrial land uses. It faces many of the same fundamental challenges and opportunities communities across the country face as they wrestle with converging forces that will determine how they grow, adapt, or in some cases decline over the next decades. These forces range from economic and social changes to technological developments that will rapidly affect building and transportation decisions. Communities that can anticipate and adapt to these changes will have the best chance of thriving.

US suburbs have increasingly begun to explore more urbanized futures in the form of walkable, mixed-use developments. This case study examines the planning process Miami Township undertook to prepare for these social and economic changes.

In the 2000s the Township launched a planning effort to prepare itself for this future, beginning with creation of a broadly representative oversight committee and initial community outreach. In 2014 the Township selected Stantec's Urban Places to work with the community to create a plan.

Context

Miami Township—an unincorporated community at the southern end of Montgomery County—sits approximately 10 miles south of downtown Dayton and is the seventh-largest township in the state of Ohio (see Figure 8.1).

The City of Miamisburg is a community of roughly 21,000 people located within the township, which has an overall population of just over 51,000 residents. The commercial

Figure 8.2. Miami Township took the lead in transforming the area surrounding the Dayton Mall—roughly three million square feet spread over 2 square miles around the mall itself—into Miami Crossing, a walkable town center. (Google Earth)

core of Miami Township is centered on the Dayton Mall, an enclosed shopping center of over 1.4 million square feet that opened in 1970. A 2-square-mile commercial district comprising an additional 1.6 million square feet of strip centers, hotels, government facilities, and a nine-story office building—all built out since the mall opened—surround the mall and make up the study district. The area is bounded by Interstates 75 and 675 and two state routes carrying some of the heaviest traffic volumes in the county. Buses and a few sidewalks provide the only non-auto access (see Figure 8.2).

Although the Dayton Mall remains successful, with four anchor department stores— Elder Beerman, Macy's, JC Penney, and Sears—it faces the same increasingly uncertain retail landscape confronting malls everywhere. The fate of the surrounding uses is tied closely to the mall's own fate (see Figure 8.3). The mall added a lifestyle center in 2006 to adapt to the trend toward mixed-use outdoor centers. However, since 2006 three mixed-use lifestyle centers with a controlled Main Street environment have entered the region: The Greene Towne Center—a relatively high-density, mixed-use development; Liberty Center; and Austin Landing (more an office development, just 3 miles away) (see Figure 8.4).

Figure 8.3. The mall, along with nearby strip retail, remains relatively successful compared with its peers, but it faces the same fundamental challenges that rapidly evolving retail markets pose for all malls. (Wikimedia Commons contributor Ed! under CC BY-SA 3.0)

Figure 8.4. Newer, more walkable developments like Austin Landing have created competitive pressure for the Mall Area. (Austin Landing)

The Township has multiple goals in moving forward. Paramount is the larger community's desire for a true center—described in community meetings as a Main Street, a town square, a place that brings everyone together like a traditional downtown. The Mall Area plan's vision statement captured this sentiment: "The Dayton Mall Area will emerge as a uniquely 21st-century 'village center' connected to the community and to itself by a network of lively, walkable streets that embrace the spectrum of community life, extending from a bustling regional mall to an intimate regional library."

But there are other goals as well. Cuts in federal and state funding are creating more pressure to raise local revenues. Nearby residents fear competition with controlled Main Streets will suck life from the district. Retail and service workers have to live far away and lack access. The site presents stormwater issues.

Working with the City of Miamisburg, the Township has developed tools to help shape change, starting with shared planning efforts. In 2009, the Township and City formed a joint economic development district (JEDD) to provide a way to capture and share income tax revenue generated within portions of the unincorporated territory. Ohio law allows unincorporated townships to create this mechanism to assume municipal powers for economic development purposes by partnering with an incorporated municipality. In addition to the JEDD, the Township also uses a tax-increment financing (TIF) district to generate funds for capital improvements within the district. Unlike the JEDD, the TIF district includes a much larger set of properties and collects revenue on the increase in value generated by property improvements. TIF funds are much more limited in how they can be used and are primarily spent on public infrastructure improvements.

The existence of a JEDD and the associated partnership between Miami Township and the City of Miamisburg provides a tremendous opportunity to accomplish plans on a larger scale than would have been attempted in the past. The planning process fully embraced the opportunity to have members of both jurisdictions involved on a regular basis and leading the way toward funding and planning for the future. One remaining challenge is the lack of federal and state economic development funding, which remains focused on bringing office and industry to communities, but still ignores the placemaking essential in many cases to attracting and retaining skilled workers and the investment that follows them.

A Mix of Opportunities and Challenges

The district faced many familiar challenges, ranging from aging buildings and auto-dependent development patterns to overreliance on traditional retail uses. Nevertheless, while many planning efforts address economic decline, the Dayton Mall remained healthy, as did many, but not all, of the surrounding businesses. This continued health was a positive sign for the area's future, but it could also make acquisition of parcels for redevelopment more difficult.

A location between the Dayton and Cincinnati markets represented one of the district's greatest opportunities, allowing it to pull from several directions and benefit from corporate decisions to locate offices in nearby centers, such as Austin Landing.

Although communities often view an aging population as a challenge, it creates opportunities and demand for other services and a lifestyle with a greater urban orientation. New empty nesters seek access to services and community in ways that once were available only through downtown living. The growth of this population presented opportunities to redevelop the area in ways that could keep and deepen established bonds of community by introducing a residential component designed to create a new suburban experience.

Standard zoning throughout much of the study area was typical of similar suburban shopping districts and had resulted in a heavily auto-dependent retail area. Planned unit development zoning had been used to accommodate some unique uses or to adjust the standard retail parking requirement and other allowances, but these planned developments also created obstacles to change because they had often been enacted with unique standards that in many cases had become outdated relative to changes in the standard codes.

One of the greatest market challenges the area faced was the uncertainty of investment in the mall itself. Developers would be reluctant to invest if they didn't see a commitment to investment by the mall and its anchor tenants. As planning efforts commenced, the mall changed ownership. Local management remained engaged throughout the planning process, but it will take some time for an overall corporate strategy to be developed.

Having no established downtown presented both opportunity—to create a Main Street environment from scratch, unhindered by historic patterns—and challenges in bringing the business community together. Place identity had focused on being near the mall, period. The lack of a historic and traditionally defined community center had also led to difficulties in establishing a cohesive business association. The area is served by at least two chambers of commerce, neither specific to Miami Township, and many businesses identify themselves with one of several neighboring communities.

Sharing a ZIP code with nearby communities is a practical challenge for many townships in Ohio. Businesses naturally identify themselves by their mailing address and hesitate to identify with a township that doesn't necessarily show up on a map and won't appear in the results of an online search. This reality introduced an impetus for creation of a new district brand that could overlay both jurisdictions and become a recognizable place for visitors to identify.

Catalytic sites could help spur the market to produce additional investment. The team's challenge was to identify the most effective locations for catalytic projects and identify the opportunities such redevelopment would create.

A developing bike network—built largely in the previous 5 to 10 years through the southern part of the township and city and connected to a regional system of more than 300 miles of paved off-street bikeway—presented an enormous, if underrecognized, opportunity to bring pedestrian connectivity into the district.

The retail environment was shifting—as seen, for example, in changing consumer electronics stores. As the physical size of the merchandise sold in these stores had shrunk, so too had the need for warehouse and showroom space. Furthermore, consumers had shown a growing willingness to purchase these smaller devices online from central warehouses or use ship-to-store and in-store ordering, again reducing the need for extensive in-store warehousing. As store leases expired, many stores appeared eager to downsize their real estate footprint. This created challenges and opportunities for repurposing former store sites. Miami Township already had experienced such redevelopment challenges; a former Circuit City store had been redeveloped as a hotel, and consolidation among office-supply retailers had created vacancies.

Competition from mixed-use centers, both within Miami Township and in nearby communities, presented both a challenge and an opportunity. Nearby centers might have competed for individual retailers and office tenants, but instead they had introduced the idea of mixed-use development and its associated density. As residents have experienced these environments and seen their success, it has become easier to see how this type of urban pattern can fit into a suburban lifestyle. This is particularly true of the mixed-use Austin Landing development, 2 miles from the study area but still within Miami Township. Austin Landing could potentially have poached tenants from the Dayton Mall Area, but to date that hasn't been an extensive issue; rather, it has often drawn tenants new to the market. As well, competition is inherent and not necessarily bad when it drives each area to improve and build upon core strengths without sacrificing one center for the other. By broadening its offerings of living, shopping, and recreational opportunities, the region becomes more attractive for employees.

Some stakeholders had concerns about the area's safety. In part this perception grew out of physical conditions in the area and in part it reflected recent events or area history. The mall is old enough that many longtime residents had heard of or experienced at least one negative incident in the area over the course of 30 to 40 years. Changing these long-held perceptions represents a fundamental challenge for many older suburban retail centers.

Ohio's climate, with its harsh winters, raised skepticism that any outdoor mixed-use development could succeed. Comments typically reflected a desire to be able to walk within an enclosed, climate-controlled facility, such as the mall. Some lifestyle centers account for this by incorporating what are in fact minimalls into otherwise largely out-door centers. In the case of the Dayton Mall Area, this concern opened an opportunity to show how an outdoor Main Street environment could be incorporated into and function alongside a traditional suburban mall.

Creating a Plan

Perhaps the most critical hurdle to moving forward was building community awareness and support for a course correction—focused on qualities like walkability, density, and mixed use—from the planning and development approach of previous decades.

Planning Meetings and Workshops

A series of public meetings took place over the 13-month master-planning period. Goals of these meetings included engaging and listening to members of the public; translating their feedback into a vision, plan, and land use map; reviewing the emerging plan with the public and various stakeholders; and further refining the plan to create a final plan built on the input of stakeholders. The planning team strove to create a plan representing of the needs and desires of the community (see Figure 8.5)

Figure 8.5. To develop the plan, the Township conducted a series of workshops with a broad-based advisory committee representing key stakeholders and held larger public meetings at key points in the process. (Stantec)

From the initial kickoff event in November 2014 to the plan-adoption meeting in December 2015, the planning team convened six public meetings and workshops. A unique planning workshop involved nearly 500 students from Miamisburg Middle School and yielded some unexpected additional community feedback. The students went home with questions to review with their families, enabling the planning process to reach many more residents than is typically possible with public meetings alone. Working with the planning team on a variety of exercises, the students provided insight into what the next generation of young adults would value in a redeveloped study area. Perhaps more important, the students themselves got an opportunity to learn about and become involved in the planning process.

A three-day placemaking workshop was held about a third of the way through the planning process to confirm and further develop the draft vision statement and planning goals drawn up after the kickoff event. Two public meetings took place, along with a day-long open house where residents could drop in to view the team at work on preliminary design concepts and interact with staff in a less-formal setting that provided ample time to explore questions and concepts.

Open houses were held to present and refine the draft plan and reconfirm that the team had adequately incorporated public comments and sentiment. A final public meeting with the Dayton Mall JEDD Board took place in December 2015 to formally adopt the plan.

Engagement Tools

The team used two digital advertising displays located along the state highways in the district to advertise public engagement events. A survey built on the Textizen mobile platform helped further engage the public in nontraditional ways. The team also received access to the results of a just-completed survey of resident perceptions conducted by the Township separately from the master planning process. Several of the survey questions had aimed to provide insight into the planning effort, such as support for a broader mix of uses in the Dayton Mall Area and general perceptions of the commercial core of the township.

A website provided information during the master planning process, featuring plan documents, publicity materials, and media coverage of the process. Township planning staff used Facebook and Twitter to announce upcoming events. (Following the plan's completion, the Township renamed the project website www.MiamiCrossingDistrict .com, based on the district brand that emerged from the process, and refocused it on promoting the planning area.)

The planning team conducted more than 45 interviews with individual stakeholders and groups, ranging from real estate brokers and chamber of commerce representatives to community leaders and business representatives. The team met with the entire Board of

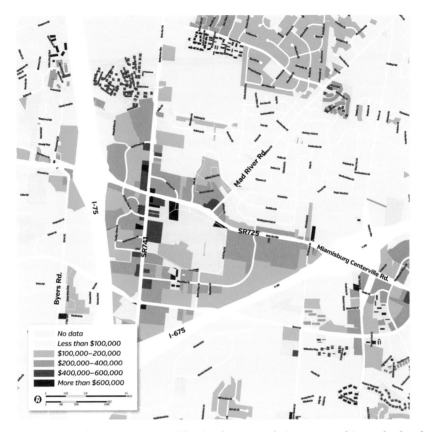

Figure 8.6. The consultant team mapped land values, parcel sizes, ownership, and other factors to identify the best potential sites for early redevelopment in response to a growing market for multifamily housing in a mixed-use setting. (Stantec)

County Commissioners during one planning workshop and discussed how the future of the Mall Area would affect the county as a whole.

Plan and Urban Design Qualities

The plan consists of three primary components: a physical plan centered on three catalytic redevelopment opportunities; a branding strategy to create a new identity for the area; and a set of ten 10-year goals for implementing the first two components.

The Physical Plan

The physical plan rested on a market analysis reflecting the area's absorption potential for residential, retail, and office uses. Real estate analyst Sarah Woodworth, principal of

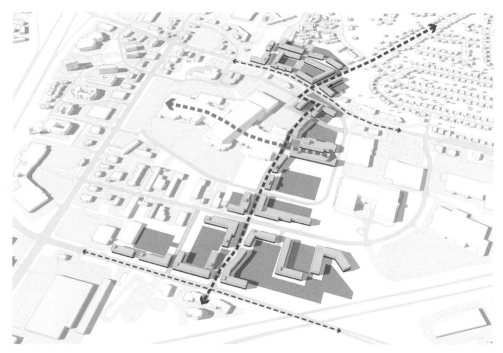

Figure 8.7. Phased redevelopment over 10 years can create a lively new Main Street along the front of the mall and become the focus for continued transformation. (Stantec)

W-ZHA (see Chapter 4), found that sufficient demand exists in the study area to support development of 1,200 multifamily housing units over 10 years. This housing, in turn, would support creation of mixed-use, urban-style density at strategic sites, a primary component of the physical plan. The plan identified three key areas as most suited for redevelopment that would encourage further extension of redevelopment to the rest of the district (see Figure 8.6).

The plan recommended creation of a downtown-style Main Street that incorporates public gathering spaces. This new Main Street can create a bridge between the suburban mall environment and more urban development nearby without requiring complete removal of the mall and its associated development (see Figure 8.7).

Improving access and walkability was a key component of the plan. Walkability was discussed throughout the planning process and meant more than just rolling out more sidewalks. The perception of the area as being inviting and accommodating to those who would prefer to walk or bike is as important as having physical routes to walk. This was a key component of the plan (and of many urbanizing mixed-use areas) that aimed to create a critical mass of community activity within the outdoor realm to make the area an appealing place to walk (see Figure 8.8).

Figure 8.8. New mixed-use development would fill in around existing retail along the new Main Street. (Stantec)

Design standards and relaxation of rigid traditional Euclidean zoning patterns were another critical component of the plan. The planning document includes a map outlining the areas to be governed by form-based zoning standards. Shifting the emphasis of the built environment from auto-oriented convenience to human-scale and human-oriented designs will not be easy. The plan recommendation for a greater mix of uses will need to be handled through design standards that address concerns that have kept Euclidean zoning in place for so many years. The plan recommends upgrading the district's public infrastructure as part of the area's redevelopment to help spur investment and provide the public commons that the area currently lacks.

District Identity

The plan recommends creation of a new brand and district identity. The planning process engaged a marketing firm working with input received during the course of meetings and open houses with staff, stakeholders, and the general public to establish a new name, Miami Crossing, and a new logo for the district. The Miami Crossing brand and its associated logo are intended to foster greater business and community partnership in marketing the district. Adoption of the Miami Crossing identity by the business community will help to promote a sense of place that is less about the mall and more about the entire district, with all its associated uses.

Ten-Year Goals

The plan outlines long-term goals, called "10 Triumphs in 10 Years," to encourage continued engagement not just by the planning staff but by elected officials and the broader community. Further grouping the goals by themes (Unlock Potential, Create a District, Improve Access, and Grow Greener) highlighted ways the final plan ties back to broader ambitions identified by residents and staff throughout the planning process.

Implementation Strategies

The plan includes multiple implementation strategies but also recognizes that the community began laying the groundwork for implementation several years prior. These efforts included creation of the TIF district and joint economic development district, and establishment of a community improvement corporation. These early measures have played a central role not only in securing funding for implementation but also in creating a political environment conducive to cooperation.

Marketing efforts for the district began in earnest shortly after the plan's adoption by the JEDD. These early efforts included further development of the brand; development of a website for the district; and creation of streetscape banners, window decals, and other print and digital marketing materials. The initial rollout of the website and marketing materials to the business community occurred less than a year after plan adoption by the JEDD Board. Initial marketing focused on groups coming into the region for special events to improve the district's capture rate for these out-of-town dollars.

Township staff is reviewing other economic development programs and incentives that can be put together to build a cohesive package of benefits designed to foster redevelopment. These efforts are being coordinated with other agencies, such as the county port authority, to maximize financing options for investors.

Meetings and tours with local developers, which have taken place since the plan was adopted, have helped staff to further refine areas of interest for potential redevelopment.

Working jointly with the Montgomery County Transportation Improvement District, the JEDD Board engaged engineering and design firms to begin planning streetscape and pedestrian improvements leading from the primary interstate gateway into the district. These efforts have already produced plans for significant pedestrian improvements and beautification within the corridor. Further studies will address other areas within the district to assist in prioritizing funding efforts going forward.

Physical pedestrian improvements are moving forward with the assistance of federal transportation funds, secured through the Miami Valley Regional Planning Commission.

The funds will underwrite the first significant pedestrian improvement project in 2018, connecting two existing apartment communities to the district with recreational paths and sidewalks. These improvements are also being actively coordinated with the state department of transportation, which also has a traffic signal improvement project planned in the same area.

Regulatory implementation in the form of design standards has already been applied to the standard business zoning districts. The design standards permit placement of buildings closer to the roadways, allow taller buildings, require human-scale architectural design, set out uniform lighting standards, and require parking areas to be placed away from primary roadways. While this initial effort is not a full form-based code, this regulatory step begins to steer the overall district toward a more urban and human-centered scale of development. The Township has previously used planned unit development standards for other mixed-use projects, but it is hoped that the new design standards will reduce the need to use the planned development standards.

Planning Lessons

Planners don't, of course, set out to produce plans that will just sit on a shelf, but this is the reality of many well-intentioned projects. To confront this problem, from the beginning we focused less on creating a plan than creating a process and program that would carry planning goals forward.

Creation of the JEDD and the partnership it established between the City and Township has been instrumental in providing the funding and flexibility not only to complete the plan but also to support ongoing marketing and implementation of the plan. Providing staff with the ability to operate within a more business-oriented environment while maintaining public government oversight has opened doors to cooperation with the business community that simply weren't available in our traditional roles.

The JEDD provides staff with the ability to directly establish a budget and work program for implementing various aspects of the plan—whether they be marketing, engineering studies, capital improvements, or grant programs—that can be directed and altered much more responsively. The projects the JEDD is undertaking, from development of a Miami Crossing District website to development of engineering plans, also allow us to reexamine the role of government in spurring economic activity.

Developing and nurturing a sense of place involves more than building public squares and creating unique buildings. It also means developing the community that will take ownership of the place. Development of the Miami Crossing brand is helping to keep this effort in focus as we continue to work with stakeholders in the area. The ongoing communication necessary to build the brand is helping to keep Township and City staff, the JEDD Board, elected officials, and the community engaged in crafting the long-term strategy for Miami Crossing. The JEDD Board is now working toward not just creating a plan that helps define a place but also redefining itself based on the brand and place called for in the plan by renaming itself the Miami Crossing Joint Economic Development District.

The value of nurturing relationships well in advance of any long-term planning effort should not be underestimated. These relationships include the business community, residents, other agencies—and, certainly in the case of Miami Crossing, the Township's relationship with neighboring jurisdictions. Building trust and confidence prior to planning allows a level of frankness and in-depth discussion that might not occur when parties come to the table with little or no prior working relationship. The ability to include businesses and residents at the earliest stages helped to establish a stronger sense of community ownership of the process than if staff had simply presented a plan to the community.

Placing development of the plan in the hands of the public and stakeholders paid dividends throughout the planning process, but perhaps most distinctly at one of the initial open houses.

The initial public meetings drew some participants who expressed suspicions of an "Agenda 21" conspiracy to instill world-government values and undercut individual property rights. Other members of the public stood up in response to these concerns and voiced their own concerns about what would happen without a plan. The public was also concerned about how the lack of a plan would affect their property values. This moment shifted the discussion in the room from what plan we, the staff, would impose on the public to how we, the community, could put together a plan that would protect the economic vitality of the area. Giving people the chance to take ownership of the status quo can be a powerful motivator for planning and putting words into action. Rising above other concerns was a genuine sense that our community needed to take control of its future and that changes would come whether we liked them or not. Any fear of planning in these moments was overwhelmed by a greater sense that the community would lose control of its destiny if we simply ignored these impending changes.

Beyond demographic and retail trends, suburbs today and society in general face dramatic technological advances that will reshape how people interact with their communities in ways unimaginable even a few years ago. Autonomous transportation systems, artificial intelligence, automated ordering and delivery services, and a host of other advances will alter the need for parking, labor, stores, and other fundamental aspects that affect the built environment.

Some systems may work against trends that have been thought to be pushing people toward mixed-use developments, such as an aging population that desires access to goods and services even if they can no longer drive, but how will this same population alter their lifestyles with access to autonomous vehicles that return this lost mobility and sense of freedom? How will building sites be altered when vehicles can simply drop off their occupants and park themselves in central parking fields or facilities? How will community finances be affected if they now rely on large pools of workers who are replaced by automated systems that don't generate an income tax? These and many other questions will challenge suburbs and urban areas in the near future, but some fundamental aspects of human behavior may also be driving this trend toward more human-centric urban form. Regardless of our technological advances we still congregate in parks, we still enjoy a night out to dinner, we still feel a fundamental pull to areas that provide a sense of community. If we can provide these basic human needs in our built environments then we will have a chance at preserving what is truly important regardless of the changes to come.

Figure 9.1. A map of Shanghai showing some prominent locations, including the case studies discussed in this chapter. (Ma Shuyun, Xumengqi, and Anushree Nallapaneni)

9

Shanghai's Journey in Urbanizing Suburbia

Tianyao Sun

Introduction

Shanghai, one of the world's largest cities, is known for its astounding economic growth and rapid urbanization. Since the Pudong New District was established, Shanghai has experienced record-breaking population growth, and most likely, the fastest urban development in human history. Within a span of 25 years, it has built the most miles of Metro track, creating a system that competes among the leading public transportation networks in the world. The majority of the city's new developments are transit oriented. As the outskirts of Shanghai have continued to grow, the municipality has prioritized building public transportation first, followed by incubating new town developments around transit stations. Xinchang and Zhoupu are two suburban towns that have recently benefited from the new Metro Line 16, which opened in late 2015. Both were considered suburbs in the past, but now they are linked to the downtown area of Lujiazui, which is Shanghai's financial district. As a result, land values around the new Metro stations have increased sharply.

Shanghai

Shanghai, the most populous city in China, is striving to be an innovative and ecologically minded global model. Today, it serves as a global financial and trade center and one of the busiest logistics hubs in the world. In 2015, the city had the largest annual gross domestic product in China (2,496 billion CNY or 379 billion USD).

At approximately 1.6 million acres, the municipal area of Shanghai is expansive (see Figure 9.1). Shanghai's downtown alone encompasses an area five times greater than that of New York City (990,000 acres vs. 195,000 acres). Though it has recently witnessed a very slight population decrease (from 24.26 million at the end of 2015 to 24.15 million at the end of 2016), Shanghai is still experiencing urban expansion. As a result, the government has put various controls on population growth in order to keep the expanding city from developing problems associated with urban development, including but not limited to a skyrocketing cost of living and the high cost of maintaining public infrastructure.

Today, as a global city, it embraces a diverse domestic and international culture. Downtown Shanghai includes both historic and modern architecture, as well as historic urban areas and many new skyscrapers. A cosmopolitan city, Shanghai embraces domestic and international culture, historic and modern architecture—even Disney's largest Disneyland, which opened in 2016.

Real estate has become a major form of investment. Housing prices inside Shanghai's inner ring rose roughly 34%, whereas those in the outer ring (Shanghai's suburban area) increased by 19% between December 2015 and December 2016. In part, this has driven people to seek cheaper housing in the suburbs.

Shanghai's rapid growth has produced a variety of environmental and planning impacts. The city is witnessing its first modernization since the introduction of the automobile. It has fallen behind other global cities in respect to its environment and livability, which city leaders realize are valuable for attracting people and investment. To address these issues, Shanghai is pursuing a number of strategies that will focus on urbanizing suburban areas. A greater focus on these strategies will help the city face the ongoing challenges of urban sprawl and create solutions to promote smart growth principles in its suburbs.

Spatial Planning Structure and Community Development

Since the 1950s, Shanghai has put significant effort into creating a "satellite city" concept in order to disperse the growing metropolis. From core city to new town typologies, Shanghai applies transportation strategies as a method of generating access to development. Within the Shanghai Municipal Area, the Shanghai Comprehensive Plan calls for four City Sub-Centers and three key New Towns (or New Cities): Lingang New City, Songjiang New City, and Jiading New City.

Shanghai implemented a series of housing and community development policies to guide the growth of its "satellite cities." In the 1950s, it built public housing communities to meet minimal living requirements utilizing limited funds. The 1980s saw these public housing communities mature into residential areas, which now include a variety of proximate uses, such as schools and commercial services.

As China's market economy began to prosper in the 1980s, the concept of commercial housing began to emerge at a time when most of the city's housing was still public. Since then, more and more market-rate housing developments with improved facilities have

Figure 9.2. Gubei Community—central pedestrian path.

emerged. Gubei District, for example, is a well-known and successful mixed-use development with high service standards catering to foreigners located on the fringe of the core city adjacent to Hongqiao International Airport (see Figure 9.2).

Ongoing Urban-Suburban Challenges

As Shanghai strives to become more innovative, livable, and ecologically sensitive, it faces many challenges from rapid expansion. As a response, the Shanghai government has implemented a number of planning tools, including developing suburban areas with an array of services, applying transit-oriented development (TOD) techniques, and ensuring a better living environment than in the central city. These communities still must deal with three questions, the answers to which will help define future growth and achieve equitable prosperity in Shanghai's suburbs:

1. How can Shanghai accommodate population growth while successfully controlling urban sprawl?
2. How can Shanghai use TOD as an effective tool for developing a sustainable suburban habitat?

3. How can planning for new livable communities meet facilities requirements while addressing environmental issues brought by a rapidly growing population?

The Shanghai Comprehensive Plan

Shanghai is working toward increasing competitiveness and becoming more ecologically sensitive. The implementation of the satellite city concept is a central method for getting the most use out of urban infrastructure and minimizing new development's negative impacts on the environment. Satellite cities are somewhat similar to London's new towns and Tokyo's subcenters—both of which distribute growth pressures away from their downtowns in a calculated way. Shanghai gives precedence to public transit and encourages nonmotorized traffic, with a goal of lowering energy consumption. In addition, the city is working toward a series of community enhancement objectives that will meet residents' demands for travel, shopping, and obtaining places of lasting value.

The Shanghai Comprehensive Plan (2015–2040) includes several strategies for reaching the city's goal. Shanghai's government is implementing these planning policies for strategic redevelopment throughout the city, including its suburban areas.[1]

*   Optimize the spatial structure of the overall metropolitan area and build a systematic spatial network. Set clear defining spatial development strategies, and adjust zoning controls accordingly.
*   Strengthen environmental protection, control carbon emissions, and reduce energy consumption by lowering energy costs, encouraging green transportation, and using new energy sources.
*   Optimize the spatial layout of land uses, and promote the integration of industrial and urban development.
*   Enhance the power of innovation, technology, and culture. Protect traditional culture as well as historical conservation areas to increase the city's attractiveness.
*   Foster diverse and harmonious urban–rural communities by proving proper housing and public services.

Two case studies have been chosen to show different approaches to adopting these strategies: the Xinchang Town Station and Zhoupu Planning Unit. Both are located in Pudong New District, outside the city's Outer Ring (the so-called suburban area). In both cases, these suburbs face the challenges of growing into compact, sustainable, and walkable communities. As development opportunities arise, the application of the principles of TOD can be witnessed firsthand, particularly given the location of the two sites near Metro Line 16, which connects to the easternmost part of Shanghai.

Some key characteristics of the two projects are different. Development in the new community in Xinchang is strong in traditional Chinese culture and needs to provide resources and activities to preserve that tradition. In contrast, the new development in Zhoupu reflects a more modern development mentality. Nearby, Shanghai Zhangjiang Innopark aspires to put a more technological and innovative spin on development trends. Both of these suburbs are on their way to adopting the principles of smart growth, including mixed-use development, while raising the demand for local office space and attracting an educated work force.

Case Study: Xinchang—Historic Preservation Meets New Development

Xinchang Town Station is a 363-acre site adjacent to Metro Line 16, north of Xinchang Ancient Town, and 35 kilometers from downtown (about a one-hour drive). Xinchang Ancient Town, rich in traditional culture, includes several tourist attractions.

Xinchang Ancient Town has approximately 100,000 residents, a minuscule number compared with the total Shanghai population. As a traditional waterfront town in the Pudong District, Xinchang Ancient Town is under the administration of Xinchang Town.

Planning Needs

Future development in the Xinchang Town Station will help shape the next generation of suburban development while providing residents a higher quality of life. The following opportunities will help the community achieve that goal:

- Using the new Metro line to relieve pressure on the transportation system and promote development around the station
- Improving and promoting local industry by taking advantage of local culture while enhancing industry innovation
- Conducting appropriate phases and intensities of development and avoiding disorderly land use
- Promoting smart growth to create urban clusters in suburban areas

Planning Strategies

Building on the available planning tools and a vision for the case study area, officials have adopted these strategies as a way to ensure the success of Xinchang Town Station.

Culture Preservation and Innovation

Xinchang Ancient Town can only accommodate limited new development due to regulations designed to encourage historic preservation. (Most surrounding new developments have not taken historical building scale and character into consideration.) Equally important, existing infrastructure in Xinchang has already met its limit, with no room for upgrades. This leaves the historical area and nearby land with little growth opportunity.

To address these limitations, Xinchang Town Station aims to create human-scaled streetscapes and landscapes that reflect the culture and traditions of Xinchang Ancient Town. The town will also make an effort to attract a variety of cultural and art industries for the enrichment of its citizens. The new development will focus on local culture, further increasing demand for local commercial services, retail, and recreation. For example, an artist village will be constructed, along with business and exposition functions.

As development of the suburb moves forward, early investments are funded by local government revenue from land transfer acquisition and rent. These investments are being used to redevelop the historic area and to hire planners and architects with the know-how to deal with the issues of historic areas. As the project takes advantage of the traditions of the community, it also rewards the old town with more revenue and a better-preserved built environment.

Multimodal Public Transit

The development uses park-and-ride and traffic-management schemes similar to those used in the core city. A key approach is to build a public transit hub that connects different travel modes—including light rail, sightseeing buses, public buses, taxis, and public bicycles. The hub consists of the Metro station, a bus terminal, and parking lots for the entire district, all of which are aimed at solving problems of daily commuters.

A similar solution in Tampines New Town in Singapore uses a mass rapid transportation transit hub to combine a Metro line and bus terminal to coordinate the transportation networks serving the blocks around the hub so that the area functions as a town center; this is a typical representation of TOD. An early land use plan for Tampines New Town reserved a block near the hub for development as a mass transport hub and a site for an increase in residents (see Figure 9.3).

Residents are able to walk to schools, the hospital, the community commercial center, and the Metro station via a dedicated pedestrian-only path. In addition, the government will use geographic information systems to aid in establishing an effective transportation network (see Figure 9.4).

Smart Growth

Starting from the Metro station and based on TOD concepts, future developments are encouraged to build more density to improve land use efficiency. However, form-based design guidelines will ensure that each development parcel meets the overall urban design objectives (see Figure 9.5).

Case Study: Zhoupu, a Growing Suburb

In terms of development, Zhoupu's situation is similar to that of Xinchang Town. Located at the easternmost edge of Pudong New District, Zhoupu Town was originally a rural

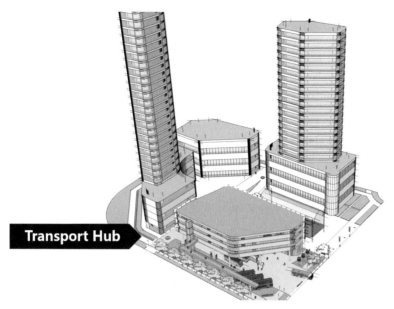

Figure 9.3. Transport hubs, a new concept in Shanghai's new towns, connect buses, transit, and parking.

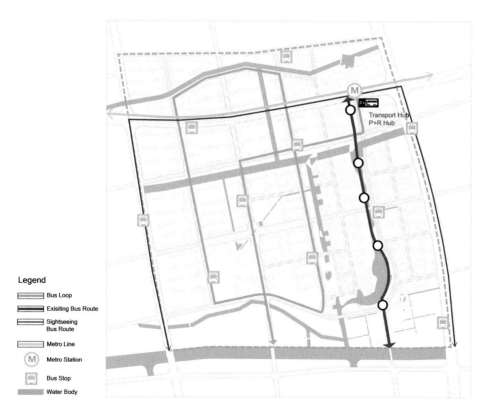

Legend

Bus Loop
Exisiting Bus Route
Sightseeing
Bus Route
Metro Line
(M) Metro Station
Bus Stop
Water Body

Figure 9.4. Public transit network planning.

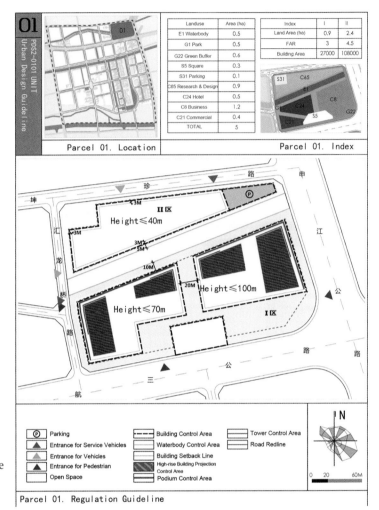

Figure 9.5. Part of the design guidelines for Xinchang.

town; however, its proximity to a city subcenter won it designation as an area to house decentralizing industries and residents. This has created great potential for new real estate ventures.

As a part of Zhoupu Town, the new town project site covers approximately 293 acres; residential areas are located to the west, and an industrial area is located to the east. It is surrounded by four vibrant town centers, including Wanda Plaza and Disneyland. The site is significant, since it connects the existing industrial park with the core city.

Planning Considerations

Overall, the community seeks to apply the principles of smart growth as it increases development adjacent to its rail transit stations. With these principles in mind, the following opportunities were contemplated and integrated into the local planning framework:

- Take advantage of Metro Line 16 to fully embody the "land-intensive, high-performance composite" TOD philosophy.
- Lay out industrial uses according to local conditions, launch a modernized innovation industry, create job opportunities, enrich public services and facilities, and increase nonmotorized traffic to make the planning area a livable and sustainable neighborhood.
- Manage appropriate phases and intensity of development to control the misuse of land, ultimately leading to a smart and compact new city.

Planning Strategies

A number of planning strategies will allow Zhoupu Town to develop into a more livable suburban community. These strategies draw on the principles of smart growth while taking advantage of existing physical and social infrastructure.

Mixed-Use Development

Mixing both working and living facilities represented the first step in building a sustainable suburban community. The project adopts a compact-city concept that integrates commercial, office, and cultural functions and forms a unique and competitive business district that is regionally significant. It is a suburban center characterized by shops, innovative working spaces, and an integrated community center.

Phasing

The phasing strategy will balance market demand and project economics. Phase 1 will incorporate facilities intended to encourage future development and help the area become a walkable suburban center. Development will include public facilities like museums and libraries, and residential development with apartments and other housing types. At the same time, connectivity to the Metro station and other public transit will be enhanced to provide increased accessibility throughout the Shanghai region. Phase 2 aims to continue strict management of the project and will incorporate additional innovative features for the development (see Figure 9.6).

Public Transit

Metro Line 16 serves two key functions for Zhoupu: it helps residents reach downtown Shanghai (and move throughout the region) and it gives tourists access to the community. As in Xinchang, this project relies on the rail station, innovative land use typologies, industrial clustering, job creation, and popular attractions to appeal to nearby areas.

Because this plan relies on connectivity and pursues sustainability, public transportation will play a key role in the evolution of the area as a walkable suburban community. Transit operators will enhance access to Metro Line 16 by establishing an internal

Figure 9.6. An international community in Shanghai–Lianyang International Community, Shanghai.

bus loop that coordinates bus services and serves car parking. The loop will serve to create "transport islands" where these modes will converge. To facilitate the blending of human and motorized traffic at these islands, a bridge will link the commercial core to the East Zhoupu Metro Station.

The design of the station and surrounding parcels establishes a link between the community's main transportation hub and strengthens the sense of belonging for residents in Zhoupu. Great attention was paid to the seamless connection of the rail station and the transport islands. Structured parking with park-and-ride hubs improves access to other communities and additional services.

Open Space

As a part of Zhoupu, the community includes typical Shanghai suburban characteristics, such as waterways and farmlands. The design of the community's open space will take advantage of the area's environmental amenities (see Figure 9.7). The local water network will be used as a resource throughout the site and create diversified water features to enrich outdoor activities. In addition, low-impact development techniques will include permeable paving to reduce stormwater runoff.

Other Factors

Adequate institutional and public facilities will be close to the site, including the Zhoupu Park, an international hospital and affiliated medical industrial park, and an international medical school, in addition to commercial uses, and a business park.

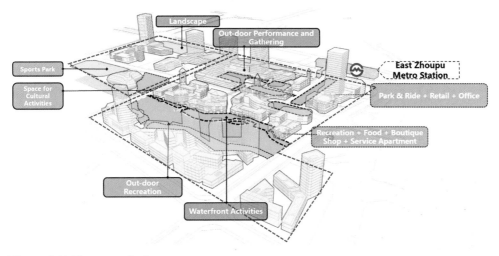

Figure 9.7. The network of open space.

Condominium prices have risen sharply in the area, which is often the outcome of rapid urban development: on one hand, urban housing prices are part of the success of population dispersion from the core city; on the other, high housing prices show that commercial housing and land use policies have not reached a healthy balance.

Conclusion

As a sprawling urban area, suburban Shanghai has a responsibility to accommodate the decentralization of city functions and population. Newly developed suburbs are mostly built on undeveloped land, and transportation plays a key role in connecting them to the remainder of the region. For planners, these projects serve as an opportunity to build new suburban communities with convenient transportation, a healthy economic and industrial outlook, and a livable environment.

Many new projects were approved or planned during the first half of 2017, and Shanghai government policies often undergo dramatic change in order to meet economic and social demands. Despite the challenges brought by rapid change, over the past 25 years, Shanghai has proved highly attractive for residents and businesses alike, with the most diversified population of any city in China. The emergence of new town projects along Metro lines that follow development models like those in Xinchang and Zhoupu should help Shanghai move closer to its goal of becoming a global model for environmentally responsible urban and regional growth.

Note

1.   *Shanghai's Comprehensive Plan* (2015–2040).

Figure 10.1. The location of North York in relation to the Toronto Metropolitan Region (Ma Shuyun and Xumengqi)

10

North York Center: An Example of Canada's Urbanizing Suburbs

Harold Madi and Simon O'Byrne

During the American presidential election in 2000, a Canadian comedian asked George W. Bush, the Republican candidate, for his thoughts on the endorsement of his campaign by "Canadian Prime Minister Jean Poutine."

"Well, I appreciate his strong statement," replied a straight-faced Bush while the cameras rolled. "We'll work closely together." Canada's prime minister at the time was Jean Chrétien. Poutine is a Canadian dish of French fries, cheese curds, and gravy.

Exploring Americans' image of Canada is something of a national pastime for Canadians. We love to tell ourselves that Americans think of Canada as a frozen wilderness. The actual Canada is a highly urbanized country with many past and recent planning successes to celebrate, of which a significant number are found in the suburbs of major Canadian cities. This chapter examines the forces driving this change and highlights best practices and lessons learned that can help decision makers in either country boost economic growth and density in their communities.

A Suburban and Urban Polarized Migration

The 2016 census revealed that 82% of Canadians live in large- and medium-sized cities, making it slightly more urbanized than the United States[1] and giving it one of the highest urban concentrations among G7 nations.

Canadians are clustered around several major city-regions. For example, one in three Canadians now lives in Toronto, Montreal, Vancouver, or their surrounding regions. Millennials' preference for living close to where they work has shifted from "emerging trend" to "new normal." Mixed-use developments are bringing the "18-hour city" to the suburbs.[2]

The explosive growth of the downtown area, predominantly fueled by millennials, has been especially pronounced in Canada's largest city—Toronto (see Figure 10.1). As background to a comprehensive planning study completed in 2018 for the downtown area, known as the TOcore Study, the City published a trends and issues report in 2014 that revealed an extraordinary shift under way, as evident in the following analysis:

- After a steady decline between the 1950s and 1976, the population of the downtown has doubled over the last 40 years.
- The rate of growth has accelerated since 2001, reaching 18% in 2006–2011, four times the growth rate for the city as a whole.
- While growth occurred across all age groups, 20- to 39-year-olds living downtown more than doubled, from 46,310 to 97,015.
- Overwhelmingly this growth is taking place in the development of high-density condominiums; 71,000 units were built between 1976 and 2011, with another 75,000 units in the pipeline.

Similar to the American experience, census data also show that for decades the suburban areas in these regions have captured a vast majority of growth relative to the core cities.[3] Unlike the "white flight" and subsequent decline experienced by many American cities, this was driven in large part by affordability. Increasingly, working- and middle-class families cannot afford to live in the center of Canada's big cities.

The outstanding example of this is Vancouver, whose housing market ranked as the third least affordable *on the planet* in the 2017 Demographia housing market survey.[4] As of early 2017, only 5% of income earners in Vancouver would qualify for a mortgage on a single-family home in the city proper.[5] In the outer suburbs the figure rises to 40%, with almost 80% of earners there able to afford a used, recently built condominium.[6]

Vancouver's market is far from unique in Canada. Toronto, which anchors the biggest urban region in the country, scored as a less affordable housing market than New York City in the Demographia market analysis. The report also found that "Montreal has seriously unaffordable housing," and that Toronto, Vancouver, and Montreal all experienced domestic outmigration in 2016.

The net effect is that urbanizing downtowns are creating "spillover" urbanization pressure in their suburbs. Large cities across Canada are becoming more polynuclear. This has created many edge cities that abut central cities. These edge cities tend to be located in areas where there is either extended heavy rail transit or suburban commuter rail lines (e.g., North York Town Centre, Metrotown, Laval).

Responding to this urbanization trend, Canadian developers are trying to create more complete communities that balance different population cohorts and lifestyles. This is principally driven by a reaction to rapidly rising housing prices and ever-increasing commuting times to downtowns. Developers are building vertical developments in suburban edge cities that cater to the middle class that can't afford to live in downtowns. These edge cities cater to first-time home buyers who are typically childless or have preschool-aged children. These areas are pluralistic and tend to have higher levels of diversification than downtown areas in Canada due to their better affordability.

Provincial, regional, and local governments across Canada have responded to growth in the suburbs with new land use controls and regulations aimed at making new developments more ecologically, socially, and financially sustainable. In this context, ecological sustainability has meant municipal policies with outcomes that reduce carbon footprints, halt the conversion of agricultural land to development, and ensure densities that will facilitate multimodal transportation choices. Social sustainability is applied in Canadian municipalities to ensure that each community has a diversity of housing typologies and a flattened neighborhood life cycle (e.g., for public school sustainability). Canadian municipalities are also applying full cost accounting on new developments to determine the tax revenue-to-expenditure burden over the long term. The latter have shown that much conventional suburban development has a multibillion-dollar liability across most regions in Canada. All of these respective public policy tools have already reshaped urban communities across the country.

Suburban Density in Canada's Largest Urban Area

Some of the most notable of these new regulations apply to the Greater Toronto Area (GTA), which is home to almost 6.5 million people—nearly one-fifth of Canada's population. In 2005, the Ontario government passed two important pieces of land use legislation.

The first is the Places to Grow Act, which sets density targets and identifies urban growth centers, strategic employment areas, and settlement area restrictions to reduce the negative impacts of sprawling, uncoordinated growth. For infill urban areas, the plan aimed for between 60 and 162 residents and jobs, combined, per acre by 2031. For suburban and greenfield developments, the goal is 20 combined residents and jobs per acre by 2031. Dense development is already flourishing in GTA suburbs like York, Vaughan, Markham, and East Gwillimbury. The Cornell neighborhood of York, for example, has more than 30 jobs and residents per acre. The plan was updated in late 2016 with more ambitious density targets. The GTA's target for all greenfield development, for instance, jumped from 20 jobs and residents per acre to 32.

The second piece of legislation is the Greenbelt Plan, which restricts development in more than 1.7 million acres of "protected countryside" surrounding the built-up GTA.

Combined, these regulations are transforming growth in many areas of the GTA. In 2006, single detached homes made up 54% of all residential construction in the area outside of Toronto proper. By 2013, that fell to 47%, as apartment and rowhouse building outpaced single detached house construction.[7]

New neighborhoods in places like Milton, a community of 84,000 an hour's drive from Toronto, blend traditional subdivision layout townhouses, skinny lots, and bike lanes. Townhouses can reach densities of up to 41 units per acre.

Another notable success is Cornell, a neighborhood of the city of Markham in the northern GTA. Cornell has been moving to higher density since the 1990s. Today it regularly appears in Canadian media as an example of suburban planning done right, achieving density in ways that promote a sense of community and aesthetic values. Cornell uses narrow streets, garages at the back of houses, and copious greenspace to create a walkable atmosphere. Mixed-use buildings, including multistory "live-work units" designed for businesses on the ground floor, with owners living in apartments above, have boosted density to more than 30 jobs and residents per acre (see Figure 10.2).

A 40-minute drive west of Cornell, the City of Brampton's Mount Pleasant Village provides a striking example of transit-oriented suburban development (see Figure 10.1). Built around a central commuter train station, Mount Pleasant Village uses a radial development pattern, with higher-density development along main transit routes and lower-density development toward the edges of the community.

Mount Pleasant Village encourages residents, in ways both covert and overt, to avoid driving. In addition to cycling infrastructure and walkable streets, the neighborhood uses design to shape behavior. For instance, while the transit hub does have a parking lot, it sits on the other side of the tracks from the station proper. Walking to the station is much more convenient.

Transit and Density Drive Suburban Success

As these case studies suggest, suburbs across Canada are growing denser by the day. This is giving a noticeable boost to the success of downtowns and newer walkable urban centers.

One key factor is that population density and availability of transit are both much higher in Canadian suburbs. This was achieved through cascading economic causes and effects, like a series of dominos knocking each other over in sequence.

The first domino is regulatory. Canadian governments have applied many more land-use controls and regulations to the development industry than their American counterparts. Tools like minimum densities and required transit options make developing new suburban homes more expensive.

Agricultural land on the edge of Edmonton or Calgary will sell to a developer for $250,000–$350,000 per acre. In the greenbelt of the GTA, similar land goes for between

Figure 10.2. Cornell, Ontario, created a mixed-use main street with live–work housing units. (NAK Design Strategies)

$1 million and $1.5 million per acre. After entitlements and servicing costs, which run between $2,500 and $4,000 per front foot for a lot, Canadian developers must sell the lots at $4,500 to $12,000 per front foot to make a profit. These higher costs are the second domino, which knocks over the third—density.

A generation ago, most Canadian suburbs were filled with single-family homes, usually with between three and six homes per acre. But rising land costs and servicing charges (i.e., the cost that Canadian municipalities force developers to pay toward the construction of off-site lift-stations, arterial roads, interchanges, sanitary trunks, reservoirs, libraries, fire stations, etc.) have pushed developers toward different housing types. Today, in cities like Edmonton and Calgary, new suburbs will average between 14 and 18 units per acre. In suburban Toronto, the figure rises to between 25 and 50 units per acre (see Figure 10.3).

The critical mass of people in these new developments makes them better able to support main streets, local retail, and new town centers. Retail in these denser suburbs is thus healthier and more financially sustainable because stores can rely less on automobile traffic. Canadian suburban businesses still accommodate vehicular visitors, of course, but

Figure 10.3. Rapid growth and rising land prices, together with public policy, have pushed suburban densities in the Greater Toronto Area to 25–50 units per acre. (IDuke and Sting under CC BY-SA 2.5)

their clientele gets a substantial boost from pedestrians and transit users. Density also makes mass transit more efficient and less dependent on subsidies.

The densification of Canada's suburbs has brought new challenges and opportunities. Housing affordability is an increasingly hot topic, with governments in British Columbia and Ontario both introducing legislation intended to address the issue. Denser communities demand new thinking on transit, with bicycle infrastructure and light rail solutions attracting much discussion in planning circles. Urban planning that encourages community activities through Canada's dark, cold winters is still nascent, but Edmonton, Winnipeg, and Saskatoon have joined Montreal and Quebec City in developing robust planning strategies for winter conditions. Planning professionals, governments, and the general public will doubtless debate these issues for years to come.

North York Centre: From Suburban Commercial Strip to Vibrant, Ever-Evolving Downtown

Toronto's North York Centre today is a striking example of how a vibrant downtown with continued robust growth and change can be carved out of a preexisting suburban context. This outcome is a result of strong public sector leadership and commitment to a clearly defined vision and implementation strategy; developers that carry out and pay for the supporting infrastructure; and the community's willingness to support density alongside higher-order public transit.

Some key early initiatives gave momentum to the establishment and subsequent growth of North York Centre:

- Early vision and planning in advance of a subway line extension into the area
- Strong public and civic purpose and presence in the form of a municipal civic center and public plaza, main offices for the school boards, federal and provincial government offices, and a performing arts center
- Early high-density senior housing and large-scale mixed-use projects
- Introduction of a service road to circle the downtown area as a means of traffic management, but also to serve as a clearly defined edge to preserve adjacent neighborhoods
- Clear and predictable policies and a regulatory framework for scale, transition, and mechanism for developer-funded public capital improvements in exchange for additional but defined density
- Continued large-scale strengthening of public transit in the form of a new central subway station and the transformation of another station into an interchange station for an entirely new subway line linking to downtown
- Broader regional, city, and provincial policies reinforcing the importance of the downtown for a sustainable regional urban structure and accordingly, directing growth to it
- The unrelenting championing of the downtown by a passionate and persistent mayor

The rolling out and notable success of these initiatives, however, did not occur overnight, nor were they all set out in one all-encompassing plan. Indeed, as with any dynamic and evolving traditional downtown, North York Centre has been 45 years in the making—a result of numerous plans and involving many hands. If this history tells us anything, it is that North York Centre will likely always be in the process of ongoing change, improvement, and refinement—and that isn't a bad thing.

From Rural Township to Rapidly Growing Suburban Municipality

Amalgamated with the City of Toronto nearly 20 years ago, the former City of North York maintains to this day a strong sense of identity rooted in a long history of efforts to emerge out of Toronto's shadow as a great urban center. First settled as a farming community in the early twentieth century, North York's transformation from a rural township to a bustling suburb with a walkable urban center that earns the title "downtown" makes for an instructive case study. It demonstrates both the challenges of creating a mixed-use, dense, walkable downtown out of an automobile-oriented suburban context, and the power of smart urban planning to engage with such challenges.

North York was initially created as a township in 1922, carved out of the much larger Township of York, directly north of Toronto. Though subdivisions laid out in a grid were created in the general area after the First World War, North York remained a mostly agrarian community for many years. However, in the 1940s, two key planning policies, adopted by governments elsewhere, played a key role in kick-starting the development of North York and eventually its downtown, known today as North York Centre. The first of these was the "City of Toronto's Master Plan of 1943." A first for the city, the document recognized that Toronto's future growth would take place in the vacant land of adjacent suburbs. Future planning would have to consider the whole metropolitan area.

The second was the provincial government's Planning Act of 1946, which required each urban municipality to form its own planning board. Toronto and the surrounding communities formed the Toronto and Suburban Planning Board. The board promoted specific projects like a suburban "green belt" system, a unified network of arterial roads, and creation of a unified public transit network in the area.

The early efforts of these boards proved mostly ineffectual. Their failures included the rejection by municipalities of a large highway extension, which would have run the Allen Expressway right through what is today downtown Toronto. This extension was the direct ancestor of the Spadina Expressway, which Jane Jacobs famously opposed in the early 1970s. However, the Toronto and Suburban Planning Board set an important precedent for regional cooperation and planning.

The culmination of that precedent was some years in the making. The next significant planning milestone, in fact, was another setback for integrated planning in the GTA. In 1950, elected officials at the City of Toronto voted in favor of amalgamating the municipal government with the surrounding suburbs. Municipal governments in those suburbs, including North York, almost universally rejected the idea.

In 1954, the municipal governments reached a compromise and agreed to form the Regional Municipality of Metropolitan Toronto. The Metropolitan government, led by a Metropolitan Council, made decisions about regionwide issues, including major roadways, drainage, regional planning, and public transport. The individual municipalities continued to administer most other services, including business licensing. North York was included in Metro Toronto, and it soon became one of the fastest-growing districts in the area thanks to its proximity to Toronto as well as the completion of Highway 401, which linked Toronto's suburban ring with the rest of southern Ontario.

The Initial Plan: Yonge Street Redevelopment Plan 1969

North York was formally declared a borough in 1967. Two years later the Borough of North York Council passed the Yonge Street Redevelopment Plan.

Yonge Street, sometimes called "Main Street Ontario," is a major regional arterial that runs from the southern boundary of Toronto on the shore of Lake Ontario to the shores of Lake Simcoe. Running north–south at the approximate geographic center of the municipality, Yonge Street essentially functioned as North York's main street. As the area evolved from a rural township into a rapidly developing suburban borough, the hamlets that once dotted Yonge Street became enveloped in continuous strip commercial uses.

In anticipation of the expansion of the Toronto subway up Yonge Street and into North York, the Redevelopment Plan focused on the area around the planned subway station at the intersection of Yonge Street and Sheppard Avenue. The plan imagined transforming the area's large commercial lots and abundant vacant lands into a node of mixed-use and transit-oriented development.

Though it did not come to fruition exactly as intended, the Redevelopment Plan's vision of a dense urban development almost 10 miles north of Toronto's downtown was the seed that would eventually blossom into North York Centre as we know it today. By the time the subway extension opened in 1974, downtown-style developments at the Sheppard–Yonge intersection, including large-scale commercial, residential, and government uses, was well under way.

The year before the subway opened, a furniture salesman named Mel Lastman was elected mayor of North York. Lastman, who had a keen sense of regional rivalry, would serve as mayor until 1997—just prior to North York's amalgamation with Toronto. His attitude that everything Toronto had, so too should North York, further boosted awareness for North York's downtown.

Reorientation: Yonge Street Centre Area Plan 1979

In 1979, North York incorporated as a city and opened its modern new city hall, called North York Civic Centre, fronted by a grand urban public space that would eventually be redesigned and named Mel Lastman Square. The planning for downtown also reached a crucial milestone with the adoption of the Yonge Street Centre Area Plan. Rather than focus downtown development exclusively at the Yonge–Sheppard subway stop, the 1979 plan proposed a larger downtown area consisting of a linear corridor along Yonge Street that linked development nodes built around the subway stops of Yonge–Sheppard and Yonge–Finch, a mile and a half to the north (see Figure 10.4). By the early 1980s a densified and diverse downtown had emerged in North York. Anchored by the municipal government headquarters and large-scale mixed-use development, the area also included an education center, federal government offices, and senior housing.

Setting Clear Parameters: Downtown Plan 1986 and Uptown Plan 1993

North York City Council approved the Downtown Plan in 1986, providing greater planning detail for the southern portion of the redevelopment area. The plan for the northern

Figure 10.4. North York, now part of Toronto, opened its Civic Centre in 1982 as a public catalyst to attract investment to a new downtown. Mel Lastman Square in front of the Civic Centre, opened in 1998, reflected a growing focus on urban design and walkability. (Flickr user PFHLai under CC BY-SA 4.0)

portion and balance of the downtown area was updated with the Uptown Plan, approved by the Council in 1993. These plans intensified development and expanded the area of suburban retrofitting to the downtown's present confines. They also set clear boundaries for the extent of the downtown, as defined by a ring of new service roads that served both to normalize the irregularity of block depths and to allay the fears of adjacent neighborhoods of further encroachment of development. All development was subject to a density and height regime that established a clear urban structure that directed the tallest and most intense development along either side of Yonge Street. On either side of the corridor, development would be required to step down in height and density subject to a combination of angular planes and buffer areas meant to ensure adequate transitions to the adjacent neighborhoods. The plan also established financial tools to make developer investment pay for new infrastructure, parks, and many other community amenities intended to benefit the neighborhoods adjacent to the downtown.

Overall, the 1980s were a period of iteration and refinement to the regulating plans. Construction and large-scale real estate development proposals boomed, led by what was coined as the "Big Five," five transformative, large-scale, mixed-use developments. This optimism for the future of downtown North York was certainly strengthened in 1985 with the Toronto Transit Commission release of Network 2011, a plan that prioritized a new Sheppard Subway line to reinforce the Metropolitan Council's plan for three suburban "subcenters" to become central business districts in their own rights, independent of Toronto's downtown. The ultimately seminal year 1987 marked the opening of the North York Centre Subway Station serving the Civic Centre area, midpoint between the Sheppard and Finch stations.

A Renewed Focus on Urban Design: North York Centre Secondary Plan 2002

Development in the 1990s steamrolled ahead, with commercial, public, and residential projects building up the corridor with a high degree of focus along Yonge Street. In 1993 an important civic and cultural milestone was reached with the opening of the North York Performing Arts Centre. However, while the downtown gained key civic and cultural functions and was growing by leaps and bounds, the quality of the public realm lagged— characterized by a "Main Street of heroic proportions" together with high traffic volumes, tall buildings, and not much to interest pedestrians.

The Urban Design Study was undertaken to inform updates to the Downtown and Uptown plans, which are required by the provincial government to be reviewed every five years. The study described the Yonge corridor and the residential areas surrounding it as "worlds apart, purposely separated from each other." The origins of this divide lay in the concerns of residents that dense development would overwhelm their residential community. The study sought to bridge this gap with more nuanced planning guidelines aimed at cultivating a more animated and inviting, pedestrian-oriented public realm. Up until this study, the evolving plans were mostly concerned with the configuration of downtown's boundaries and enabling development subject to blunt controls on density and heights, but they offered no clear and coherent vision for the public realm, and minimal guidance was given on how development ought to contribute to its improvement.

The Urban Design Study recognized that the success of a dense and mixed-use downtown ultimately hinges on a distinct sense of place and high-quality pedestrian experience. Accordingly, it introduced principles, policies, guidelines, and strategies that were subsequently integrated into the regulatory plans and have continued in force through today. Numerous key outcomes of the study have reshaped North York's downtown and are evident today:

- Softening the transition between the downtown and neighborhood areas to make it less abrupt
- More interactivity and continuous retail uses along Yonge Street and the side streets
- Broad, animated, and appealing pedestrian promenades with double rows of street trees, a center landscaped boulevard, and consistent paving treatments to reinforce the primacy of Yonge Street as the central downtown spine

- A fine-grained pedestrian network through the introduction of midblock connections on larger blocks
- The design and treatment of the service roads such that they connect, rather than divide, the adjacent neighborhoods from the downtown
- Streetscapes enhanced with street trees and continuous building frontage at heights no greater than the width of the street
- Setbacks and build-to-requirement that ensure appropriate edge conditions
- Protection of heritage buildings
- A continuous green network generated by linking parks, streetscape improvements, and private but publicly accessible open spaces
- Protecting and reinforcing special identity areas
- Directed grade-level access to buildings from streets or public spaces
- Establishment of a Business Improvement Area to expand and maintain public realm improvements

From amalgamation to the present day, planning policies have continued to strengthen North York Centre. Notable milestones include:

- The Sheppard subway line, opened in 2002, was the only line identified in the Network 2011 plan of 1985. The new line boosted the accessibility and appeal of the area for businesses, attracted private investments, and raised awareness of North York Centre.
- The 2006 City of Toronto Official Plan, among other things, expanded the possible land uses for suburban centers like North York to boost population and employment growth.
- The provincial Ontario Growth Plan for the Greater Golden Horseshoe, also in force since 2006, is a regional plan for the expansive urban area centered on Toronto. It applies policies to all municipalities in the region to mitigate the environmental, economic, and public health impacts of urban sprawl. Notably, it contains minimum-density targets and prioritizes urban growth centers like North York Centre.
- The Yonge Street North Planning Study, completed in 2014, articulates a plan for development between North York Centre and the city's northern boundary. It coincides with the planned extension of the Yonge subway line. As of this writing, the study is embroiled in political opposition rooted in fear of the speed and scale of its proposed changes.

Modeling of Potential Development from the Yonge Street North Planning Study

North York Centre today is dotted with dense development and local landmarks. These include the North York Civic Centre and Mel Lastman Square; the Toronto Centre for the

Figure 10.5. The Toronto Centre for the Arts, opened in 1993, added a significant cultural dimension to North York. (Flickr user abdallahh under CC BY 2.0)

Arts (formally the North York Performing Arts Centre) (see Figure 10.5); Empress Walk, a large mixed residential and retail complex that includes the longest unsupported escalator in North America; the Hullmark Centre, a large mixed residential, office, and commercial complex with a public plaza; and, the Emerald Towers, distinctive skyscrapers that have redefined the skyline. Job growth in the area is robust, with a 15% rise in 2016 alone, as is development, with 1.2 million square feet of nonresidential development in the pipeline. It has also met its density targets for people and jobs under the 2006 Growth Plan, a rarity for the region.

The year 2016 brought a sorely needed study for the reimaging of Yonge Street to introduce a "complete street" approach that will include a dedicated cycle track. This re-visioning will also serve to finally realize the splendid public realm first imagined 20 years ago. As of this writing, the Council has held back funding, but it appears likely to be reinstated eventually.

Despite great successes, challenges will continue to confront the ongoing planning and refinement of North York Centre. Key initiatives ahead include the completion and improvement of the public realm, addressing housing affordability, expansion northward in coordination with transit, and overcoming the fractured ownership of a number of the remaining undeveloped sites in the corridor. But planners know that their work is

Figure 10.6. A succession of plans clearly delineated North York as a high-density, transit-oriented urban center set among low-density residential neighborhoods. More recent planning has focused on enhancing walkability, use mix, and design quality. (Harold Madi)

never truly complete. How the planners in the area deal with these issues will determine whether North York Centre's status as a successful suburban downtown will be abiding or temporary (see Figure 10.6).

Notes
1.   CIA World Factbook. 2015, accessed August 9, 2017, https://www.cia.gov/library /publications/the-world-factbook/fields/2212.html.
2.   Susan Pig, "Urbanization Is 'New Normal' for Canada, Report Says: Drive to Live Downtown Reshaping Much of Real Estate Industry," the star.com, October 28, 2014, ac-

cessed August 9, 2017, https://www.thestar.com/business/2014/10/28/urbanization_is
_new_normal_for_canada_report_says.html.

3. Statistics Canada. "Population Size and Growth in Canada: Key Results from the
    2016 Census," February 8, 2017, accessed August 9, 2017, http://www.statcan.gc.ca/daily
    -quotidien/170208/dq170208a-eng.htm.

4. 13th Annual Demographia International Housing Affordability Survey: 2017 Rating
    Middle-Income Housing Affordability, Data for 3rd Quarter 2016, accessed August 8,
    2017, http://www.demographia.com/dhi.pdf.

5. Tracy Sherlock, "UDI/Vancity Housing Affordability Index: Statistics Show Homes Get-
    ting Even Further Out of Reach for Most," *Vancouver Sun*, February 11, 2016, accessed
    August 8, 2017, http://www.nationalpost.com/m/vancity+housing+affordability+index
    /11713933/story.html.

6. Ibid.

7. Dakshana Bascaramurty, "Places to Grow: Ten Years Later, Is This Progressive Act a
    Success or Failure?" *Globe and Mail*, October 6, 2016, accessed August 8, 2017, http://
    www.theglobeandmail.com/news/toronto/places-to-grow-ten-years-later-is-this
    -progressive-act-a-success-or-failure/article23886492/

Figure 11.1. Muirfield Village, built around a golf course designed by Jack Nicklaus in the mid-1970s, typifies the development model Dublin pursued from 1960 well into the 2000s. (Erin Hull photo; Muirfield Village Association)

11

Dublin, Ohio:
Bridge Street Corridor

Terry Foegler

Dublin, Ohio, outside of Columbus, is the quintessential suburban success story. Although its small village core was established in the nineteenth century, Dublin today is the product of the explosive suburban growth that accompanied urban decline elsewhere. It grew from a village of just over 600 in 1970 to a city of over 45,000 in 2015, with an employment base today of more than 50,000 workers.

Jack Nicklaus's development of Muirfield Village, home of the PGA's annual Memorial Tournament, and the focus for high-end residential development were catalytic (see Figure 11.1). With the opening in 1970 of the outer belt for Columbus, I-270, Dublin became the region's premier suburban office and attracted Wendy's International and other corporate headquarters. By the late 1970s Dublin was on its way to becoming a national model for suburban success (see Figure 11.2).

The influx of jobs and attendant payroll taxes built an extraordinary tax base while stimulating demand for rapid single-family housing development. During most of this rapid growth, Dublin enjoyed a growing tax base, a strong dedication to planning (demonstrated by a planning staff larger than that of Columbus), and excellent schools.

Like many Ohio municipalities, Dublin's tax revenues derive largely from a payroll tax, paid primarily by an estimated 50,000 workers concentrated within 9.3 million square feet of office space. This tax base supported levels of services and resident satisfaction that ranked among the highest in the United States[1]—and attracted affluent residents.

In the early 1990s, after doubling its local payroll tax rate to 2% (City officials stressed to voters that most workers in Dublin did not actually live in Dublin), the City began

Figure 11.2. Metro Center, shown here shortly after it opened, was once the region's premier office address. It risks losing tenants to newer mixed-use, walkable centers. (City of Dublin)

formalizing its approach to economic development. This effort culminated in the Mt. Auburn Economic Development Strategy, completed in 1994, which guided the City's approach to economic development for many years. That analysis showed that the continued growth in the city's tax base needed to maintain the high level of services and facilities residents had come to expect would require a sustained focus on office development, for which the city was extremely well positioned (see Figure 11.3a, b).

With extraordinary fiscal health, highly satisfied residents, a national reputation, and the second-highest household income in Ohio, why would Dublin tinker with success and consider an entirely new tack for future development? Simply extrapolating past success into the future produced a very rosy picture. Further complicating the consideration of any new approaches was a deep-seated opposition to multifamily development in general on the part of many city officials and residents, and a view that a density of more than five dwelling units to the acre was inherently undesirable.

Change on the Horizon

Until the early 1990s Dublin stood as Central Ohio's premier suburban office location. The community prided itself on its strict development standards, often applied through

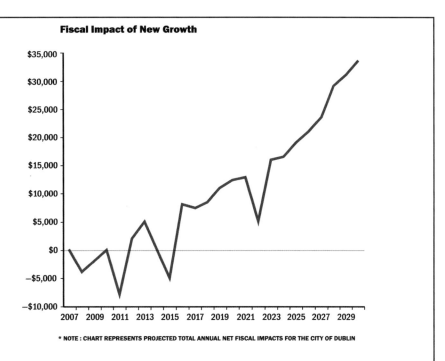

Fiscal Impact of New Growth

* NOTE : CHART REPRESENTS PROJECTED TOTAL ANNUAL NET FISCAL IMPACTS FOR THE CITY OF DUBLIN

Figure 11.3a, b. Office parks generated robust fiscal benefits for Dublin because Ohio allows host communities to tax employee earnings. The result was an unusually high level of local services such as the community's recreation center, shown below. Concerned about slowing growth in legacy office parks, Dublin adopted a plan in 2007 that proposed denser, walkable, mixed-use developments in some areas as a way of restoring employment and revenue growth. (Chart: Stantec. Photo: Wikipedia contributor Analog Kid under CC BY-SA 3.0)

"planned" zoning districts that usually incorporated a set of highly customized, negotiated development standards for each project.

Dublin had long prided itself on staying "ahead of the economic development curve." While Central Ohio had experienced slow population and employment growth for several decades, Dublin had succeeded by becoming the "go to" suburb for high-wage employers and high-income residents—adding more than 7.5 million square feet of suburban office space in the 1970s, '80s, and '90s.

By the late 2000s changing demographics and household characteristics posed an increasing threat to its competitive position—particularly in two areas. First, as baby boomers aged and began selling their homes in increasing numbers it was unclear if there would be enough buyers for those homes. The spread of larger-format, lower-density, single-family detached subdivisions that had defined much of the region's growth over four decades, driven largely by the baby boom housing bubble, was likely over.

Second, other suburbs were developing more competitive office parks. More worrisome, the region's largest developer—Nationwide Realty (an affiliate of Nationwide Insurance, headquartered in Columbus)—had taken an active role in creating large, mixed-use urban districts like the Arena District and Grandview Yards close to Columbus's increasingly desirable downtown. Meanwhile Dublin's office space was aging. Given the importance of employment tax revenue, Dublin needed new strategies to keep its office market competitive. Contrary to the 1990s when CEOs chose suburban office locations based on where they and their middle-aged executives wanted to live and work, employers found themselves increasingly driven to attract talent and by the desire of that young mobile talent for more urban, walkable, mixed-use environments in which they could both live and work. Dublin needed new economic drivers to take over the roles once played by golf courses and class A office parks.

Third, the city council wanted to make sure that it was taking the needed actions to prepare Dublin for its changing future, although the path and its implications weren't initially clear. Protecting the existing tax base—which meant renewing Dublin's appeal to well-paid knowledge workers—remained a critical priority. This meant making sure that employers could attract workers to Dublin well into the future. The city council also welcomed learning about changing demographic and housing patterns that would drive residential development in coming years. Council members were hearing bits and pieces of this message in their own lives: they had empty-nester constituents who wanted to remain in Dublin but couldn't find housing options. Council members also heard their own adult children say they wouldn't choose to live or work in Dublin.

An early outgrowth of this discussion was council support for the City to explore ways to create a denser, walkable, mixed-use—more dynamic—core. People quickly grasped some advantages of this approach. Dublin could introduce new types of housing that might appeal both to the young knowledge workers that employers sought and to the

growing pool of empty nesters. It seemed likely to bring new types of "urban" office settings with more walkable choices for food, shopping, and entertainment.

Sharing recent research by Dowell Myers, Richard Florida, and others helped frame
the issues for the city council, the City administration, and the broader community. Several central ideas emerged from these discussions and eventually framed many of the
City's first efforts:

- How can Dublin respond to substantial demographic shifts that will change hous-
  ing demand, and in ways that strengthen Dublin as a place to live and work?
- How does the city maintain and expand its strong employment base? How important is attracting young talent?
- How can the city help preserve the value of existing single-family homes, given data
  suggesting substantially fewer home buyers than future home sellers?
- What are the policy and housing implications of a growing pool of empty nesters?
- What are the opportunities for developing new living, working, and shopping environments that respond to these trends; improve the city's economic competitiveness; create a more vibrant core; and help preserve or enhance the values of existing
  homes?
- In summary, how could a suburban community like Dublin position itself for success in a changing world?

The City retained David Dixon FAIA, then at Goody Clancy and currently at Stantec,
to lead this initial planning effort, which kicked off with a speaker series that included
Christopher B. Leinberger (see Chapter 1) and Carol Coletta, then head of CEOs for Cities.
The series was designed to encourage public dialogue about these subjects, help build an
understanding of their implications, and focus on target areas for redevelopment.

The consultant team also included experts who assessed potential market demand for
newer types of housing and commercial uses that would locate in a denser, mixed-use
neighborhood. The team helped explore the incentive structure Dublin would need to
become more walkable. Reliable market data were deemed critical to framing and informing this public policy discussion. Interviews with human resources directors elucidated
their companies' views of the challenges in drawing talent to Dublin and strategies the
City might consider to help them attract and retain talent. Public input was gathered at
the speaker series, at other public presentations, and from citizen surveys.

The Bridge Street District

Early in the planning effort, the focus for studying the possibilities for a densely developed, walkable, mixed-use core settled on a 1,000-acre area around "Old Dublin," the
community's small historic center. Quickly labeled the Bridge Street District (BSD), it

represented about 6% of the city's land area and was bisected by the scenic but little-used Scioto River. Although the BSD included multiple developed parcels, many sites appeared ripe for redevelopment—particularly struggling, outmoded strip centers and office parks. Because the district included few residential neighborhoods, it was relatively insulated from widespread resident pushback. The BSD also benefited from direct interstate highway and busy arterials on all four sides.

Still other features strengthened the logic of focusing on this area:

- Dublin residents liked recent smaller-scale redevelopment that had occurred in the historic village (especially the restaurants) and clearly wanted more walkable environments—in fact the most frequent comment from nearby residents who saw early plans was, "Will I be able to walk there?"
- Residents desired more access to green space along the Scioto River.
- Residents noted that several strip-retail centers had clearly been distressed for years despite Dublin's favorable demographics.

However, the idea of "redevelopment" was foreign to a community where more than 95% of development had occurred since 1975, and initially many community leaders were highly skeptical that "density" and a new "downtown" were natural to Dublin's DNA. The consultant team helped paint a picture for the community of the walkable BSD not as undoing Dublin's suburban character but rather as adding a new "layer" to it. This new layer would introduce complementary housing, office, and retail options that would improve and expand choices in Dublin; enhance and preserve competitiveness; and provide desirable new places that would improve quality of life and add value to the other 94% of Dublin. The team also reminded residents that they had planned well for four decades of baby boomer–driven growth. Now the city needed to plan for new demographics and economic-development dynamics that would shape the community for four decades to come.

What Mattered Most?

I would ascribe the city council's eventual embrace of the BSD initiative to several key factors:

- Council members believed that successful implementation of the BSD vision would improve Dublin's economic competitiveness and the health of its tax base—a core element of the City's economic development strategy.
- The city would benefit from new housing options and environments attractive to young professionals working in Dublin and new types of urban office environments the district would offer. Dublin's largest employers reinforced these ideas.

- Dublin's livability would be enhanced by new parks and green space along the river that would be activated by the new mixed-use development.

- The growth of Dublin's urban core from a small village center to a substantial mixed-use city center befitting a dynamic city of 45,000 would provide a much wider array of housing, restaurants, hotels, and other retail, as well as new public spaces.

- Apartments that attracted young professionals would help create a "feeder network" of potential home buyers. One of the region's most respected market analysts noted that communities should find ways to offer the last apartment young professionals rented before buying their first home. This demographic group, he noted, typically rented that last apartment in more urban, mixed-use environments.

- Successful implementation would enhance the city's overall quality of life. The addition of new mixed-use development for all residents would benefit broad subsets of the community. (Market studies performed for the BSD plan showed significant retail sales leakage, demonstrating that Dublin could capture substantial unmet demand with walkable, mixed-use environments that included the right retail choices.)

Other studies in the region reinforced the importance of initiatives like the BSD. Most notably, Insight2050 brought in Peter Calthorpe's firm to examine the impacts of various growth scenarios for Central Ohio over the coming decades.[2] That study's demographic analysis, which built upon another influential regional study by Arthur Nelson, reached conclusions that mirrored the findings of Dublin's planning efforts.[3]

At the end of the initial planning process in 2013, the city council approved the Vision for the Bridge Street District. The document included a concept for the BSD that reflected much higher development densities than Dublin had ever built—a dynamic mixing of land uses and the establishment of an urban, multimodal street grid that would provide the development framework for the district. It included an illustrative plan for such a roadway and building layout framework; a mix of land uses based on preliminary market assessments and projected development capacities; and renderings that dramatically conveyed the exciting nature of the district's multistory, mixed-use development and public spaces.

Communication

With a robust internal communications infrastructure, the City organized extensive outreach throughout the planning and public engagement processes. Although surveys reflected a high level of resident support for the BSD initiative, some residents continued to express concern about issues such as traffic impacts, building heights, and proposed densities, especially the number of apartments contemplated. The input helped identify where additional planning and study were needed (such as better understanding of the nature and timing of roadway improvements, especially where the new urban grid would meet the suburban arterial system).

Resident surveys demonstrated over time that the more residents knew about the planning effort, the more likely they were to support it. That understanding helped guide the City's ongoing communication, social media, and community outreach efforts, with the result that residents reporting strong familiarity with the BSD plan rose from 12% in 2013 to 73% in 2016.

In the 2016 survey, 87% of residents indicated they were supportive of the BSD, with 88% believing the BSD would strengthen Dublin's economy, 86% believing the BSD would make Dublin more attractive to young professionals, 87% believing it would enhance the city's reputation, and 66% believing it would make Dublin more attractive to residents planning to retire. The efforts of the previous five years had resulted in a transition from a population with little to no apparent interest in high-density, mixed-use planning and development, to one that broadly understood and supported it.

The City also invited developers to become involved in the BSD planning effort, both to test their interest in the development types being discussed and to stimulate their interest in exploring opportunities for potential development.

From Vision to Implementation

Following official adoption of the BSD Vision in 2013, the City launched more detailed analyses of transportation (conducted by Nelson\Nygaard), fiscal impact (Tischler Bise), and development regulations to include a form-based zoning code (Farr Associates) for the BSD. These studies would both further test and prepare for implementation of the BSD Vision. Studies ultimately determined that existing infrastructure could accommodate the proposed development patterns, demonstrated positive fiscal impacts, and provided a new form-based code to facilitate implementation.

Traffic congestion loomed as the biggest concern in these analyses. How could the BSD's denser urban development not create havoc on Dublin's roadways? How could existing, heavily used roadways safely welcome pedestrians and cyclists? Eventually, information on the functional advantages of dramatically increased connectivity and a greater understanding of the internal trip-capture rates envisioned for the BSD became critical to acceptance of the overall concept.

The studies showed that sewer, water, stormwater, and other utilities were all adequate to meet the needs of new development types, with no adverse impacts on other parts of the city. The fiscal-impact analysis demonstrated a net benefit for the City, but it later became clear that to finance the structured parking and roadway improvements required to serve the planned intensity of development, the City would need more robust financing incentives.

Public Investment

Early in the implementation process it became clear that key infrastructure—including parking garages (in order to achieve the desired density and likely unable to charge user fees at first), streets with more urban finishes, and enhancement of the public realm in general—would need the City's financial support. This meant the City and the Dublin City School District would need to reach agreement on the parameters of the incentive structure needed to stimulate BSD development. Ohio law allows cities to capture a portion of incremental real estate taxes generated by new development. It also makes provisions for school boards to negotiate alternate revenue-sharing arrangements with a city.

In Dublin, the school district receives about two-thirds of real estate tax revenues, but sending two-thirds of the incremental revenues from BSD development to the district would have rendered new development financially infeasible.

The City began with several key assumptions. First, the new tax revenues from the proposed BSD development would not occur without incentives, and there was no way to fund those incentives without the lion's share of the new revenues. Second, significant portions of the BSD district had experienced stagnant or declining tax valuations for several years, and there was no reason to think that traditional suburban development could stimulate meaningful reinvestment. Third, the City collected extensive information from similar higher-density developments, all of which strongly suggested that the housing would add little demand for space in district schools. Finally, the City demonstrated that the floor area ratios achieved by BSD redevelopment would create per-acre valuations many times higher than those under conventional suburban development. Once the incremental revenues had paid for the needed infrastructure, the school district would reap the benefit of these windfall valuations.

Where to Begin the BSD?

With council approval of the BSD Vision in 2013 and a BSD form-based code in 2014 to ensure that development embodied the Vision's walkable, street-oriented, urban qualities, Dublin was ready to move to the last step: where and how to get started.

While residents expressed growing excitement and began asking how soon redevelopment would start, many in the development community expressed doubt that Dublin, known for its restrictive development-review processes, low densities, and quintessentially suburban character would move forward with a 1,000-acre, urban vision. It was also not clear that property owners would fully support the transformational projects envisioned for these sites. The City decided to encourage initial implementation along the Scioto River in the BSD by concentrating its planning focus and key capital improvements within this high-priority area. Several reasons drove this choice:

- The historic village center, already established in this area, represented a well-loved piece of walkable urbanism. New development could build on this base.
- Dublin residents had long expressed a strong desire to make better use of the river, an extraordinary natural amenity.
- With three of the city's busiest roadways crossing it, the corridor had excellent vehicular visibility.
- Several prime parcels, if assembled, could provide excellent development sites.
- The City had begun considering several parks and roadway-improvement projects in this corridor. These projects could give a strong boost to the desired types of private investment.

The BSD Scioto River Corridor Framework, adopted in 2016, grew out of these efforts. It laid out initial planning concepts for three public-improvement projects proposed for this area, together with conceptual plans for a new walkable urban center to launch redevelopment of the larger corridor.

The Framework included several key elements:

- Definition and location of key public improvement projects in the corridor. These included construction of a roundabout, relocation of a roadway along the east side of the river to free up land for a new public park, concepts for the new river park along both sides of the river, and an iconic pedestrian bridge that would connect the west side of the river (including the historic core) with the urban core being developed on the east.
- Definition of the character, scale, and location of new privately developed buildings and the street grid that formed the transportation framework for the development
- Renderings that showed the desired character of this area and demonstrated how the public and private investments would mutually reinforce one another and collectively yield the parks and vibrant urban environment envisioned by the community

One element particularly captured the public's imagination early in the planning process: an iconic pedestrian bridge crossing the Scioto. The $17 million bridge, designed by Paul Endres of Endres Studios in San Francisco, quickly became a symbol of the enhanced connectivity that the BSD would bring to the traditionally river-separated east and west sides of Dublin (see Figure 11.4).

The parks on both sides of the river, connected by the new bridge, also represented important citywide amenities that appealed to many Dubliners.

Implementing the Bridge Street District Vision: Bridge Park

As the City's focus became clearer to the development community, and interest began to build, Columbus-based Crawford Hoying determined that the emerging plan for urban,

Figure 11.4. An iconic pedestrian bridge connects Bridge Park to historic Dublin Village and a new riverfront "Central Park." (Endres Studio)

mixed-use development types and the public improvements aligned well with its own vision of creating a new generation of walkable urban places in the region. The company began aggressively acquiring land before final adoption of plans by the City and in advance of any agreements with the City on cost-sharing for new streets and other infrastructure. Crawford Hoying's boldness reflected an acceptance of a higher-than-normal level of development risk—at least by the standards of most midwestern, suburban developers. These aggressive moves, however, quickly established the developer as a very credible BSD player. Perhaps more consequentially, they gave Crawford Hoying control over much of the prime developable land in the BSD river corridor (see Figure 11.5).

Crawford Hoying named the new district Bridge Park and immediately began working with the City on creating a public/private partnership—early on cooperating to buy a struggling strip center whose location blocked progress on the district and new roadways. From the City's perspective, this transaction required upfront public investment but unlocked significant value. Counting both already approved capital-project investments

Figure 11.5. Bridge Park, roughly 3 million square feet of mixed-use development, launched the first phase of a walkable new downtown that could reach 10 million square feet, reversing decades of sprawl. (Crawford Hoying)

by the City in the river corridor, and committed investments from two major developers, the BSD vision and planning will have stimulated well over $450 million of new investment in this area by 2019.

As this book is being finished, the first 1 million square feet of mixed-use development is under construction and scheduled to open in 2017. By 2020 another 2 million square feet will open. The 30-acre district will include more than 300,000 square feet of offices, close to 200,000 square feet of retail and restaurants, a grocery store, more than 700 units of rental and ownership housing, two hotels (both new "flags" geared to walkable urban locations), a 500-person event space, a 4,000-seat arena, and a recreation center. The district will include roughly 3,000 structured parking spaces in addition to curbside parking (see Figure 11.6).

Determined to meet Dublin's and its own goal of creating a lively, walkable district rather than a freestanding development, the developer organized Bridge Park into seven blocks of mixed-use development with a street grid that can connect into future blocks as the larger Bridge Street corridor continues to develop. Bridge Park faces the new Scioto

Figure 11.6. Bridge Park is organized along an urban grid of streets that mix retail, restaurants, housing, offices, a hotel, and a performance venue. (Crawford Hoying)

Riverfront Park across Riverside Drive with a mix of housing and offices located above retail together with the new arena. However, the district really comes to life along four blocks of Longshore, a new street that extends the length of the district one block in from Riverside Drive. Longshore is lined with cafés and restaurants, stores, hotels, and similar uses that animate the street. To infuse the district with a more dynamic live/work quality and attract start-ups and creative businesses not interested in conventional office space, Crawford Hoying introduced a floor of "above the store" work space on the second floors of buildings along Longshore that also include three floors of housing above the office.

Notes

1.   National Citizens Surveys, conducted by the National Research Center, Inc., 2012, 2014.

2.   Calthorpe Associates, Insight 2050 Scenario Results Report. Columbus: MORPC, Columbus 2020, and Urban Land Institute Columbus, 2015, accessed April 24, 2017, http://getinsight2050.org/about/.

3.   Arthur C. Nelson, "Columbus, Ohio, Metropolitan Area Trends, Preferences, and Opportunities: 2010 to 2030 and to 2040," Washington, DC: Natural Resources Defense Council, 2014, accessed April 24, 2017, www.nrdc.org/sites/default/files/columbus -metro-area-trends-report.pdf.

Figure 12.1. Decades of far-sighted policies, which it frequently fine-tunes, have helped Arlington County create a high-density spine of walkable urban places, like this area near Metro's Clarendon Station. One measure of the success of this strategy: 12 percent of the county's land generates 50 percent of its revenue.

12

The Arlington Experiment in Urbanizing Suburbia

Christopher Zimmerman

The urban county of Arlington, Virginia—today one of the most frequently cited exemplars of transit-oriented development (TOD)—is a first-ring, auto-oriented suburb of Washington, DC, that successfully transformed itself into a model smart growth community and has become a magnet for millennials. Though much of this transformation has occurred since the 1990s, the foundation was laid much earlier, and the planning process (in terms of both policy and implementation) took several generations. In fact, Arlington was beginning the practice of "smart growth" long before the term was invented. As a result, Arlingtonians had to invent a lot along the way—making plenty of mistakes, both in substance and in process. Arlington's success story is one of learning through experimentation.

Arlington is notable for what it did—and did not do—to realize its success. The County made almost no use of tax abatement or other financial incentives. Public money was spent heavily, but on public property, for public goods. (Most obviously, on the Metro system, for which 11 stations were opened in Arlington by the early 1980s; but also on elements of pedestrian infrastructure, parks, affordable housing, and others.) In fact, in Arlington many public amenities were paid for by private development, a reversal of the usual pattern.

The transition of Arlington from suburban bedroom community to a model of walkable urbanism evolved over several decades, in distinct phases. Rather than the execution of a grand plan, it reflects a series of adjustments, of learning through trial and error, a process in which there were shifts of focus and in which new approaches and techniques were devised based on the experience of the previous phase. In rough terms, three phases can be discerned: (1) an initial period focused on Metro planning and development, in the 1960s and '70s; (2) a middle period, encompassing the initial sector planning for Metro station areas, extending from the 1970s to the '80s, focused on the location of density relative to rail stations (the "bull's eye" plan); and (3) a culminating period in the 1990s and 2000s, which produced detailed urban design; changes in transportation planning, design, and operations; and, finally, the extension of urban concepts (walkability and use-mix) beyond the Metro corridors.

Evolution of Arlington: From Rural to Suburban to Urban in Less Than a Century

Separated from the District of Columbia ("retroceded" to Virginia) in the mid-nineteenth century, as Alexandria County, and divided from the City of Alexandria after the Civil War, the county began the twentieth century as a sparsely populated, rural backwater that didn't even have its own name. (In 1920 frustrated county residents ended confusion by getting the name "Arlington" adopted—at a time when the population was less than 20,000.) With the New Deal and the Second World War, Arlington experienced explosive growth as a bedroom community. Population peaked at roughly 170,000 in the 1960s, then fell 12% in the 1970s. The County's embrace of Metro in the 1970s reversed decline, and today Arlington's population tops 230,000.

The Role of Rail Transit

Arlington's transformation was the work of several cohorts of elected officials, citizen activists, and county planners working over several generations. Without question, the key driver was the introduction of the Metrorail subway system (planned in the 1960s and constructed in the 1970s and '80s), and the key transformative act was the decision to shift Metro's planned Orange Line from a highway-median alignment to an underground corridor through the heart of the county. This farsighted action by Arlington's leadership in the late 1960s, at variance with the approach taken in every other jurisdiction outside of Washington, made possible the creation of a new, linear downtown (see Figure 12.1). In 2002, the US Environmental Protection Agency recognized the Rosslyn–Ballston Corridor with its first Award for Overall Excellence in Smart Growth.

The development took decades, and the County had much to learn along the way about how to make TOD work, but this fundamental decision to build the Metro underground made possible everything that has distinguished Arlington since. Those making the decision at the time did not have all the tools to create successful TOD.[1] The regional scheme for Metro was basically for the expensive underground portions of the system to be concentrated in downtown Washington. Outside of the District, the plan contained costs by running track on the surface, largely in the medians of major highways.

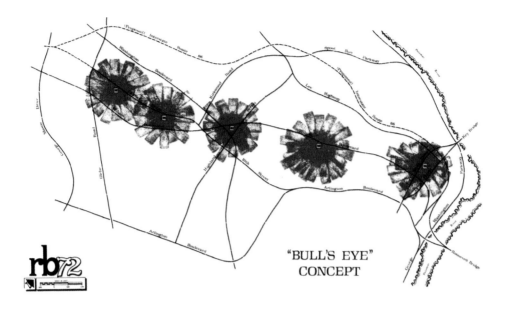

As these areas are delineated the "Bull's Eye" concept develops.

"BULL'S EYE"
CONCEPT

Figure 12.2. The "bull's eye" concept for the Rosslyn–Ballston Corridor. (Arlington County)

The suburban stations would be surrounded by parking lots and would function as a commuter rail service. In Virginia, the Orange Line was to run along a new highway, I-66, all the way to the Vienna terminus in Fairfax County. Had this plan been followed, the Orange Line would have provided little more than commuter service through Arlington, as it did in Fairfax and other suburbs.

But Arlington's leaders in the late 1960s made the bold (and decidedly more expensive) decision to bring the line underground and create five stations along a corridor less than 3 miles long. The stations were spaced closely enough (about a half mile on center) to allow them to be reached by a short walk from anywhere in the corridor. Highly dense development was placed "on the bull's-eye" of each station entrance (see Figure 12.2). This enabled walkable developments and the creation of synergies among them. Ultimately, it would produce tremendous economic benefits, with nearly 60 million square feet of office, retail, and residential development along the Rosslyn–Ballston (R-B) Corridor, and more private office space than the downtowns of Atlanta, Dallas, Denver, Los Angeles, Seattle, or Miami.[2] Seven station sectors (the five located in the R-B Corridor plus two on the Blue–Yellow Metro corridor in the southern part of the county) contain about one-tenth of Arlington's land area, but generate more than 50% of its tax revenue.

However, Arlington still had to learn how to execute the concepts of "urbanization" (in the best sense of the word—alien to Arlingtonians of the time). They had gotten the "macro" decision right; learning the "micro" concepts would take more time, and processes. Placing the Metro line underground; locating stations on roughly half-mile centers; and focusing planning for high-density development in the immediate prox-imity of station entrances were "big picture" decisions. These set the necessary, but not sufficient, conditions for TOD. The full formula for the transformation of a car-dependent residential suburb to a walkable, mixed-use community required the integration of spe-cific design features, covering a myriad of details, into the planning and implementation process. Only with the incorporation of good urban design requirements[3] into station sector plans could the Metro station areas become truly transit oriented, and not merely transit adjacent.

Learning these details, and establishing standard practices for the station sector plans and the approval of individual site plans, was the work of later citizens, planners, and elected officials. This took place over many years, through much trial and error. The learn-ing process can be seen in the built environment as it emerged at different points along the timeline. In some ways, Arlington's Metro sectors offer a showcase for both best prac-tices and bad practice.

Mistakes Made, Lessons Learned

Not surprisingly, early efforts brought mixed results, resulting in a built environment that displays an uneasy compromise between late twentieth-century auto-centric planning and walkable town building. This is most evident in the first station area to develop.

Rosslyn, at the east end of the corridor (and the closest to Washington, DC), was an early magnet for high-density office development (owing to a decision by the federal gov-ernment in the 1960s to lease significant office space) in the years preceding the opening of Metro. From the standpoint of density, Rosslyn's development was consistent with the bull's-eye plan. Unfortunately, the execution of dense development resulted in a decid-edly pedestrian-hostile environment, and the creation of a sterile cityscape lacking any "sense of place." There were two fundamental flaws: insufficient use mix and pedestrian-*unfriendly* ground-plane design.

Initially Rosslyn wasn't really a mixed-use sector. Office development was concen-trated in the center, with residential on the periphery. By the time the Rosslyn station opened in 1976, 4 million square feet of office space had been developed, but only 184 residential units. And these were pushed farther from the station, along with a few hotel sites (see Figure 12.3). Moreover, retail was located on the second-floor level, with "sky-walks" bridging high-volume one-way streets below. Construction costs were reduced by allowing parking to be included in buildings at ground level, resulting in extensive blank walls along street sidewalks. Garage entrances and loading docks occupied large expanses of midblock sidewalk (see Figure 12.4). This approach to development guaranteed that

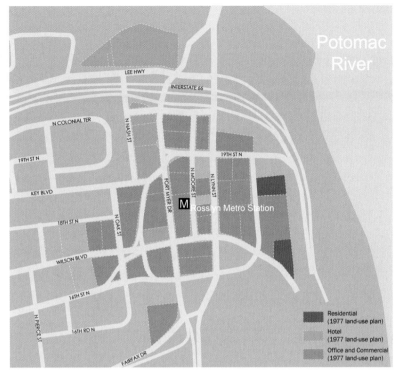

Figure 12.3. Rosslyn land use, mid-1970s. Concentration of office space in the center, minimal amount of housing at the periphery. (Ma Shuyun and Xumengqi)

Figure 12.4. Early streetscapes in Rosslyn featured extensive blank walls along sidewalks, giving little consideration to activation of the street and sending a clear message that pedestrians didn't belong there. In 2013, the county launched an ambitious plan to correct this problem with rebuilt streets, new parks and plazas, and other measures to add life to Rosslyn's realm. (Chris Zimmerman)

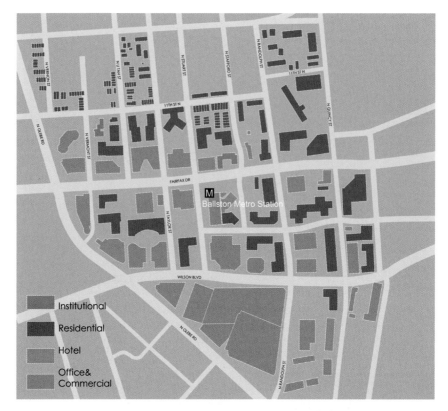

Figure 12.5. Ballston station area land use, showing contrast with Rosslyn. (Ma Shuyun and Xumengqi)

the heart of Rosslyn would be dead at night and on weekends, with minimal street life, even during the weekday lunch hour.

By the 1990s, Rosslyn's built environment was recognized as a problem that needed to be solved, if the full potential of its real estate were to be realized. Approved solutions included large-density bonuses for the redevelopment of building sites consistent with pedestrian-focused design standards, and the insertion of residential properties into the core. But from the early days of the R-B Corridor in the mid-1970s, Rosslyn became the symbol of what Arlington did not want for the corridor.

Lessons learned from Rosslyn benefited subsequent station areas, informing later sector plans and second-generation sector plan rewrites. The major downtown center at the other end of the corridor, Ballston, demonstrates that Arlington learned the critical importance of diversifying the use mix. The blocks surrounding Ballston's station entrance display an almost checkerboard pattern of alternating office and residential development (see Figure 12.5). Parking is below grade, allowing for active interface between street wall and sidewalk. Even in Ballston, however, the earliest buildings (approved and constructed in the early 1980s, soon after the station's opening) still sported a few noticeably blank facades along sidewalks, frontages that pulled back from the sidewalk, and even a drive-way between the sidewalk and building (see Figure 12.6a, b).

In some respects, the initial planning goals for the five station sectors show signs of the residual impulse from Euclidean zoning to separate uses, with each having its own "theme," which restricted the mix of uses within. The Virginia Square Metro station area for instance, was slated to be primarily residential, while neighboring Ballston would be an office center. It is fine to aim for "unique character" for each neighborhood; however, enabling a non-car-dependent lifestyle means providing destination variety within walk-able distances. If we think of walkable distance from a rail station as something between a quarter and a half mile (as Arlington's planners did), then the planning focus is an area of roughly 125 to 500 acres. When areas of this magnitude are designated for one principle use (e.g., residential), destinations are pushed beyond a walkable distance (the fundamental problem of suburbia). The result can be a community with density and transit access, but

Figure 12.6a. A 1980s-vintage office building in Ballston displays the era's uneasy compromise between a suburban office building and an urban site. Note the setback with a driveway in front, a withdrawn facade with landscape planters, and the drive entrance in the foreground (leading to surface parking and cut for below-grade parking). (The building also contains ground-floor retail space, none of which faces the street.) (Chris Zimmerman)

Figure 12.6b. A pedestrian-friendly Ballston building from the early 2000s. (Chris Zimmerman)

still dependent on automobile use for daily life. Over time, both the growing understanding of the importance of mixing uses in close proximity and the force of the real estate market led to a greater balancing between residential and office uses in each station area.

A midcourse review conducted in 1989 examined concerns about the achievement of Arlington's goals for the R-B Corridor, especially in terms of "quality of place." It identified shortcomings in the process, finding an "overriding need is to evolve a more complete approach to design decision making." Specifically, "guidelines and procedures have to be developed and tested for negotiating future development proposals within the context of a detailed design framework. . . . The types of tools most needed are: zoning that permits greater control over specific uses, offers the transfer of development rights in certain situations, and designates setbacks, build-to lines and building-to-building relationships" and "Sector plans with thorough design guidelines including information on materials, scale, and diagrams showing how buildings should address the sidewalk and street."[4] (See Figure 12.6b, for an example of the improved streetscape resulting from the more refined approach.)

This "moment of reflection" presaged a period of robust dialogue among leaders and the general public about how to ensure that development would generate not just an enhanced tax base but the kind of place that people wanted to live in. The outcome was a change in consciousness among Arlingtonians about the character of their community, and their relationship to development. Where before the understood goal of policy was "managing growth," now it became a matter of shaping the built environment to achieve a highly specified model of community design. It became less reactive and more intentional. And a community that had seen itself as suburban came to identify itself proudly as urban.

A contributing factor was the emerging New Urbanism movement by the mid-1990s, which took root not just among County planners, but in the ranks of informed citizenry.

Through the 1990s and early 2000s, there was a steady course of refinements to plans and processes that not only raised community benefits but cemented the County's commitment to good urban design. Sector plans and other overlays became more specific and detailed. Site plan conditions grew in number, often in reaction to disappointments with prior approvals. For example, to animate the sidewalk environment, the site plan for a building above the Court House Metro station required significant fenestration for ground-floor retail. When a pharmacy occupied the space and placed the back sides of shelving units against the windows, frustrating the intent of the site plan, subsequent site plan conditions became more specific to ensure transparency.

Because the economy in the 1980s and 1990s was strong and the demand for density was growing, the County and its citizens were in a relatively strong position to set high standards and expect them to be met. They could afford to say no to development proposals that fell short. When they did so, the bar was raised for subsequent project consideration. (A major turning point was the rejection in 1995 of a plan to put a suburban-style Home Depot on a 10-acre site a few blocks from the Clarendon Metro station.) Design features that had been aspirational amenities came to be standard expectations, starting points for a proposal rather than items to be negotiated as benefits. Buildings with blank walls along sidewalks became nonstarters; garage entrances and their associated curb cuts were minimized; and contributions to open space, public art, and affordable housing were now routine.

By 2005, the R-B Corridor had become a model of desirable TOD, the new hip place, where every young professional (millennials) longed to move to, if only they could afford it. It became hard to remember that just a few years earlier there was considerable frustration that the vision was taking so long to realize. Yet many residents felt that they lived with the negative impacts of intensive development, without enjoying the benefits. There were a lot of big buildings throughout the corridor, but too much space between them and not enough life along the street. The necessary "critical mass" was not yet attained.

It would take some time before the station areas achieved sufficient density to generate the active street life and support a high level of retail service. The fact is that the insertion of five rail stations and the associated comprehensive plan changes put a lot of potential density on the table. The very high densities may have contributed to a delay in reaching "critical mass." Individual projects, soaking up large amounts of market demand vertically, slowed the extension of horizontal development. Rather than being concentrated, private development occurred scattershot, with some very large buildings going in early, and standing relatively alone for years. After 2000, development levels reached a threshold, enough spaces were filled in to create extended sequences of good blocks, and everything started to click. But it is worth remembering that, even in a strong economy, the achievement of plans is subject to market limitations.

Going Beyond the R-B Corridor, and Metro

In this "third phase" of Arlington's evolution, the goals of walkable urbanity began to extend beyond the R-B Corridor.

In 1997 a plan filed for a 13-acre tract near the Pentagon City Metro station (on Metro's Blue and Yellow lines) proposed to replace a previously approved scheme for tall, single-use residential towers with a mixed-use plan of ground-floor retail topped by several stories of residential units, wrapping around a public square. Pentagon Row overcame initial community opposition to become extremely popular with the surrounding neighborhoods, providing them with convenient services and a kind of "town center," injecting vibrancy into a previously sterile ambiance. It was a significant success, both as an improvement to the built environment and in terms of public engagement.

One consequence of the Pentagon Row breakthrough was a proposal by the same developer for a site away from the Metro corridors. Shirlington Village sits adjacent to a major interstate highway and includes an express facility for buses. In addition to being well placed to serve as a bus hub, it lies along one of the most heavily traveled bicycle trails in Northern Virginia. The roughly 25-acre site included a 1940s-era two-sided retail strip, a movie theater, and an old-style department store surrounded by parking. By the late 1990s, the retail strip contained a number of fairly successful restaurants, which depended on the movie theater as a draw, but little else, except many acres of surface parking. The resulting development, approved in 2000 and completed by 2008, extended the existing strip to create a two-block-long retail street, with apartments above (rental and condo). Parking was moved to structures behind the buildings. Two office buildings were added. Residents enjoy a grocery store and a post office near their doorstep. Partnership with the County brought a climate-controlled transit center that accommodates hundreds of buses each day, connecting residents to Metro and elsewhere, and a public library and live theater fronting on a small plaza. Shirlington Village brought new commercial and public services to the surrounding residential neighborhoods, while creating a compact, walkable, lively, mixed-use center at a more modest scale than that along the R-B Corridor.

Concurrently, a major initiative was undertaken for the Columbia Pike Corridor, a major thoroughfare lacking Metro service, that had evolved as an auto-dependent, pedestrian-hostile strip. Among other things, the initiative (discussed in more detail later in the chapter) sought to bring walkability to the Pike, and walkable access to services to the surrounding neighborhoods.

With the jelling of the Rosslyn–Ballston Corridor, and the addition of walkable centers in Pentagon City and Shirlington, the idea began to take hold that walkable urbanity should be the norm throughout the county, not just peculiar features of very high-density Metro station sectors. People started to demand that their neighborhoods (even the single-family "suburban" ones) have complete sidewalk networks, that basic services be reachable on foot, and that transit accommodate more trips within the county. The County's transportation master plan was completely rewritten, with dedicated elements for bicycles, pedestrians, transit, transportation demand management, and a "complete streets" policy.

Although most of Arlington is still relatively low scale (high-rise development being concentrated on the 10% of land in the Metro corridors), today most residents regard their community as urban, and they expect that every part of the county should be walkable. The community and its government learned that much of what works to make a Metro station area function well and become a desirable place could be applied to areas that are not served by rail transit. Arlington learned to build walkability (and livability) throughout the county.

Process Stuff: "The Arlington Way"

Arlington is a community with a peculiarly strong commitment to active participation by citizens in the policy process—so much so, it acquired its own name: "The Arlington Way." Beginning in the 1970s, civic engagement became an institution of development policy. Whether or not this is a good thing has itself been an ongoing controversy. Nonetheless, without it, the kinds of decisions that were made—and maintained over many election cycles—would not have been politically feasible. Nor would development achieve such a high level of quality.

Developers don't always like to be told that "if you want to build in Arlington, the public is going to help design your building." Nonetheless, they have often found (and admitted) that their projects were improved as a result. This process can be messy, and sometimes protracted. It can be demanding on staff, who spend more off-hours in meetings with citizens than in most jurisdictions. It is demanding on elected officials, who must frequently work as intermediaries to resolve conflicts. And it is demanding on citizens, especially volunteers, who are often key negotiators for both specific neighborhood concerns and community-wide interests. It would be hard to overstate the significant role private citizens (those who are neither elected officials nor County staffers) have played in the transformation of Arlington over the past four decades. This is true both in the development of broad policies and in the process by which proposals for specific sites are approved.

In addition to its legacy of experimentation with urban design treatments, Arlington has also been a laboratory for planning and approval processes. There are three principal methods by which development has been entitled as alternatives to by-right zoning: (1) the "site plan process," (2) the phased-development site plan, and (3) form-based code. The most important in terms of development along the Metro corridors is the site plan process, which is in fact a special exception process based in the zoning ordinance.[5] Under certain zoning categories, the County board has wide authority to make exceptions to what would otherwise be required by the ordinance (in terms of things like setbacks, building height and density, parking, etc.). The vast majority of dense, high-rise development in Arlington has been facilitated through this process.

There are two key elements of the Arlington strategy that set the stage for the site plan process. The first is the sector plans adopted for each station area, which provide overall goals and expectations for private development and indicate the potential for increased density in specific locations. The second is that pre-Metro zoning was retained. Parcels would not be "up-zoned" (to realize the increased density indicated by the sector plan) unless and until a site plan is presented consistent with requirements of the sector plan. The board then approves the site plan simultaneously with the requested zoning change.

The site plan is the instrument through which community benefits are secured. Each site plan approval includes a substantial list of conditions—some standard and some specific—including construction requirements, one-time developer contributions, and permanent, ongoing responsibilities that run with the land. The terms of each site plan are developed through the course of many public meetings with broad community representation, discussions with staff, hearings before the planning commission, and, finally, hearings and action by the County board. The time and difficulty with which a project moves through the process can vary greatly, depending on the degree of controversy that may attach to it. Generally, projects that hew closely to the sector plan achieve expeditious approval. Projects that seek exception from sector plans may experience a much more arduous path, with no certainty of success. Thus there is both cost and risk to a developer in entering the process. Nonetheless, the creation of Arlington's TOD, with millions of square feet of office space, housing, and retail and much of the public improvements around seven Metrorail stations, is largely the result of such site-by-site negotiation on hundreds of plans over the past four decades.

A related process called the "Phased-Development Site Plan" (PDSP), is essentially a master planning technique that the County has used with large properties under single ownership. Development of individual parcels is then approved under the aforementioned site plan process. By negotiating major goals beforehand, a developer may expedite the subsequent approval of site plans, showing that they are in conformance with the PDSP. This approach has been important in the development of Pentagon City, Potomac Yards, and Shirlington Village.

Finally, in 2003 Arlington instituted its first form-based code (FBC). This was for the Columbia Pike Corridor in the southern part of the county. The densest commercial corridor in Arlington without rail service, the Pike maintains the highest level of bus service and ridership in Virginia. As new development burgeoned in the Metro corridors in the 1980s and '90s, the Pike lagged behind. Residents became frustrated with a lack of services and the car dependence imposed by the existing built environment. In 1998, the County board launched the Columbia Pike Initiative and began an extended community dialogue that developed a vision for the transformation of the Pike from its character as a typical suburban commercial strip (developed under by-right zoning), into a traditional Main Street.

Transforming the built environment to something walkable would require considerable redevelopment; however, the method used for the Metro corridors, with sector plans and individual site plans negotiated for each parcel, was unlikely to be effective on Columbia Pike, for two reasons. The site plan process depended for its success on the incentive offered by tremendous value for real estate generated by proximity to the Metro, and the County's willingness to provide significant increases in allowable density. On Columbia Pike, the community desired compact development on a smaller scale than the Metro corridors (6-story building maximums, rather than 16, 26, or 36). Also, land values were insufficient to draw much development into the arduous and time-consuming site plan process. A form-based code offered a method of encouraging investment of the type desired, through lower procedural cost and risk to the developer, consistent with a master plan based on creation of a walkable environment. Following the adoption of an FBC for commercial nodes in 2003, the Pike saw its first mixed-use developments in decades, and walkable centers began to emerge. With plans approved in 2013, development for the entire 3-mile corridor was regulated by the FBC.

Final Lessons

The Arlington experiment in urbanizing suburbia generates some important lessons that may have wide applicability.

- Rail transit is a powerful tool to drive development, and to help shape it—but its effectiveness depends heavily on the accompanying approach to land use and urban design.

- The importance of the built environment means both the design of private buildings and the design of public space. To elevate the design of private buildings is to confront a regulatory challenge—and frequently to confront landowners and development interests.

- Designing quality public space is a lot about transportation. It means aligning transportation philosophy with the planning approach—making the streets match the buildings.

- Density can also be a powerful tool, but it must be conserved. Its effectiveness is subject to considerations of time, absorption, and critical mass.

- Transformative development takes time; in any given period, only so much density can be absorbed by the market. The more density you throw out there, the longer things take.

- There is a minimal level of concentrated development necessary to generate the urban dynamic that creates high real estate values, and the quality of place that is the objective driving the whole effort.

- Process matters. Transforming the built environment from car-oriented to compact and walkable requires many years of development, with a sustained commitment to plan goals. This is only possible with the sustained support of the community. And it is only possible to win and maintain the support of the community with processes that are open, transparent, and participatory. By involving members of the community from the beginning, and throughout every stage, from long-range planning to individual project approvals, credibility is won. Even more importantly, the plan goals become rooted in the community and have a chance to endure through political changes over time.

Notes

1. In the 1960s and early '70s, there was no new "theory of TOD" to guide planning; there was "modern" planning (based on zoning), which was aimed at creating car-oriented places. The associated regulatory apparatus was not geared to create traditional, walkable development (i.e., zoning regulations requiring setbacks, high amounts of parking, etc.).

2. Arlington County Profile 2014, Urban Design Research, Department of Community Planning, Housing and Development, https://arlingtonva.s3.amazonaws.com/wp-content/uploads/sites/31/2014/04/demographics_Arlington_-Profile-2014.pdf.

3. While a full elaboration of the principles of good urban design is beyond the scope of this chapter, many of the key elements that relate to buildings are identified in the discussion that follows. These are the features that distinguish auto-oriented suburban

development from walkable urbanism, which includes characteristics like varying use-mix, bringing buildings to the sidewalks, maintaining permeable (not blank) walls along streets, minimizing curb cuts across pedestrian right-of-way, taking care with placement of loading docks, and so on.

4. "Rosslyn–Ballston Corridor Mid-Course Review," Arlington County, May 1989, accessed August 6, 2017, https://arlingtonva.s3.dualstack.us-east-1.amazonaws.com/wp-content/uploads/sites/31/2014/03/RB-Mid-Review1.pdf.

5. This usage of the term "site plan process" is somewhat idiosyncratic to Arlington. As used in other places, the term typically refers to an administrative process, often a fairly routine matter. In Arlington the term refers to a very public process by which the terms of approval for a development proposal are negotiated. The latter include changes in the general land use plan, zoning, and use permit conditions for the specific "site plan," with its associated community benefits. A more generic descriptor for this type of policy instrument is, "use permit for special exception."

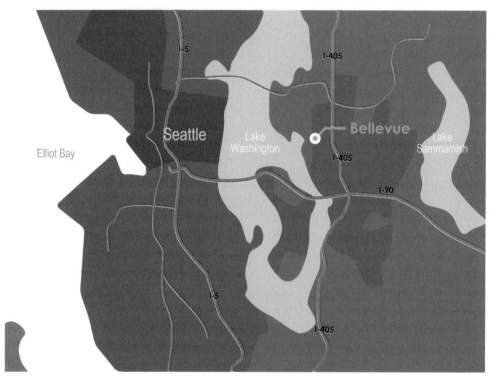

Figure 13.1. Bellevue in relation to the Seattle region. (Ma Shuyun, Xumengqi, and Anushree Nallapaneni)

13

From Village to City
Bellevue, Washington

Mark Hinshaw

Looking at the Bellevue skyline from Seattle across the waters of Lake Washington, filled with 50-story towers, it is difficult to imagine that not too many decades ago it was a tiny hamlet. A sort of American Dubai, the urban center of Bellevue virtually came from whole cloth over a span of 30 years. But not unlike similar communities—such as Tysons Corner, Virginia; Bethesda, Maryland; Stamford, Connecticut; and Glendale, California—its transformation was both accidental and intentional, a convergence of geography, demographic change, and measured public policy. What took most suburbs well over a hundred years to achieve—the classic urban attributes of size, density, and diversity—these cities acquired in less than 50 years. Each one has its own unique story; this is Bellevue's.[1]

The Village: Fruit Farms and Ferries (1900 to 1950)

Until World War II, Bellevue barely registered on any maps. A main street four blocks long anchored a tiny, unincorporated village surrounded by vast fruit farms and tree orchards. To this day, the plat maps for downtown Bellevue read as they originally did: Cheriton Fruit Gardens. Lying in the midaltitude foothills west of the Cascade Mountains, Bellevue was virtually cut off from Seattle by 22-mile-long Lake Washington (see Figure 13.1).

For more than 50 years, residents and visitors had only two choices for traveling between Bellevue and Seattle—make the long trek around the lake or take a small passenger ferry from a dock at the end of Main Street. In that era, the metropolitan area's

Figure 13.2. Thirty years ago downtown Bellevue had virtually no skyline. It now surpasses both Tacoma and Spokane as the second most intense urban center in Washington. (Chuck Wolfe)

many connected lakes, canals, and waterways were crisscrossed by scores of diminutive, steam-powered vessels—nicknamed the Mosquito Fleet. Either way, it was a major effort to travel to or from Bellevue. So Bellevue sat, a quiet tiny town with dirt roads that penetrated the flat farmlands and rolling, leafy hillsides.

Bellevue's isolation, agriculture, and quietude began to change with the opening of a floating bridge between Seattle and Bellevue in 1940. The war years delayed any immediate impact. But once veterans returned home to start families and buy cars and houses, Bellevue was, quite literally, open for business.

The one part of downtown Bellevue that has not changed much is the original Main Street. One-story buildings still flank its short length, occupied by stores, cafés, restaurants, and other locally owned businesses. Although not a true historic district, the zoning for that area precluded high rises. Nevertheless, the pressure to redevelop is intense, and already dense mid-rise buildings pack both ends of the street (see Figure 13.2).

Quintessential Bedroom Suburb (1950 to 1980)

In the early 1950s, one of the region's first suburban shopping malls was built. With the area's mild climate, Bellevue's mall followed the example set by previous malls, with several local department stores loosely arranged on a 30-acre superblock. Smaller shops, restaurants, and a movie theater were scattered in between, with parking lots accessible from all directions. Bellevue Square now anchors one side of downtown Bellevue, but it is by no means the only shopping destination.

Textbooks of the time praised the efficiency of superblocks for laying out streets and parking. Indeed, it was "the bigger the better." In that dismal planning philosophy, streets were for cars; the needs of pedestrians barely even registered. Wanting to be cutting-edge, Bellevue's planning director laid out streets on then-languishing farms with blocks that measured 600 feet by 600 feet. A wide right-of-way, eventually intended to be six lanes wide (with essentially no sidewalks), framed each of them. And it came to pass: for decades no one walked in "downtown" Bellevue. If anyone dared to be out on sidewalks that were a miserly 5 feet wide (where they existed at all), they were deemed suspect. Police would stop walkers to—depending on your point of view—inquire if they needed help or make sure they weren't criminals or vagrants.

The City even eschewed parking on streets, because streets were viewed as conduits for only *moving* vehicles. The head of the planning commission at the time vowed that only over his dead body would Bellevue allow on-street parking. For years in a dusty back room of the city hall sat a cardboard model built by the first planning director. It depicted a raised circulation system for pedestrians only—with bridges and platforms and ramps. Thankfully, that aspect of downtown Bellevue never was implemented.

Two more crucial ideas kept Bellevue from ever becoming more than a tepid version of Frank Lloyd Wright's idealized "Broadacre City." In case the city might need even wider streets in the future, all buildings had to be set back 20 to 40 feet from the property line. Moreover, all commercial development had to provide five parking stalls for each 1,000 square feet, a minimum standard then recommended by the America Society of Planning Officials. This combination of autocentric standards resulted in most buildings being no taller than four stories. The few that were taller sat surrounded by acres of asphalt.

Finally, for at least three decades (1950–1980) Bellevue benefited greatly from "white flight." Middle-class white residents could use VA loans to help buy houses; they would be in enclaves separated from blacks located in Seattle. Although by the 1980s the community began to shed its racist roots, Bellevue's reputation as a bastion of segregation hung on. Bellevue served as the constant butt of cocktail-party jokes throughout the region for its classist, neowealth attitude. Some of that remains today, despite the entirely different demographics that exist.

If there is a single legacy of that era that (inadvertently) pointed Bellevue toward its future as a dense urban center, it was freeways. Bellevue was flanked by three of them. In classic transportation formulas, there is nothing like access to attract investment.

Laying the Foundations (1980 to 1995)

Bellevue could have followed many other examples of suburban growth. Every metropolitan area from Los Angeles to Denver to Dallas to Atlanta has them—miles of wide arterial roads extending in every direction, with low-rise buildings dotting the landscape and an occasional high-rise office or hotel tower poking up near a freeway interchange. Unexpectedly, though, Bellevue did something different.

In the early 1980s, Bellevue had become a politically conservative stronghold that revered private property, detached houses, and parks that served the *local* population. This political attitude, however, produced what we might today read as a liberal outcome when the city council adopted a sweeping set of policies and laws designed to clamp down on development everywhere but downtown. Rather than frittering away major public investments in infrastructure scattered all over, the idea was to focus public spending in an area less than a mile square. That would be the new downtown (see Figure 13.3).

Accomplishing this required several procedural steps. First the Citywide Comprehensive Plan was revised to clearly state the policy. By intent, no "pop up" development could occur near freeways or along arterial streets outside of downtown. The tool assured that a floor area ratio (FAR) no greater than 0.5 applied everywhere outside the downtown boundaries. (With the exception of a recent light-rail station area, this policy has held fast for more than 35 years.) In a sense, this decision presaged the state's Growth Management Act, a decade later, which established clear boundaries to define where growth should occur and severe limits everywhere else. (This did not stop development in other locations; it just limited it in size and intensity.)

Once policy makers made clear what they did *not* want, their attention shifted to what they *did* want. Owners of properties in the nascent city center area lobbied hard for greater development potential, given visibility and access from the adjacent interstate freeway.

First, the City set downtown boundaries, defining an area of approximately three-quarters of a mile on all sides. This came from the notion of maximum walking distances—a surprising consideration for the time, since almost no one actually walked.

Second, the City eliminated required setbacks along streets and replaced them with the idea of "zero setbacks," or what are now popularly called build-to lines. (This occurred many years before New Urbanism introduced this notion on a broad scale.)

Figure 13.3. In the early 2010s, the transformation from a suburb of Seattle to a densely built city center in its own right became especially pronounced. (Chuck Wolfe)

Third, the City replaced parking *minimums* with parking *maximums* (3 stalls/1,000 square feet). Robert Cervero of the University of California at Berkeley has long used Bellevue as a case study in applying parking codes strategically to alter the form and intensity of development. It may sound bureaucratically wonky as a tool, yet it had a profound effect on development. Essentially the limit said there would be no more suburban-style projects. No longer would there be any buildings surrounded by parking. Current lots would be phased out as development occurred. Furthermore, the City used specific tools to wean people away from standard suburban forms, such as prohibiting drive-through windows. Banks and finance agencies called City staff repeatedly to verify these standards. Some were stunned. A few declined to build. But most developers got with the program. Indeed, once they realized that there would be no exemptions or variances from the parking maximums, it was viewed as a level playing field. The days of marketing ample parking were over.

This quickly set in motion a market system for parking. As with textbook economics, when a supply is constrained and demand is high, price goes up. Within a few years parking went from free to costly. Now it is very costly. Donald Shoup's hypothesis was tested in Bellevue long before he wrote *The High Cost of Free Parking*. Reduced parking also proved an incentive for developers, albeit an unusual one. Most suburban developers provide free parking (although as Shoup points out, nothing is really free). Now they could save many millions of dollars by not building parking, they had more land to develop, and, they could charge for the parking they did provide.

With many millions of square feet of development and dramatically increased property values, charging for parking quickly began to make sense. Above-grade garages that initially replaced surface parking eliminated the potential for much greater income from office buildings. Instead, parking was built underground. Given the cost of $50,000 per stall, the quantity of parking is considerably below market demand, and prices have escalated. Developers are pleased that the City now caps parking supply through code maximums, assuring that no competitor will come in offering more parking. This development pattern is markedly different than what one sees in larger cities, where parking structures of many stories are clearly visible. With the exception of Bellevue Square mall, all parking in downtown Bellevue now sits underground and out of sight. Commercial uses line the sidewalks—a far cry from the situation a few decades ago.

Recall the 0.5 FAR set for properties outside downtown. New FARs set for properties inside downtown ranged from 3.0 to 8.0—an order-of-magnitude difference. Furthermore, building heights were allowed in some areas up to 450 feet. In a sense, this was akin to opening up a gold mine or issuing a license to print money. Although it took at least a decade for the development community to fully understand the "new regime," they finally got it. In three decades downtown went from having 3 towers to having more than 30. Bellevue has a population of less than 140,000, yet it has a skyline that rivals that of Portland, Oregon, which has a population of 600,000.

Other tools were added to the mix. The City instituted design review, a function that was carried out by staff using a set of standards and guidelines. A series of dramatic legal challenges all resulted in findings in favor of City-imposed standards. After a rather tumultuous beginning, the development sector has a predictable process and clear guidelines to follow. The regulatory system makes use of a bonus approach: the more public amenities in a project, the more development rights it receives. Parks, plazas, day care, through-block pathways, theaters, grocery stores, and museums all qualify for development bonuses.

The City also recognized its responsibility in achieving a mixed-use urban center. It worked with the regional transit authority to increase bus service and is now working to build a light rail station. It talked the county library district out of building its typical suburban-style branch, persuading it to build a multistory structure with underground parking.

Perhaps the most significant public investment was a 15-acre downtown park. What might have been another block of high rises is now a verdant civic place that is regularly used by families and visitors for both pastoral respite as well as organized events. It is a civic park on the European model, not a park filled with recreation fields (see Figure 13.4). Famed architectural historian Vincent Scully headed the panel that selected the design through an international competition. His first words when he saw the design concept were "I want to meet these people. They understand urban parks." The winning design was by a "dark horse" team—the architecture firm of Beckley Myers, based in Milwaukee, Wisconsin.

Towers Replace Strip Malls (1995 to 2010)

Over a period of 15 years—spanning two booms and two recessions—downtown Bellevue saw a fundamental shift in the scale, form, and intensity of development (see Figure 13.5). Smaller and midsized properties were purchased and consolidated. All but a couple of the original, long-standing landowners were bought out. Some of them tried to do deals with themselves as equity partners or by offering long-term leases, but in the end, most developers insisted on fee-simple ownership.

In the 1980s few people lived in downtown; indeed, the entire idea was roundly mocked by the real estate industry. The City subsequently recalibrated its zoning to create incentives for building housing downtown. Developers were slow to take advantage of the incentives, but ultimately embraced them, and today downtown counts dozens of residential towers—some in the range of 50 stories. And in contrast to an expected pattern in which those would be outside the core, many are dead center, where one would normally find office buildings. It is now not uncommon for residential towers to sit cheek by jowl with office towers. There is virtually an equal demand for both. In fact, since the zoning was put in place in the early 1980s, downtown Bellevue's residential population has grown from a few hundred to over 10,000. Most of that increase has occurred in the last decade. This aspect, of people living downtown, has been responsible for the most radical social change that Bellevue has ever experienced. More on that later.

Bellevue Square was the city's first big development in the early 1950s. It followed the typical spread-out pattern, with parking laced between freestanding, single-story structures. In the last two decades, the mall has added multiple towers of offices, hotels, and residential units. It now contains theaters, restaurants, and other places of entertainment.

Figure 13.4. The City invested significantly in a 15-acre downtown park to stimulate the development of urban housing. (City of Bellevue)

Figure 13.5. The City has put great emphasis on the design and activation of public spaces. (Mark Hinshaw)

It flanks the street in a manner not unlike Rockefeller Center. The Bellevue Art Museum sits squarely in the middle of this swirling urban complex, and on one block, a large performing arts center has been proposed. After years of feeling like a singular island of retailing, Bellevue Square (renamed The Bellevue Collection) is now barely distinguishable from the rest of the high-rise development in downtown (see Figures 13.6 and 13.7).

In a symbolic gesture, Bellevue City Hall moved in the early 2000s from a location outside of downtown to a spectacularly rehabilitated former fortress-like building built by the old Bell Telephone conglomerate on downtown's east side. A small city in itself, it sits across the street from the expanding convention center. Between both sits an elegant urban park built atop parking. This part of downtown now functions as a true civic center.

Density and Diversity (2010–)

In contrast to other densely urbanized suburbs, such as White Plains, New York, and Walnut Creek, California, Bellevue's transformation did not originate in a public investment in

Figure 13.6. Designated sectors of downtown have added new dense urban housing, ranging in scale from townhouses, to midrise buildings, to high rises. (Mark Hinshaw)

rail transit. Rather, land-use changes appeared first through private-market actions. Other than traditional investments in streets, parks, and public buildings, Bellevue's story is mainly one of directed private development. Nor was there any development agency involved; tax-increment financing is not a legally available tool in the State of Washington. Nonetheless, regional bus service was arranged to simulate the frequency and capacity of rail. Now, rail transit is fully supported by the focused intensity of development located within walking distance of stations.

So committed was the City to making downtown work that it consistently said *no* to intensive development in other areas of the community. Downtown has succeeded so well that this policy has changed. The Spring District, east of downtown, will be served by a future rail line. This district is slated for midrise, mixed-use development. It is important to note that the City might have stymied the development of downtown had it followed the same path that cities elsewhere did in allowing "pop up" towers near freeway interchanges.

Figure 13.7. Height and stepback standards have rigorously controlled the scale of Old Bellevue, the original town center. (Mark Hinshaw)

Probably the most surprising element of Bellevue's transformation from a suburban model to an urban one has been the infusion of multiple cultures. After all, for several decades the city encouraged and benefited from the white flight of the postwar decades. However, in the last decade, cultural diversification has occurred at an almost exponential rate. Dozens of languages are now spoken, with a large and growing number of residents from China and India.

In some ways, downtown Bellevue resembles some burgeoning cities in China, with gleaming towers and great densities. Thus familiarity may be a factor, as well as less fear of density than many Americans seem to have. In addition, Bellevue as a downtown is relatively safe and clean. That might help attract a growing workforce of single women from many parts of the world.

One fascinating phenomenon has been the shift in the city's politics. For much of the suburban era, Bellevue was solidly Republican. An occasional liberal would win election, but that was an exception. The entire cluster of cities east of Seattle, including Bellevue, has become increasingly more Democratic. Although the rest of Washington tends to vote as a conservative bloc on statewide issues, Bellevue voters today typically vote in ways similar to Seattle voters. Perhaps with increased density, there is a collective sense that there are strong roles for government to play in society. In a place where elected officials used to champion rights of individuals, there is a clear swing to embracing the importance of shared responsibilities.

Finally, one of the effects of policies and regulations that have spanned multiple decades is that Bellevue now has a dramatic skyline. Set against the backdrop of the Cascade Mountains and with a foreground of Lake Washington, Bellevue's glassy spires are impossible to miss. One can literally see the expression of programs that encourage development while maintaining the verdant, low-rise understory of the older context (see Figure 13.8).

Conclusion: Transferable Tools

Every city possesses a particular mixture of people, politics, setting, and history. Simply applying what works in one city doesn't guarantee that it will work in another. However, it is possible to learn from another's experience. The dramatic transformation of downtown Bellevue—from a loose collection of strip malls strung along wide arterial streets to a dense, mixed-use, walkable, transit-oriented urban center—was the result of multiple actions, which can also be taken by other cities.

Adopt Clear, Consistent, Continuing Policies

The City adopted a simple, easy-to-understand diagram and set of public policies. The concept has provided a consistent framework that has not changed significantly over several decades, providing predictability for investors.

Establish a Strong Regulatory Framework

The land use code has provided a solid set of development standards, design guidelines, and incentives that have worked well over time. Projects need to be approved for design quality, but the basic entitlements have not changed. Moreover, it is now understood that no variances or exceptions will be made for particular circumstances; it is simply quid pro quo.

Institute a Design Review Process

The process is administrative, using skilled staff, and recommendations and rationale have generally survived challenges. Appeals go to a hearing examiner, who acts as a judge and allows cross-examination of witnesses. Some appeals have been denied because they were deemed to simply object to the intensity. Appeals must be supported by claims of misapplied design standards.

Figure 13.8. Bases of buildings reflect the scale of older existing structures. Upper floors must be set back. (Mark Hinshaw)

Figure 13.9. Considerable attention has been given to the street level, using high-quality and well-designed paving materials, furnishings, plantings, and storefront design. (Mark Hinshaw)

Pursue Catalyst Projects, Both Public and Private

The City did not rely on merely changing its codes. It invested its limited funds in five or six strategic projects intended to inspire responses from the private sector, including a 15-acre downtown park, a large regional library branch, a convention center, a multi-modal transit center, and enhanced streetscapes (see Figure 13.9).

Calibrate Impact Fees

The City levies impact fees to capture some of the costs of various public services and infrastructure improvements that a new development requires. But one size doesn't fit all. The fees reflect data showing that denser, mixed-use developments have fewer impacts, especially on peak-hour traffic. Auto-oriented uses have the highest impacts, so impact fees act as an indirect inducement for urban, not autocentric, form.

Not all of these tools would necessarily work for every community, and most took years to apply, refine, and adjust to account for changes in the marketplace. Neither redevelopment funds nor tax-increment financing was used. Bellevue's downtown was transformed by a carefully crafted bundle of public investments and clear, consistent regulations.

Note

1. In describing Bellevue's transformation, the author drew from the following two publications, in addition to his own early participation and subsequent observations:

   Cervero, Robert, *America's Suburban Centers: The Land Use–Transportation Link* (Boston: Unwin Hyman Press, 1989); Shoup, Donald, *The High Cost of Free Parking* (Chicago: APA Planners Press, 2005, revised 2011).

PART IV BRINGING IT ALL TOGETHER

In Part IV the editors lay out core lessons based on new understanding of markets and on the case studies. **Planning** starts with meeting threshold requirements for leadership, inclusive community engagement, and a transformational planning process. It moves on to creating the right foundation in terms of market support, compact critical mass, and the right site, and finishes with five core principles and a discussion of how to achieve them. **Placemaking** picks up these principles and talks about how to translate them into places that people love—and where they choose to live, work, and invest.

Figure 14.1. Mayor Eva Galambos led politically conservative, affluent Sandy Springs, Georgia, through a planning process to create a new downtown, dubbed City Springs, that will serve as the civic and social heart of the community. (Copyright City of Sandy Springs)

14

Planning

David Dixon

As the case studies in this book indicate, there is no single magic formula for creating walkable urban places in suburbia. However, their collective message demonstrates that, for a diverse mix of communities, in very different regions, successful walkable urban places share common threshold characteristics:

- An initial *process* defined by
  - ◊ *leadership* willing to challenge long-held truths while bringing those who for years held those truths to be self-evident to the table;
  - ◊ *inclusive engagement* across the entire community that brings traditional movers and shakers together with grassroots activists; and
  - ◊ extensive *planning* that provides a community-wide platform for translating leadership and engagement into a blueprint that shapes change.
- An essential *foundation* that incorporates
  - ◊ *market-driven feasibility*—backed by fiscal opportunities that support public/private partnership;
  - ◊ *the right site*—one or more contiguous parcels with owners who want to partner;
  - ◊ a *compact critical mass*— often 3 million square feet or more, on largely contiguous sites of roughly 50 or more acres; and
  - ◊ a *commitment to equity*—housing, retail, public space, and mobility choices that invite diversity and make the promise of inclusivity real;
  - ◊ *flexibility to adapt to rapid technological change*—particularly, a transition to automated mobility.
- Core urban design *principles* that, in addition to universal qualities of sustainability and resilience, include

237

◊ *walkability* marked by the kinds of activities and amenities that bring streets to life and invite people to walk;

◊ *connectivity* that encompasses both convenient accessibility and integral links to the life of the community;

◊ a *multilayered public realm* that extends from places for personal reflection to community-wide gatherings;

◊ a *diverse mix of choices* for living, working, and playing geared to diverse lifestyles; and

◊ *authenticity* that captures the spirit of the community, its people, and its setting today.

Process: Leadership, Engagement, Planning

Leadership

Building a new walkable urban place begins with a civic leader—a mayor, a community or business leader, a property owner, or a potential developer—who sheds specific affiliations and steps forward as a leader for the entire community. Leaders must sometimes preach a message that is not initially welcomed by the community: change may be uncomfortable, but it has arrived, and the future of our community lies in building denser, mixed-use, walkable—in other words, urban—places. Support rarely comes immediately. The ideas of "urban" and "dense" can produce reactions that range from skepticism to strong opposition. Leadership, it turns out, is less about raising an idea than about patience, commitment, listening, building a fact-based case, and then making that case in terms that speak directly to a community's concerns (see Figure 14.1).

Making the case means

- explaining the potential benefits that merit significant investment of scarce public dollars, already-strained staff resources, and thousands of hours of community time.

- helping the community understand fundamental demographic, economic, and other shifts—and tapping growing support for sustainability—to bring elected officials, city staff, businesses, advocates, and neighborhood leaders to the table.

- enabling people to visualize "urban" and "density" and analyze the trade-offs in terms of creating value to support greater public amenities and managing impacts like traffic.

- once these stakeholders sit down at the table, leading an intensive community conversation that builds the essential political will to move forward.

Engagement

Beyond being inclusive, there is no single "right way" to engage stakeholders. An inclusive process that speaks to the needs and aspirations of the full community is critical to

Figure 14.2. Roanoke County, Virginia, engaged the full community at every step in planning to transform the strip commercial development along Route 419 into a walkable town center. (Stantec)

building the political will essential to implementing the project. Different approaches to engagement will work in different circumstances. A politically divided community may require a series of workshops and charrettes over a year or more to find common ground. An advisory committee that represents diverse points of view across broad economic, social, racial, and other lines of difference and that meets (and debates) regularly can play a valuable role by making shared recommendations as planning progresses, and if needed realigning the planning process itself.

No matter the structure, however, certain ground rules strengthen the process and the product:

- Treat a planning process as a community-education program. Openly shared data and analysis—about real estate markets, transportation impacts, public realm design, public/private partnerships, the prerequisites for walkability, and other formative issues—combined with workshops that explain how to interpret the data and the analysis, are essential to turning stakeholders into informed decision makers (see Figure 14.2).

Figure 14.3. Fontana, California, used a range of methods—from small workshops to keypad polling—to help residents build consensus for more compact growth. (Stantec)

- Make information sharing and decision making transparent.
- Empower stakeholders to understand and make meaningful trade-offs (e.g., increased density can pay for more amenities and an enhanced public realm—or affordable housing).
- Commit to granting every participant the right to speak freely without retribution in a public forum.
- Use social media in innovative ways to invite people into the process and reach people who don't normally participate in meetings and public events.

The most persistent barrier to gaining support for transformative change is NIMBYism (not in my backyard). The architect Michael Pyatok, admired for his provocative proposals for mixed-income urban housing, argues that the term oversimplifies neighborhood concerns. "Today . . . the increasingly uncharted nature of urban growth brings change to people's front doors . . . and in most cases that change is not exactly familiar or instinctively welcome" (see Figure 14.3).

Dublin, Ohio (see Chapter 11) offers a useful illustration of how to engage people to move beyond NIMBYism. A broad cross section of community, business, developer, property owner, and other stakeholders came together to take stock of themselves and their community. Did they still hold the same values and seek the same lifestyle as they had when they arrived in Dublin? Did Dublin offer the housing, shopping, recreation, and work opportunities that they sought today? Was Dublin doing what it needs to remain economically competitive? To attract new generations? As they answered these questions together, they crafted a bold new vision for the city.

Planning

Transformative change requires transformative planning. A plan becomes transformative only when it empowers a community to make transformational decisions—working with stakeholders to frame the right questions, provide the right choices, and make achievable, informed decisions—which ultimately are the only decisions that lead to the right plan and sustain the political will to go forward. The ultimate test of the plan is how well it achieves principles described below. The ultimate test of the process is how well it informs and supports this decision making.

Planning for significant suburban redevelopment does not assume incremental change. For example, it requires asking a community to explore—and grow confident about—demographics that break the mold of the previous 50 years, innovative solutions to transportation that require a 180-degree reversal from funding highways to funding transit, planning for automated vehicles, and bold new partnerships with developers. Asking a community to make decisions about change that can appear antithetical to everything that has defined the community and shaped its growth over decades is not a casual exercise—but it is an eminently doable exercise.

Foundation: Feasibility, the Right Site, Compact Critical Mass, Equity

Market-Driven Feasibility

Change starts with greater value and greater density. No community can assemble enough public funding—federal, state, or local—to make development of a new urban center feasible in the absence of market demand. The potential to create walkable urban places in suburbs starts with two realities: first, walkability creates value today, and second, auto-oriented development no longer does. Strip centers, malls, office parks, and similar "gray-field" sites with far more surface parking than actual built space represent today's prime redevelopment opportunities (see Figure 14.4). Higher-density, higher-value redevelopment can include office, research, hotels, and other uses that all pay more for walkability, but multifamily housing mixed with retail often represents the strongest market response and often serves as the "anchor" for new walkable urban places. As a rough rule of thumb, Sarah Woodworth of W-ZHA (see Chapter 4) estimates that when a mix of market-rate housing and retail more than triples the density of existing auto-oriented development, the stage is set for potential walkable redevelopment (see Figure 14.5a, b).

Figure 14.4. A former industrial site outside of Dallas is being planned as a walkable urban center to outcompete nearby office parks. (Stantec)

Transit is the new highway interchange. For decades, opening a new highway interchange caused suburban retail and office development seemingly to pop from the ground. Today transit plays this role. "High performance transit"—generally heavy or light rail—generates the best results, pushing up residential and office values by 10–25% or more.[1] However, commuter rail—and in some regions bus rapid transit (BRT) when supported by dedicated lanes (thus not competing with other traffic)—also stimulates significant investment. This premium is most pronounced within a quarter-mile of a transit station.[2] Stewart Schwartz, executive director of the DC-area Coalition for Smarter Growth (and author of Chapter 6), reported that in 2017 "for the DC metro area, almost 90% of new office development in the pipeline . . . sits within a quarter-mile of Metro."[3] He notes that one of the factors that pushes employers and developers to seek transit-accessible locations is the appeal to knowledge workers for whom transit accessibility can significantly reduce household transportation costs (see Figure 14.6).

A "transit ready" walkable urban place can help build the case for extension of an existing light rail or BRT line. A rough review of current literature suggests that having between 6,000 and 8,000 residents and workers within a half mile of a new station (with a majority within a five-minute walk) represents a threshold for considering a service

Figure 14.5a, b. A phased, 10- to 15-year redevelopment plan will replace the Tanglewood Mall parking lot with a walkable, mixed-use town center serving the Route 419 corridor in suburban Roanoke County, Virginia. (Stantec)

Figure 14.6. Emeryville, California, developed a lively new downtown around its BART rapid transit station. (Mercurywoodrose under CC-BY SA 3.0)

extension to serve a new walkable urban place.[4] Adding a stop on an existing transit line with frequent peak-hour service would require a lower number of new riders.

Fiscal benefits unlock public/private partnerships. Both the public and the private sectors have a fundamental stake in promoting the denser, mixed-use redevelopment of out-moded grayfield sites. While walkable urban places unlock significant private value, the public sector benefits from a dramatic increase in assessed values. There is a compelling logic of shared benefit to public/private partnerships (see Figure 14.7).

Increased density and value per square foot together produce substantial fiscal benefits. Compare two suburban sites along Route 128, in the suburbs of Boston. In 2016, on one site, outmoded office buildings surrounded by surface parking commanded rents of $25 per square foot. Less than 1 mile away, a new office building in a mixed-use, walkable redevelopment of older office and industrial parks commanded rents of $45 per square foot—at four times the density of the first site. The newer office space includes more expensive structured parking, which modestly reduces the fiscal value of its rent premium, but it yields an assessed valuation eight to ten times greater for the redeveloped site.

Figure 14.7. Sarah Woodworth (see Chapter 4) helped the City of Rockville, Maryland, develop a public/private partnership with Federal Realty to create Rockville Town Square. (Federal Realty Investment Trust)

Sarah Woodworth (see Chapter 4) notes that tax-increment financing (TIF) or similar strategies can tap this fiscal premium to pay for the new grid of streets, structured parking, utilities, and additional infrastructure that a new walkable urban place requires. In a public/private partnership the public sector can use the proceeds of bonds—sold on the basis of the increased tax revenues tied to denser, higher-value development—to cover the front-end infrastructure costs of wholesale redevelopment that trades acres of surface parking for the grid of streets and public spaces that characterize urban life.

Landing on the Right Site
Affordable doesn't always mean available. While values may appear to *justify* market-driven redevelopment, apparent availability does not guarantee the *ability* to redevelop.

Figure 14.8. Northland Center, in suburban Detroit, represents a classic grayfield site without complex ownership obstacles. The largest shopping mall in the world when it opened in 1954, it closed in 2015, and its host city bought the site with a plan to clear and sell it to a developer.

Woodworth advises clients that, even when grayfields with declining land values appear to be ready, less obvious constraints can stymie redevelopment efforts. In the midst of otherwise declining strip development, some auto-oriented retailers and office buildings remain highly profitable and carry high land values that make near-term redevelopment infeasible. In other cases, retail tenants may hold long-term leases with decades to run that prevent an owner from selling. And while rents may be stagnant for outmoded developments, the owners may lack incentives to redevelop because the properties still produce steady, predictable cash flow, and the mortgage is fully paid. A large corporation may own a very attractive, theoretically affordable site but have other priorities and not be willing to devote the time and attention necessary to making the site available (see Figure 14.8).

Leadership comes into play—finding the right owner in the right location. Developing new walkable urban places, then, requires a willing partner: one or more property owners interested in making a site available to get started. Unless an owner is a larger development company familiar with the process and risk profile of higher-density, mixed-use redevelopment, these owners will likely need a developer partner to move forward. A mayor or community or business leader can play a critical role by approaching property owners, providing information (and often commitments of political and/or economic support), and exploring potential interest.

Compact Critical Mass

A walkable urban place needs a critical mass of people, disposable income, and activity to draw the full community and function as a center for community life. There is no one-size-fits-all formula for creating a new walkable urban center. But the case studies and other examples suggest some meaningful rules of thumb.

At least two blocks of an active Main Street, lined with 40,000 to 80,000 square feet of shops, restaurants, and entertainment—often in conjunction with a "town green," civic destinations like a city hall, and/or cultural destinations such as a regional performance center—can bring a place to life. The goal is not simply to relocate the same large-market retailers who occupy malls, but to build a mix of businesses—some national, others locally owned—that reflect the needs and aspirations of the community.

Located within a five-minute walk of Main Street, 2,000 to 4,000 units of housing can offer the critical mass of market support to attract unique, independent businesses geared to the values of the community rather than a franchise geared to drive-to consumers coming from a 5- to 10-mile radius. This same concentration of households can typically activate a small park or town green.

Office space can play the same role, but the rule of thumb here holds that it takes twice as much office area as housing area to support the same amount of retail space.[5] In addition, Woodworth sees only limited demand over the near term for the kinds of speculative offices or new corporate buildings that represent the majority of new office space in most suburban markets. This said, as already noted, demand exists for "cool" office space geared to creative businesses, tech start-ups, research-oriented companies, and similar "innovation" businesses. These companies seek environments that appeal to their highly educated workforce. As a result, they routinely avoid suburban office parks and thrive in mixed-use, walkable environments.

Determining a threshold size for a new walkable urban place that comes to life as a lively, diverse community is not a science. Every case is different. This said, rules of thumb exist in this area too. Housing is likely to constitute the largest component and can provide a critical mass of demand to support a couple of blocks of Main Street retail (2,000,000–4,000,000 SF or more). Add a city hall or similar civic use (50,000–100,000 SF); preferably enough office or research space to contribute at least 1,000 to 2,000 jobs to the mix (200,000–400,000 SF); a mix of unique local and franchise and larger-format retail (100,000–250,000 SF or more); and a variety of other activities, and 3 to 5 million square feet becomes a reasonable threshold for creating a successful new walkable urban place. In regions with robust real estate economies, a walkable urban place of this size can reach this build-out within 5 to 10 years of receiving zoning and other approvals during strong market cycles. Fifteen years or more represents a more reasonable time frame in less robust markets.

While suburban residents often worry about height, the realities of most markets limit feasible development to frame construction atop one to two floors of masonry construction or similar lower-cost models that avoid more expensive high-rise construction. These considerations generally limit building heights to between five and seven floors.

Accounting for streets, a square or town green, and other public spaces while concentrating 3 to 5 million square feet to promote walkability, new walkable urban places usually require 60 to 100 acres. A larger area—200 acres or more—can readily accommodate potential future growth.

Rental housing plays an essential role in getting started and accelerating phasing. It would not be surprising for a development of this scale to take place over three or four phases. Very few projects involve the kind of patient capital or public investment that eliminates a need to design for the market from the start. Designing for the market means quickly establishing an inviting sense of place with a critical mass of activity and choices to support walkability—which can represent a significant challenge in the absence of a significant rental housing component. As a rule of thumb, rental lofts and apartments fill up three to six times faster than comparable for-sale housing. Historically, many communities viewed rental housing as the last resort of those who couldn't afford ownership and saw owners as people with a much stronger commitment to the community. Today, by contrast, rental housing has a different profile: as a stepping stone to ownership, as a preferred choice for empty nesters, and as a smart choice for a young professional who may have to move to pursue career advancement. A substantial portion of millennials (25–34 years old) and empty nesters (55 and older) prefer rentals, and together they represent a majority of the North American housing market—and the strongest housing market for walkable urban places.

Innovative parking strategies play an essential role in getting it right. Walkable density requires structured parking—in suburbs or cities. Maintaining standard suburban parking ratios (number of spaces required by zoning per 1,000 SF of office and retail or per unit of housing) can add 40 to 50% or more to the cost of developing office or retail space and 15 to 25% or more to the cost of housing compared with suburban developments that rely on surface parking. Putting parking below grade can add 50% to these cost premiums. Communities can reduce the cost premiums by following a series of strategies:

How Different Uses with Differing Peak Demand Times Can Share the Same 100 Parking Spaces

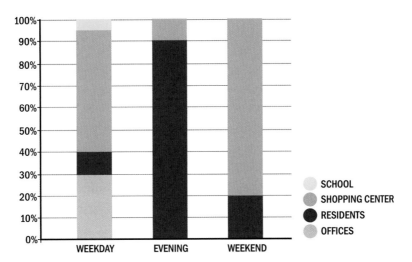

Figure 14.9. Parking shared by multiple uses (housing, office, retail) reduces the total number of spaces needed and lowers development costs. (Stantec graphic, based on data from the Institute for Transportation & Development Policy)

- *Rightsizing parking requirements*—transportation planner Jason Schreiber reports that his experience in planning for new walkable urban places in suburban settings suggests that conventional parking requirements can be cut by a third or more for office, housing, and retail.[6]
- *Providing access to transit*—Schreiber further suggests that a transit stop located within a quarter-mile (five-minute) walk of a development can reduce these requirements by an additional quarter or more and that this reduction can top 50% for office and housing.[7]
- *Promoting shared parking by different uses*—the next target is creating the ability for different uses to share the same parking space. Jeff Wolfe, owner of The Car Park and former president of the National Parking Association, uses data that indicate actual parking usage by office, rental, or ownership housing, and different types of retail for each hour throughout the month to identify opportunities to share the same parking spaces. His experience suggests that sharing between housing and office can cut the combined total by a quarter or more. Retail is more difficult to gauge but can also share spaces. He notes that shared parking works best when the different, sharing uses are located within at least one block of the parking; the spaces are not assigned to individuals or businesses; and the housing is rental rather than ownership[8] (see Figure 14.9).

Taken together, these reduced ratios can lower the cost premiums associated with structured parking for office and retail from 40 to 50% to 20 to 25% or less and for housing from 15 to 20% to 10 to 15% or less—reducing development costs by tens of millions of dollars.

Equity

The greatest success a walkable urban place can offer is to emerge as a true "downtown" that functions as the heart of the larger community. The greatest failure is to stand socially and economically apart, a sort of urban gated community. Equity defines the difference. In addition to amenities, lively retail, civic activities and places, and other ingredients that make a place the heart of a community, achieving equity requires one more key measure: inclusion—making everyone feel welcome and at the same time removing economic barriers to full participation in the community. Put another way, a walkable urban place's public realm should be programmed and designed not just to welcome but to extend an active invitation to the full spectrum of the community. Its private realm should include affordable housing options, lower-price-point retailers, and services geared to people of all ages, incomes, and backgrounds.

Equity is at least as pragmatic as it is moral. A socially and economically inclusive walkable urban place builds broader political support for controversial new zoning. As housing analyst Laurie Volk notes, economic, racial, and cultural diversity attract growing numbers of potential residents and workers who value diversity in choosing where to live or work. Equity also represents an honest recognition that even in the strongest real estate markets public dollars fund private success. They pay for the roads and transit that provide access, the new grid of internal streets, and often structured parking.

As public resources grow scarcer, neither private markets nor public policy alone can make equity happen. Tax credits and traditional affordable housing programs are already stretched too thin. There are no public programs to promote economic diversity in retail or local services. Strong markets can achieve many things, but equity and inclusion also require active public partnership in the form of policies, incentives, and funding through tax-increment financing and similar strategies that tap the value premiums created by higher-density, mixed-use urban places. This funding can help promote mixed-income housing; offset the risks and reduced rents that come with accommodating retail start-ups and community services for families and older residents; and support similar activities that make sure a walkable urban center serves the whole community.

Core Principles

Every walkable urban place emerges from a unique context defined by markets, landownership patterns, politics, community culture, environment, topography, leadership, and a long list of other characteristics. Yet walkable urban places share core principles that bring them to life as the civic, economic, and social heart of community life. As described in the Introduction,

1   they are walkable,
2   they are connected to their community,
3   they enjoy a multilayered public realm,
4   they offer a diverse mix of choices, and
5   they are authentic to the community and its setting.

These principles may be broad, but they're not just feel-good slogans. They require a great deal of strategic planning and thoughtful design to achieve. The good news is that we can frame widely applicable and effective guidelines based on underlying metrics, years of experience, and well-documented evidence. The better news is that, rather than representing a generic straitjacket, these principles suggest objectives and strategies for creating a successful walkable urban place invite planners and designers to bring their own inspiration to celebrate the unique qualities of each place and community. And finally the best news—principles not only enhance quality of life and promote a sense of community but they also boost economic value.

1. Walkability stands as the defining, threshold ingredient of successful urban places. *The term doesn't just refer to the comfort and ease of walking but also to how enjoyable walking is in terms of a variety of experiences, how engaging in terms of interaction with the larger community, and how practical in terms of access to the things people need or enjoy. In turn, walkability enhances community life when it produces a critical mass of people along public streets to support shops, restaurants, and other activities that reflect the local community's values and aspirations; to bring parks, squares, and other public places to life; and to mark a place as the heart of a community* (see Figure 14.10).

Strategies include the following:

- ***Start with the basics.***
  - ◊   *Walkable streets are tree lined, well lit at a pedestrian scale,* and rarely require pedestrians to cross more than four lanes of traffic.
  - ◊   *Urban streets are complete streets that serve all modes*—but precedence goes to walking and biking. Pedestrians and cyclists can stop to engage a friend, drop into a bakery or bookstore, decide to hang out in a square, and do the many other things that bring a walkable urban place to life. Vehicles matter, trucks bring goods, and cars and buses bring people, so walkable urban places must also meet their needs without giving them priority. Until autonomous mobility renders

Figure 14.10. Creating new walkable streets in a big-box retail center requires density, a mix of uses, and uses that animate the pedestrian experience. (Stantec)

curbside parking obsolete, streets should incorporate a parking lane to provide a buffer between pedestrians and traffic and "calm" passing traffic. Streets should be planned and designed for those who make a place a destination, not for through traffic.

- ***Develop walkable density.*** 1,500 to 2,000 housing units within a 5- to 10-minute walk can generate support for a block of Main Street retail that reflects the values of its immediate community—as opposed to a generic chain store serving a larger, auto-dependent market. These businesses reflect the character of the area, and they attract others in the community and region seeking an alternative to a one-size-fits-all approach. This walk-to market will matter much more going forward as e-retailing competes with mass market (drive-to) retail. As a rule of thumb, 2 or more square feet of office, research, and hotel space provide the same amount of support for retail as 1 square foot of housing.

- ***Make transit the handmaiden of walkability.*** Where possible develop transit-oriented walkable urban places—concentrated within a 5- to 10-minute walk of a station—or transit-ready walkable urban places. A compact walkable urban place can provide sufficient ridership to justify extension of a nearby light rail or BRT line.

- ***Create a "grid" of streets and squares programmed and designed to invite walkability.*** A hierarchy of public *streets* assigns each type of street a role in the life of a walkable urban place:

  ◊ *Main Streets*—the single most significant street and often "signature" feature. The fundamental goal is to create a place where people expect to meet—the now almost mythical "third place"[9] that promotes a sense of community. To achieve this goal requires a street designed to invite walking (street trees, sidewalks sized to permit outdoor dining and curbside parking), animated with uses that engage pedestrians and programmed with activities that attract a cross-section of diverse lifestyles. When there aren't enough stores, cafés, and restaurants to animate Main Street, artist workspaces, dance studios, entertainment, and similar activities can serve the same role.

  Main Streets also benefit from a civic dimension—a city hall or library and parades and other community-wide celebrations. Main Street can also become an entertainment venue in its own right—for example, weekend street performances, a farmer's market, interactive public art—but this requires active management and dedicated funding.

  A core walkable Main Street experience rarely extends for more than three to four blocks, constrained by the dual reality of how much retail the market supports and how far most people are willing to walk (see the "five-minute rule" discussion later in the chapter).

  ◊ *Squares*—a public place whose primary role is to enhance the appeal and community-building qualities of a Main Street. Not surprisingly, a square should embody the same qualities as a Main Street. In contrast to a town green (see "public realm" discussion later in the chapter), a square is an active public space that offers more opportunities for enjoying Main Street's amenities (e.g., a weekend beer garden, a children's play fountain)—and a wider variety of programming and civic opportunities. To avoid breaking walkable continuity along a retail street, limit its maximum dimension to around 200 feet—about a one-minute walk for a typical pedestrian.

  ◊ *Primary streets*— "front door" streets for housing and other uses not located along Main Street; organized into a network (often a grid) of small blocks; designed to invite walkability with trees, curbside parking, and attractive materials; and where possible lined with human activities. Where active uses such as retail aren't feasible, define the street with a rhythmic pattern of front doors (signifying neighbors) offered by narrow-lot houses, row houses, or townhouses built into the base of multifamily buildings. Where possible connect these streets to adjacent neighborhoods.

◊ *Secondary streets*—while these often act as service streets providing access to parking, loading, and other maintenance functions, they may also serve as "mews," entertainment streets, and similar unique roles that add variety and unique character.

◊ *Small blocks*—offer pedestrians multiple options and promote a sense of connectivity among all activities. Without a compelling reason, no block should be longer than 400 feet and preferably 300 feet or less.

◊ *Parking structures*—should not face directly onto public streets or squares but sit behind buildings or be wrapped with housing, stores, or possibly offices, where they face a public way.

- ***Invite walkability in every season***. Every walkable urban place can celebrate regional climate and ecology with native trees, landscaping, and other natural features that remind people of the joys of being outdoors. Every region offers climate-related challenges—rain, cold, heat, humidity—but a walkable urban place must function well every day. Enclosed malls solved the climate problem but in the process created an artificial environment that has proved less inviting over the long term. Urban places "manage" weather by creating the best place to be outside any day of the year:

    ◊ *In cold climates*—"winter cities" cannot afford to take winter off, and many have devised intriguing ways to lure people to come together in public places. Edmonton's mantra has been to make virtue of necessity: It says, "climate is our ally" and treats winter as an opportunity to reconnect with the fun and whimsy of childhood. Warming huts and pop-up patios appear in parks, where people gather around fires with hot drinks and music. Instead of getting rid of snow, the city collects it to fill parks with sledding hills, snow labyrinths, and snow walls that kids of all ages paint. Because darkness comes early, fire and light help make even drab blocks feel enchanted. Artists from around the world convene to create "firescapes"—huge wooden structures that are set ablaze.

    ◊ *In hot, humid climates*—the challenges "summer cities" face can be just as daunting. The narrow passageways and frequent fountains that characterize the medinas (historic centers) of historic Islamic cities in North Africa represent centuries-old ways of creating shade and enlisting the cooling effect of water. Together they compound their benefits. While supplementing the shade provided by awnings or an arcade with "misting" does help, it consumes significant energy. Fountains, watercourses, and other features that animate as well as cool offer a more sustainable approach that adds far more value to the public realm.

Figure 14.11. The first form of automated vehicles likely to enter wide use will be on-demand shuttles hailed from mobile devices. In mass production by the early 2020s, these shared automated vehicles (SAVs) will be more convenient and less expensive than today's Uber or Lyft ride-sharing services and provide an economical new tool for connecting new urban places to transit and to the larger community. (Stantec)

2. Walkable urban places succeed when they are connected both to the community's *mobility networks—by car (conventional or automated) and by bike, walking, transit—and to the life of the community with uses and activities that make it a destination for everyone.*

Strategies include the following:

- ***Plan now for autonomous mobility.*** Look for opportunities to use shared autonomous vehicles (SAVs) to make the walkable urban place transit oriented—and to provide convenient access to job centers, universities, and other major destinations. Build in sensors and other technology, and work with local and state transportation departments to prepare for SAV technology to appear widely by the mid-2020s (see Figure 14.11).
- ***Focus density around transit.*** Transit is most effective at sparking development and drawing riders within a 5- to 10-minute walk (a quarter to a half mile) of a station. Office and housing parking requirements (and costs) should be reduced within a 5-minute walk of a transit station.
- ***Park once.*** Minimize the need to drive anywhere after parking—whether for a resident, worker, or visitor.

- ***Make connections that enhance a walkable urban place's accessibility, and make it a welcome neighbor.*** Where possible—particularly for sites designed to be reached only by car—introduce pedestrian, bike, and transit connections to adjacent neighborhoods, the larger community, and the region. In many cases cars will remain the primary connection between a new walkable urban place and the larger community. Transportation connections should not translate into traffic impacts. While extending adjacent neighborhood streets into a new walkable urban place might seem to make sense, such connections need to work in practice. Any new street connections must reflect a comprehensive traffic-management strategy that moves traffic (trucks as well as cars) efficiently into and out of the walkable urban place from and to the regional network without drawing significant traffic through adjacent neighborhoods. In many cases a pedestrian connection to a nearby neighborhood will make more sense than a through roadway.

- ***Incorporate uses and activities that connect a walkable urban place to the life of the community.*** Community members will value a new walkable urban place more highly if it functions as more than just a place to live, work, or spend money. Locate uses here that belong to the entire community. A new city hall, library, town green, recreation center, health center, or early-childhood education center will draw a wide cross section of the community. Cultural and performing arts centers not only enhance a new walkable urban place and boost the community's "brand" but also draw customers to shops and restaurants. In turn, because these facilities rely on regional audiences they thrive in mixed-use environments whose mix of food, entertainment, and other amenities creates a regional destination.

3. Successful urban places enjoy a multilayered public realm including a full spectrum of places ranging from "active" squares to places of quiet reflection and often including a town green and other civic space. Whether owned by the public sector or not, the streets, squares, parks, and other components of the public realm are open to all without qualification. The art of public realm has always involved more than "beautification." Today, when cities and suburbs alike struggle to make diversity and equity work—and to compete in a knowledge-driven economy that values community—that mission ultimately means promoting community, bringing people together, and encouraging everyone to share their stories (see Figure 14.12).

Public realm is at once about providing a variety of places that make walkable urban places central to lives differentiated by culture, age, income, and other sources of diversity, and equally about bringing people together around a shared experience. At the same time, public realm traffics in both the joys and the tensions that accompany diversity—a place equally appropriate for celebrations or protests.

Figure 14.12. Jamison Park in Portland's Pearl District combines grass, shade, and water with enough nearby density to make it the heart of a lively new neighborhood. (David Wheeler under CC-BY SA 3.0)

Strategies include the following:

- ***Build a hierarchy from fully personal to fully public places.*** This range should begin with quasi-private, personal places, such as stoops or shared courtyards. These spaces should connect to quasi-public places shared by neighbors or affinity groups—for example, quiet streets, tot lots, or small parks primarily used by neighbors, or shared-interest places like bark parks or the equivalent of Miami's "Domino Park" along Calle Ocho, which attracts older Cuban immigrants by drawing on their cultural heritages. Toward the more public, interactive end of the spectrum are places that bring diverse people together—a few people in a pocket park or public garden, larger numbers along an active Main Street or public square, and potentially large weekend crowds at a large park programmed to attract the entire community.

- ***Tell the diverse stories of those who live and work in the community.*** Traditionally many suburbs, like older urban neighborhoods, shared one major benefit: homogeneity. Community came more naturally in part because most people carried around a shared story—shaped by broadly similar economic, racial, ethnic, and other shared backgrounds.

- ***Program and design Main Streets and squares to celebrate a sense of interactive community:***

  ◊ *Kids of all ages play together in fountains*—they represent the single most effective way to animate a place, inviting people to interact and bringing diverse people together. On a warm day, in a fountain full of kids of every color, laughing, chasing each other, and inventing water games, kids discover each other . . . and so do their nearby parents.

  ◊ *Public realm "furniture"*—can promote interaction and be fun. For example, bus shelters can substitute swings for fixed seats and provide interactive information about the Main Street, the neighborhood, or local events. The shelters themselves can tell the community's stories through digitally programmed changing—and always current—words and art.

  ◊ *The power of interactive public art to enrich the public realm by promoting community is rapidly expanding. Pedestrians can orchestrate water, light, and sound using their smart phones* (see Figure 14.13):

    – Audio/video installations can put people in touch with each other—5 feet or 5 miles apart. John Ewing's Boston-area installation in 2010 invited people in urban Roxbury and suburban Brookline to communicate live via storefront-sized video screens.

    – Games like "ActiWait" can connect people. A touch-screen game, it lets strangers play a Pong-like game as they wait for a pedestrian crossing signal in the German cities of Oberhausen and Hildesheim.

Figure 14.13. Color Commons, created by New American Public Art, allows people to text one of 900 color names from a smart phone to *Light Blades*, along Boston's Greenway. LEDs in the sculpture, by Dennis Carmichael, then transmit the chosen color. (New American Public Art)

- Information can be interactive art. An installation in Seattle invites people to talk about what residents in a large apartment building—and across Seattle—are tweeting, in real time.
- Fountains can be a form of interactive public art—beautiful both for their physical form and the ways they invite children of all ages to interact with friends and strangers.

- An artist has designed laser installations that would, for example, engage strangers along Boston's Greenway in playing together by "painting" the facades of nearby dark office buildings with stunning digital graphics.
- A promising new frontier is not installations, but interactive events. Tactical urbanism quite literally redefines the temporal and spatial boundaries of the public realm. The impact has been exciting, profound, and unsettling: unlocking redistributions of space in which car-choked streets undergo an almost surreal/sublime transition to informal, people-focused beer gardens; spontaneous programming draws communities of like-minded people together to create events and uses that no one had imagined for those spaces; and at a deeper level, interactive events provide opportunities for people concerned about issues like gentrification and social inequity to push for social change (such as Black Lives Matter "die ins" in 2015 and 2016 that walked a fine line between protest and programming).
- Looked at another way, using public art to bring the public realm to life can democratize the public realm. It turns the traditional top-down model, by which a public entity or developer funds and installs street trees, lighting, or art, on its head. Anyone who is willing to invest his or her hard work in a new inspiration has the potential to launch a work of tactical urbanism that can be magical—or unnerving—but almost never dull. But unleashing this bottom-up potential can still benefit from management (coordination, scheduling, help with funding, etc.) that comes from above—ideally from a downtown manager but possibly from city hall.

- **_Incorporate a civic dimension._**
  - ◊ *A civic space*—a town green or similar public space that welcomes people from every walk of life and accommodates a wide range of activities, from lying on the grass, to events sponsored by members of the community, to community-wide events, such as potluck dinners.
  - ◊ *A civic place*—an iconic city hall or library that symbolizes the importance of a new walkable urban place to the life of the community and communicates that the place "belongs" to the entire community.

4. Expanding choices enhances quality of life *by expanding a suburban community's options for living, working, shopping, entertainment, culture, and core elements of life across different lifestyles, incomes, ethnicities, and other differences. This same inclusive variety of choices draws a diverse community when it touches aspects of daily life—eating with friends, shopping, consuming culture, celebrating. This multidimensioned variety is central to establishing a walkable urban place as the social heart of a community* (see Figure 14.14).

Strategies include the following:

Figure 14.14. Belmar in Lakewood, Colorado, designed the street level of a parking garage as artist work/sell space, creating a one-of-a-kind attraction that brings people from throughout the region who might not otherwise visit the development. (Clark Reader/The Lakewood Sentinel)

- ***Offer new choices for living, working, playing, culture, and other core components of livable communities.***
  - ◊ *A walkable urban place can align a community's housing choices more closely to its changing age, economic, and social profile.* An urban place can meet a burgeoning demand for rental lofts and other types of multifamily housing that meet the needs of younger and older residents. At the same time, walkable urban places can also fill other market niches, serving families who want to raise their children in a walkable environment, people who want to walk to work, live/work options for entrepreneurs ranging from the arts to technology, affordable housing that serves the needs of older residents who want to age in their community, and newer residents who can't afford single-family houses.
  - ◊ *Urban environments increasingly represent a necessary choice for established knowledge-industry companies.* As businesses vie for scarce knowledge workers, these companies increasingly seek urban environments that match their workforce's lifestyle preferences. These companies will trade convenient parking, lower office park rents, and highway visibility for amenity-rich, walkable places, particularly if these places mix in housing and offer opportunities to walk to work.
  - ◊ *Mixed-use urban environments are a natural choice for many emerging companies.* Many start-ups and other "creative" businesses strongly prefer a mixed-use

urban environment and will head to the urban core if suburbs don't offer urban options. These smaller companies represent a substantial share of job growth for many suburbs and a valuable source of longer-term, high-quality jobs.

◊ *Unique retailers, restaurants, and entertainment venues that fail to take root in regional "drive to" markets seek out walkable urban places.* These businesses range from clothing boutiques to chef-owned restaurants, brew pubs, and music venues that thrive in the unique markets shaped by the personality of urban neighborhoods. At the same time a higher-end, niche supermarket or even a mass retailer drawn to a "cool vibe," such as an urban-format Target, may choose a walkable urban place location, which in turn draws more activity.

◊ *Cultural venues, artists, and similar uses can find a home in a walkable urban place* that often eludes them in drive-to locations that lack a synergistic mix of unique food, unique shopping, and entertainment.

◊ *A mix of entertainment, arts, and culture broadens a walkable urban place's appeal.* Cinemas, music venues, community theater space, art galleries, and similar uses make these environments more than a place to live, work, and shop. These uses can occupy ground-floor space not required for retail. Belmar, outside of Denver, retrofitted a parking garage with ground-floor artists' workspace/galleries to bring the adjacent street to life. Regular "gallery walks" now attract thousands to Belmar's restaurants and shops. These amenities can animate a walkable urban place on evenings and weekends. Concentrate these activities strategically around a square or town green.

- ***Program-in entertainment and vitality.***
  ◊ *A regionally significant performance or cultural space* can represent a strategic investment. For example, a city council chamber that doubles as a venue for theater or musical performances can go a long way toward shaping a place's image and support the restaurants, cafés, cultural events, and other activities that bring a walkable place to life.

- ***Follow the five-minute rule to make choices accessible.***
  ◊ *Most people will walk about a quarter of a mile—five minutes—unless headed for a transit station or work.* To make the benefits of walkability real, a walkable urban place needs to offer a diverse mix of live/work/shop/play choices that support diverse lifestyles within a five-minute walk of one another.
  ◊ *Compact development is particularly important for the early phases of development.* The diversity of uses and density that the five-minute rule suggests producean early identity for a walkable urban place that may take a decade or more to develop. Empty spaces that interrupt walkable connectivity, such as undeveloped sites, surface parking lots, or even a large park, can undermine an urban place's greatest amenity—walkable choices.

Figure 14.15. Galleries and workshops along Makers Alley showcase Tampa's artists and makers, bringing life to Water Street Tampa, a new nine-million-square-foot urban district. (Stantec)

5. Authenticity means seeking inspiration from, and embodying, the unique traditions, arts, innovation, culture, diversity, landscape, or other qualities that define a community and its setting today. *Authenticity embodies what is genuine, distinctive, and defining about each community and place today.*

Authenticity can remain a challenge even when all the foregoing principles are fully achieved. No matter how walkable, connected to the life of the community, enriched by a lively public realm, and full of choices suited to diverse lifestyles, new walkable urban places share defining traits. They are developed at roughly the same time and are subject to the same design aesthetic; they are subject to the same construction economics, which produce the same predominance of four- to six-story frame-over-podium buildings; they exemplify the same contemporary retail trends, no matter how "cool," that repeat again and again. Nor is this sameness resolved by different histories, architectural heritages, or other elements of a unique past. These are new places, and mimicking the past is generic, even if the physical manifestations differ (see Figure14.15).

Strategies include the following:

- **Program and design in the people who make a community unique.** Draw on the artists, musicians, performers, makers, chefs, innovators, and others whose creative skills represent the community's contemporary spirit and living history to program, design, and bring their contributions directly to the life of the new walkable urban place.

- ***Tell the story of the community, its diverse constituencies, and unique individuals.*** Public art can tell the story of an entire community—and the distinctive constituencies that together make the community what it is. Racial and ethnic groups, immigrants, artists, and musicians, and many others can speak in their own voices. As demographics and a dynamic economy change our society at an increasingly rapid pace, it becomes more important for those who built our neighborhoods, raised families, practiced our arts, fought the good fights—and in other ways shaped who we are today—to tell their stories. In the past we have done this with murals, statues, and plaques. Today we can add video, audio, and music installations to the tools we use to bring these stories to life in compelling ways in parks and squares and along city streets.

- ***Respond to the natural environment in every aspect of planning, programming, and design.*** Walking distances, mix of uses, architecture, and every element of the public realm should reflect the opportunities and challenges posed by the public realm. Climates with extremes of temperature and humidity should provide frequent relief than milder climates, with much shorter walks between destinations and constant opportunities for shelter. Building and public realm design should not only embody standard "green" practices—but *be* green in the ways most relevant to each place. The natural environment can always be an inspiration, not an obstacle.

- ***Seize opportunities to create the social, economic, and cultural heart for the community.*** The most important form of authenticity is to represent the genuine heart of a community, a place "claimed by us and about us." Creating a place that speaks to the values and sensibilities of an entire community and invites its member to come together can't gloss over the realities of life in the community. How diverse are sensibilities and values? How easily can they be embodied in the same place? Is the community divided along lines of race, income and social class, town and gown, or other differences? What would encourage people to cross these lines and come together? Are there gaps in the shared life of the community that a new urban center might offer a unique way to fill, perhaps with a civic center, cultural center, or other form of common ground?

If nothing else, planning a new walkable urban place requires the integration of multiple perspectives. A wonderful tree-lined Main Street with the walkable pattern of the 1920s won't come to life without enough nearby density to support twenty-first-century shops and cafés that bring it to life. Achieving this density will require an inclusive public process that fosters a genuine understanding of density's benefits and that makes it clear that tools exist for managing traffic and other potential costs. Density and a strong market by themselves often can't unlock change without civic leadership and broad public engagement. Those elements can build political support and set the stage for a public/private partnership (P3) that can fund the infrastructure of walkability—new walkable blocks, parks and public spaces, and, potentially, expensive structured parking. Even with enough density, effective leadership, strong community support, a great market, and a robust P3 in place, a walkable urban place won't be worth the immense investment of energy, dollars, and political capital if it doesn't embody the principles that make it the welcoming heart for everyone in the community.

Notes

1. Multiple conversations with real estate consultants Laurie Volk (Chapter 3), Sarah Woodworth (Chapter 4), and Michael J. Berne (Chapter 5), 2015–16.

2. Eric Jaffe, "What Does Living 'Close' to Transit Really Mean?" CityLab, January 12, 2015, accessed August 6, 2017, https://www.citylab.com/solutions/2015/01/what-does-living-close-to-transit-really-mean/384421/.

3. Conversation with Stewart Schwartz, April 24, 2017.

4. Conversation with Yolanda Takesian, transportation planner at Kittelson Associates, July 15, 2014.

5. Conversation with retail consultant Michael J. Berne, June 5, 2016.

6. Conversation with transportation consultant Jason Schreiber, April 15, 2017.

7. Ibid.

8. Conversation with parking consultant Jeff Wolfe, April 15, 2017.

9. The "third places" (Main Street, cafés, city sidewalks, public parks) described by sociologist Ray Oldenburg that offer spontaneous opportunities for diverse interactions outside of home and work.

Figure 15.1a, b, c. The figure grounds show how each development fits into its context and how its internal connectivity helps create a walkable urban place. (a) Reston Town Center, (b) Bethesda Row, (c) Rockville Town Square. (Justin Falango)

15

Placemaking

Jason Beske

We end this book with a chapter on placemaking—giving shape and character to the places we create. Long confined to planning and design jargon, "placemaking" and the ideas behind it began seeping into the mainstream in the early 2000s. Today mayors, developers, and neighborhood leaders talk as easily about placemaking as do urban designers. The mainstreaming of placemaking took place at the same time as a shift in demographics, the rise of a knowledge economy, and a longing for more social interaction. These forces have come together to make the shape and character of communities matter more than at any time since World War II.

Defining the Term

How you define "placemaking" depends on whom you ask. A planner or urban designer might call it the planning, design, and management of public spaces to benefit the people who will inhabit them.[1] That means working with community members to create places of lasting value guided by the belief that the social aspects of the community and personal well-being are of utmost importance. Meanwhile, a developer or builder might see placemaking as a tool for marketing an idea or call it the act of designing and creating a place where people want to live. This definition focuses on the act of creating places, in both a physical and a social sense—bringing together a diversity of interests to create places of lasting value.

With an eye on our topic—the creation of new walkable urban spaces in suburbs—we treat placemaking as the physical expression of the unique look, feel, and heritage of a community. Drawing freely on local history, geography, ecology, culture, and values, placemaking seeks to reinforce a sense of character and to give the buildings and public spaces of new development a distinctive quality. To adapt Gertrude Stein's dictum, placemaking puts the there there.

Why Placemaking in the Suburbs?

Placemaking as a conscious practice first made its presence felt in the 1980s, long before the term itself was coined. Some of the most influential thinking on the topic emerged from the New Urbanism movement, which worked to develop a more human-centered approach to the forms and organization of buildings in suburbs. The movement arrived in cities in the early 2000s in response to the damaging legacy of midcentury planning and urban renewal. Young planners and grassroots activists sought to shift the focus of city-building from cars back to people, in part by recapturing traditional urban values and in part by finding urban forms to celebrate new urban values.

Aside from its community-wide social value, placemaking has become a powerful way for suburbs to differentiate themselves for attracting residents, development, and jobs. Driven in part by changing demographics and lifestyles that favor denser, more urban development, the desire for community identity in suburbs continues to increase. More than ever, community members, elected officials, and developers agree on the importance of creating walkable urban places, whether to enhance quality of life, attract jobs and investment, or generate fiscal benefits. After the much-discussed revival of cities, the rise of walkable urban places is rapidly shifting the focus back to suburbs.

Several of the case studies in Part III illustrate how much development occurred in suburbs before anyone recognized placemaking's absence from the equation—even, as we've noted, before the term even existed. Placemaking doesn't just create a livable, culturally sensitive built environment, it holds the key to succeeding in the marketplace. This chapter examines the importance of placemaking as an economic development tool, one increasingly adopted by leading developers to create walkable urban places in suburbs.

As the introduction notes, this book doesn't attack sprawl. Instead, it focuses on how continued suburban growth can strengthen existing suburbs by creating walkable, mixed-use urban places that both add character and make these communities more economically competitive. Placemaking channels community aspirations, ideally relying on time-tested principles of urban design. Suburbs are almost always newer and less layered than the cities they spring from. Few will rival their city for placemaking—a sense of character that blends history, topography, design, and culture—but many can develop their own histories and an urban fabric of their own distinctive places.

Key Placemaking Characteristics

Placemaking reaches every aspect of the public and private realm, but no community or developer has the resources or the control required to get everything right. Suburban communities need to look for priorities and opportunities—and seize the opportunities that represent the highest priorities.

Every community needs to solve this equation in its own way. That being said, the five principles laid out in Chapter 14 represent a great place to start:

1. **Walkability**—Planning and designing development in ways that encourage pedestrians to interact and connect with each other and their surroundings is fundamental to placemaking. Organizing development around the needs of pedestrians—comfort, safety, ease of movement, and visual interest, ranging from architectural details to opportunities to watch other people—gives new development a sense of activity that attracts people and helps assure economic success.

2. **Connectivity**—Do people have lots of options for moving easily and safely from any point A to any point B within a development? Are there lots of ways to travel (on foot, by bike, in vehicles like shuttles, in cars)? Does the development provide the same ease of connection and range of choices for getting to nearby neighborhoods or destinations in the wider region (transit joins the list of options but shouldn't displace any of the other methods)? In short, does a place provide easy access to daily needs, community amenities, and activities throughout the region?

3. **A multilayered public realm**—From quieter places for contemplation and reflection to larger settings for community-wide gatherings, the public realm should provide a range of possibilities. Parks, plazas, squares, and sidewalks should support activities that most residents want to pursue, but some elements—such as skate parks, playgrounds, and dog parks—should also allow pursuits that might only appeal to a small subset.

4. **A diverse mix of choices**—Walkable urban places need to provide for varied activities that appeal to diverse populations and lifestyles, while offering a range of choices well suited to the community they serve. This diversity makes good economic sense as well—the more kinds of activities and choices a place offers, the broader the potential market it can serve.

5. **Authenticity**—The design of a walkable urban place should draw on a community's unique qualities. Those can include topography, climate, history, cultural traditions, food, and artistic expression. Any or all of these sources can help capture the spirit of the community, its people, and its setting.

The five principles serve as the foundation for creating thoughtful, walkable urban places. This chapter devotes particular attention to the principles of walkability and connectivity in placemaking, particularly in the way we design streets and sidewalks. A brief consideration of walkability and connectivity precedes examples of communities using placemaking to create walkable urban places. Then we take a look at how the other principles—multilayered public realm, diverse mix of choices, and authenticity—relate to placemaking by suburban communities to create new urban places.

This story is told through a series of vignettes that the author knows well. Please note, in the spirit of Chapter 14, not only do these examples celebrate the principles, they also reflect the value of processes defined by leadership and community engagement, many of which were achieved through innovative public–private partnerships.

Walkability

Streets serve as the backbone around which a community grows. They move people and goods, and they constitute a large proportion of the built environment and public space. How well people can move around is intrinsic to a community's success and the quality of life it offers. The historic approach to suburban street networks—streets laid out without coordination and engineered to move as many cars as fast as possible—presents a significant challenge to communities looking to create walkable urban places that can serve all modes of transportation.

Even with rising demand for walkable places, people who live in suburbs still demand—and need—convenient automobile access. Attempts to create places designed first for people often runs up against a decades-long accumulation of policies and infrastructure designed to meet the needs of automobiles. Treating streets as *places* helps people see streets in their entirety, not just for their function in moving people and goods but also for the vital role they can play in animating a community's social and economic life.[2] Suburbs that want to create walkable urban places must start at the very foundation of suburban form—streets—and reimagine them for the convenient blending of transportation modes, while giving equal weight to community aspirations and the pedestrian experience.

Connectivity

Successful suburban placemaking takes into account access to and through developments—the creation and regulation of a good street network are essential to success. Properly designed street networks can reduce land consumption and increase multimodal access. New accessible and walkable urban places gain a greater chance of succeeding when they connect to multiple transportation modes, particularly when they incorporate a balance of uses and density that reflects market demand.[3] Providing efficient connections between modes is key to achieving a functional multimodal system and a successful, walkable development.

Connections within walkable developments, as well as to surrounding communities and regions, provide access for people. Conventional suburban street networks typically have minimal or no through streets or sidewalks. Traditional urban-style street networks, on the other hand, promote walkability with short blocks defined by numerous through

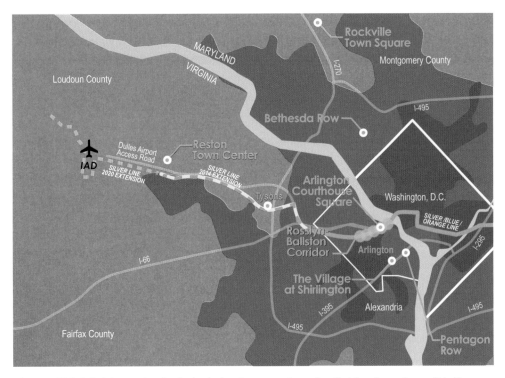

Figure 15.2. Washington's suburbs include a large number of walkable urban places. (Ma Shuyun, Xumengqi, and Anushree Nallapaneni)

streets. This provides pedestrians with multiple access points and routes by which to reach a destination.[4] Whether a grid of streets or a local transportation network, access to place is an important foundational element of creating walkable suburbs (see Figure 15.1a, b, c). Connections can be provided by regulating urban block dimensions, and incorporating sidewalks, trails, bike lanes, and bike shares (further discussed in Chapter 14, "Planning").

Reston Town Center–Reston, Virginia

As the transition to walkable urbanism becomes increasingly popular in the suburbs, Reston has been at the forefront of the movement (Reston Town Center is used throughout to illustrate the linkage of the physical and social realms of placemaking). Roughly 20 miles west of Washington, Reston is a planned community in Fairfax County, Virginia, founded in 1964 (see Figure 15.2). Part of the postwar New Town movement, it was developed to follow guiding principles that stress quality of life. Citizens would be able to live in the same community through all life stages, with different housing types available as they aged. It was hoped that Restonians could live, work, and play in their own community, with common grounds and scenic beauty shared equally regardless of income level.[5]

Extension of Metro's Silver Line—which connected Reston to downtown Washington in 2014 and continued in another phase on to Dulles International Airport (5 miles west of Reston) and beyond—has begun to influence Reston's historic suburban pattern development. Instead of focusing on the demands of the automobile, developers have begun embracing patterns and densities that support multimodal transportation, particularly walking, to a greater degree.

Reston Town Center (RTC) includes more than 2 million square feet of offices, 60 retailers, and nearly 30 restaurants. It contains about 2,500 residential units, with several hundred more on the way. The Town Center will grow to include 5,000 housing units and nearly 10,000 residents by the late 2020s. With the expansion of the Silver Line to its front door by 2020, population and jobs in the Town Center will come closer to the 1:1 ratio that Town Center leaders strive for.

RTC has garnered an identity and reputation as a regional destination (a fact I can attest to, having lived and worked there). Part of its distinctiveness comes from a relatively diverse population and patronage, as well as a thoughtfully planned network of streets and public spaces. These elements create the backdrop of a holistic community that effectively serves its members.

RTC is connected both internally and on its perimeter to the region. While the street grid and pedestrian pathways create good internal access throughout, the perimeter streets create a series of additional access points for multiple modes of transportation access from beyond. Both a regional trail (the Washington and Old Dominion, which begins in Alexandria, Virginia) and a bus transit facility on the southern edge of the core allow connectivity from across the community and region, creating equitable, multimodal access.

The heart of RTC includes a rich mixture of residential, office, and retail uses situated on a roughly 20-block, connected street grid of relatively short blocks. The grid makes access to RTC's various elements more efficient by providing multiple choices for pedestrian and vehicular travel. In order to avoid inefficient street patterns, a development should connect wherever practical to everything around it, even if its neighbors are nothing but single-use pods.[6] Market Street serves as the central spine of the Town Center; it often closes for special events and at times of greater pedestrian activity (see Figure 15.3).

As RTC continues to grow, the street grid establishes the ability for future expansion beyond the core (see Figure 15.4). Future expansion to the north and south (toward the future Metro stop) will add a substantial amount of office, residential, and retail development. Future phases will continue to integrate new public spaces and cultural amenities. Learning from past lessons, future designs will also be more mindful of the design of the pedestrian realm and overall placemaking experience.

Every year, dozens of programmed events attract thousands of people to the Town Center, none more popular than the annual arts festival, which draws 220 artists and over

Figure 15.3. As Reston Town Center's main street, Market Street connects varied open spaces and hosts a variety of community events, including the Northern Virginia Fine Arts Festival, which attracts more than 30,000 visitors and over 200 artists from across the United States and beyond. (Flickr user Warren in the Weeds)

Figure 15.4. Market Street in Reston Town Center anchors a comfortable street grid that provides multiple ways to move within the center and multiple peripheral points for access to surrounding areas. (Google Earth Pro)

30,000 visitors. The event introduces thousands of people to the arts while spilling into the streets and open spaces of the Town Center. The event is organized by the Greater Reston Arts Center (GRACE), which has a full-time headquarters on Market Street adjacent to Reston Town Square Park. As a cultural venue, GRACE augments the visitor experience in RTC and contributes to a distinct sense of place in the Town Center. More recently, GRACE has begun investing in international artists, and both indoor and outdoor exhibits have drawn increasing numbers of patrons to the Town Center. GRACE serves as an authentic cultural venue that plays a vital placemaking role for the community at large.[7]

The Village at Shirlington–Arlington, Virginia

Opened in 1944 as one of the first retail shopping centers in the United States, Shirlington has since reinvented itself as a walkable, mixed-use Main Street. The introduction of hundreds of residential units, cultural amenities (Signature Theater and a community library) (see Figure 15.5), and additional retail to Shirlington's historic urban pattern has established a critical mass of residents and created a local destination in a relatively isolated portion of Arlington County. To connect to the broader region, Shirlington established a transit center with robust bus service, enabling convenient and regular connections for its residents and visitors from throughout the region.

Roughly 50 restaurants and retail establishments, situated along a series of well-designed streets and sidewalks, support street life in Shirlington. Sidewalks are wide enough to accommodate outdoor dining, trees, street furniture, and pedestrian pathways (see Figure 15.6). Buildings along sidewalks and streets maintain a high level of transparency at ground level, making it easy for passersby to watch activity within stores and restaurants and for customers to look out onto a changing street scene. A popular destination for office workers, residents, and visitors, Shirlington is a suburban *place* that has grown in size and identity since the 1980s. A combination of its widely recognized cultural venues, walkable streetscape full of retail, and regularly programmed events ensures that Shirlington is not only a destination but also a place.

Pedestrian Streets as Public Space

While suburban streets occasionally serve as a venue for public events, until recently their design—and public policy—have made them primarily a way to maintain the flow of automobiles. When properly integrated, retail environments are more successful when directly accessible and viewable by people in automobiles. Nevertheless, developers have increasingly recognized the marketability (and placemaking potential) of public space solely dedicated to pedestrians, and have added pedestrian streets in an increasing number of walkable urban places in suburbs.

Figure 15.5. Cultural venues such as a library and community theater help define Shirlington's character. (Flickr user Dan Reed)

Figure 15.6. A vibrant restaurant scene keeps Shirlington's sidewalks full of pedestrian activity and chance encounters. (Federal Realty Investment Trust)

Figure 15.7. With a mix of uses, active storefronts, and programmed events, Bethesda Lane offers residents, workers, and visitors a vibrant public space for entertainment and leisure. (Federal Realty Investment Trust)

Although some critics argue that pedestrian streets lack activity and vibrancy, they can serve as an effective connecting element and placemaking strategy in, and placemaking strategy for, a healthy network of streets and open spaces. When planned as part of a larger urban design framework, pedestrian streets can connect multiple destinations and offer choices to the pedestrian. Additionally, they offer great flexibility for programmed events and special activities. As a caution, pedestrian streets should be viewed as a reward based on the success of surrounding mixed-use activity, not a placemaking panacea.

Bethesda Row–Bethesda, Maryland

Bethesda is a first-ring suburb of Washington. A mixed-use redevelopment that spans four city blocks, Bethesda Row includes 183,000 square feet of office space, 347,000 square feet of retail (including restaurants), and 180 apartments. The development's location within two blocks of a Metro station and adjacent to the Capital Crescent Trail provides convenient connectivity to Washington and other parts of the region (see Figure 15.1b). As a midblock connection in Bethesda Row, Bethesda Lane serves as the central pedestrian spine in the community's downtown. It is well integrated into the pedestrian network and hosts regularly programmed events ranging from fashion shows and concerts to arts festivals and dining. Bethesda Lane successfully integrates a retail block within a space that is comfortable, flexible, and aesthetically pleasing (see Figure 15.7). It includes a diverse mix of uses, primarily retail, at the ground floor. Depending on the weather and events, the space can be used for a leisurely stroll or relaxation, and at the same time allow for restaurants to spill out and activate the space.

Typically, pedestrian streets are more successful at a smaller scale, and their limited scale makes them easy to implement; most are between one and three blocks long. Their more intimate settings offer retail on a human scale, with sufficient points of interest, and places to linger, encouraging customers to browse at their own pace and make connections with shop proprietors.[8]

At 350 feet long and 55 feet wide, Bethesda Lane is roughly the length of one city block. Although relatively narrow, it provides a powerful placemaking gesture that ties together two active retail streets that run perpendicular to it at each end. By comparison, the Promenade in the denser RTC measures approximately 240 feet long and 50 feet wide (see Figure 15.8). Both streets are retail oriented and provide a comfortable pedestrian environment and sense of enclosure—each functions as an outdoor living room in its respective development. Although each is successful, Bethesda Lane has a more intimate, pedestrian-oriented feel—in part because of the adjacent uses (upper-floor apartments line Bethesda Lane), scale of adjacent buildings (Reston's are four to five times taller), the fact that Bethesda's pedestrian street incorporates programmed events, and the variation and rhythm of retail frontages on Bethesda Lane.

As the popularity of shared and pedestrian streets has grown, some suburbs have integrated these forms into urban design guidelines. The result of a considerable amount of community engagement and input, the recent Envision Courthouse Square initiative in Arlington, established an urban design framework that will guide the future retrofit of the community's government center (see Figures 15.9 and 15.10). The framework unites two shared streets via a central pedestrian street (the Promenade) that will serve as a foundational element to the plan and connect retail, public transit, various open spaces, and a series of local government buildings. As in many other walkable suburban places, the Courthouse Square pedestrian street will function as both a circulatory and an open space element—and when properly executed as an element of the built environment, it will be central to providing a new walkable urban place in Arlington.

Figure 15.8. The Promenade adds to the open-space network in Reston Town Center, while providing a varied pedestrian experience. (Jason Beske)

Figure 15.9. The vision for Arlington's Courthouse Square creates vibrant pedestrian spaces, including shared streets and a pedestrian promenade. (Arlington County)

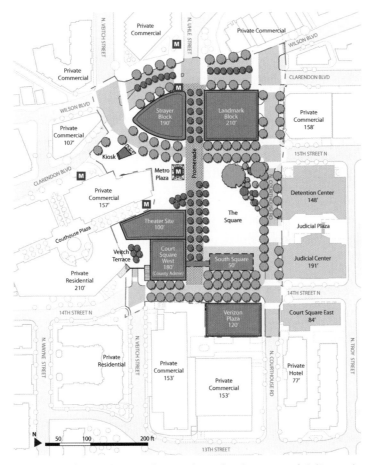

Figure 15.10. The Courthouse Square plan guides redevelopment of Arlington's government center as a place focused on people. (Arlington County)

A Multilayered Public Realm

Open space has many meanings in the planning of suburbs. Not only do open spaces contribute to the environmental and aesthetic quality of the communities in which we live, perhaps more importantly, they also contribute to social and mental well-being. A good open space system includes a range of possibilities keyed to activities that most residents want, but that also reflect the tastes and needs of small subgroups that might not necessarily appeal to a majority.

Incorporating designated open space is a key component of placemaking for walkable suburban redevelopment. Effective public spaces tend to attract people in groups, and formal social programming offers one of the best ways to do that.[9] Great public spaces are comfortable and accessible—they encourage social interaction.[10] Planning for open space in the form of parks, plazas, or squares, where people can congregate and experience a place, remains essential for suburbs making the shift to more walkable urban places.[11]

The design process should incorporate careful planning for open space based on meaningful input from community members as a way of producing a design and shaping programming that will win community support and make these spaces successful. Functionally, open spaces provide physical and social leisure through both recreation and social engagement. In a walkable environment, intensified use of public space raises the frequency of informal interactions among residents, building ties among neighbors. Additionally, many successful suburbs incorporate open spaces that are flexible enough to serve a diverse, ever-changing population throughout the year because their designs grew out of the active involvement of community members (see Figures 15.11 and 15.12).

Reston Town Center–Reston, Virginia

The open space network in Reston Town Center includes three primary spaces: the Promenade (described in "Pedestrian Streets as Public Space"), Reston Town Square Park, and Fountain Square. These open spaces provide variety and flexibility for activities in the Town Center.

An expansive open plaza, Fountain Square was designed to feel comfortable when inhabited by a few people or by a festival crowd. Market Street bisects Fountain Square; closing the street during outdoor events converts the square into a single large plaza, as opposed to the more intimate, human-scaled spaces that it typically comprises. The Mercury Fountain acts as a central landmark that serves as focal point and destination for vistors to the Town Center (see Figure 15.13). Also in the square is a glass-roofed pavilion that serves as an ice skating rink during the winter months and a multipurpose performing arts venue throughout the remainder of the year.[12] Early in Reston's development, the site of the pavilion was slated for a cultural venue (i.e., museum), but following the success of impromtu activities in the space prior to the acceptance of a design by the developer, the idea of a pavilion for community activities stuck.

Figure 15.11. Pentagon Row has proved a popular fair-weather destination for dining, relaxation, and community events. (Federal Realty Investment Trust)

Figure 15.12. Flexibility, imaginative programming, and cheerful lighting have helped Pentagon Row draw significant volumes of wintertime visitors. (Federal Realty Investment Trust)

Figure 15.13. Reston Town Center's Fountain Square serves as the backdrop for programmed events, dining, leisure, and relaxation year-round. Mercury Fountain, which symbolizes communication and commerce, has become a symbol and focal point for the Town Center. (Reston Town Center Association)

Reston Town Square Park provides an urban park experience to suburbanites who previously lacked access to this kind of asset. Designed as a complementary public space primarily for the use of nearby residents in the Town Center, the park also serves the day-time population of office workers and teleworkers. At roughly 1.25 acres in size, the park includes roughly seven distinct but connected spaces, within which a variety of activities and encounters take place. The size, proportions, and variety of these "outdoor rooms" support a variety of experiences for all ages.

The park distinguishes itself with the integration of art, with the adjacency of GRACE, a variety of seating options, and a balance of soft and hardscape elements. The park is also built with quality materials and employs a palette of materials chosen so that it blends

Figure 15.14. The Reston Town Square Park adds to the public space network of the Town Center while providing a varied pedestrian experience. (Jason Beske)

easily into the surrounding blocks and feels seamlessly integrated into the Town Center. The space is comfortably enclosed on all four sides by mid- to high-rise residential and office buildings. On the ground floor, retail rings three sides of the Town Square, and GRACE and residential buildings anchor the fourth. The resulting high level of pedestrian energy and "eyes on the street" makes the park feel extremely secure throughout the day and offers visitors a comfortable respite within the Town Center.

Repeated observation suggests that the life of the park directly correlates to the amount of sunshine on a given day—more sun, more park activity. As RTC's residential and office populations continue to rise, the park only grows more valuable as an asset and a placemaking opportunity in the Town Center (see Figure 15.14).

A Diverse Mix of Choices

Walkable urban places need to provide varied activities that appeal to diverse populations and lifestyles. They should offer a range of choices that are best suited for the community they serve. The following communities provide a diverse mix of choices, representing a departure from conventional suburban development.

Rockville Town Square–Rockville, Maryland

Previously the site of a mall that opened in 1972, Rockville Town Center has emerged as an exemplar of a walkable urban center in the Washington suburb of Rockville. Development on the 12.5-acre town center began in 2004 with the construction of the Rockville Town Square. At the heart of the Town Square is a 28,000-square-foot public space that serves the important role of bringing the people together for community events, socializing, and relaxation. In the winter, a popular ice skating rink maintains the square's function as a focal point. Midrise development surrounding the square provides a comfortable sense of enclosure and includes a library (the result of a public/private partnership), an arts and innovation center, and dozens of shops and restaurants with apartments and condos above.

Rockville Town Square includes 180,000 square feet of retail and restaurants and nearly 650 residential units. The Town Square is considered a success on many levels, not least of which is the role it plays in the daily lives of Rockville's residents. The city has made an effort to program regular events at the Town Square and to integrate it as the central gathering place for the community—through festivals, parades, formal gatherings, and live music. Part of the success of the Town Square is the ability to close adjacent streets and expand the usable pedestrian space.

The Town Square represents the first phase of a master plan for the center of Rockville. Connectivity to and through the development establishes the framework for a walkable pedestrian environment throughout the rest of the 60-acre planning area. Proximity to a Metro station offers a direct link to regional amenities and workplaces for car-light or car-free households, and three parking garages include nearly 2,000 parking spaces to accommodate visitors and workers. Rockville Town Square provides a comfortable and flexible pedestrian environment. The library, well-designed open space, programmed events, and lively streetscapes combine to create a community gathering place that serves both residents and visitors (see Figure 15.15).

Santana Row–San Jose, California

Santana Row is an 18-block development situated on 42 acres. Its first buildings opened in 2002, launching the conversion of a failing 1950s strip shopping center into a walkable, mixed-use center. Completion of its sixth phase, now under way, will give Santana Row 650,000 square feet of retail and restaurants, 1,200 residential units, 350,000 square feet of office space, a hotel, and a theater. It will also include roughly 3,500 parking spaces located either on-street, or in center-block parking garages.

Modeled on the Ramblas de Catalunya in Barcelona, Santana Row (the street) serves as the central spine of the development and provides a richly layered public realm and diverse mix of choices for pedestrians. While the street serves as an active linear park, it

Figure 15.15. Rockville Town Square serves as the town green for Rockville and as a backdrop for community events, social gatherings, and leisure. Locally owned shops, restaurants, and a community library add to the vitality of the Square. (Federal Realty Investment Trust)

also links a series of other public spaces. Although it could improve on integration with public transit and surrounding development, plans for a future Santana West call for another 1 million square feet of retail, residential, and office uses. Santana Row establishes a grid that will support connectivity to surrounding areas. Its future expansion as a walkable urban place will also expand placemaking opportunity for the City of San Jose.

Santana Row integrates well-designed, walkable streets with public spaces in a mixed-use environment (see Figures 15.16 and 15.17). Its regional popularity demonstrates the broad desire for walkable urban places in suburban locations and represents a classic instance of the market shift to walkability from a site once defined by automobiles and economic decline.

Figure 15.16. Santana Row provides pedestrians with a memorable and vibrant space in which to linger. A variety of architectural designs and sophisticated landscaping details lend to the European atmosphere of the street. (Federal Realty Investment Trust)

Authenticity

The words "suburb" and "authentic" rarely appear together in a sentence. Following World War II and continuing to today most suburban development has responded to mass markets—whether residential subdivisions, retail malls, or office parks. The results have been far more generic—responding to one-size-fits-all stylistic and cultural preferences—than place-based. Infusing new walkable urban places in suburbs with authenticity represents an exciting opportunity to assert local climate, culture, and, ironically for significant new development, traditions. The examples in this chapter highlight strategies communities have used to capture local spirit and create genuine places of lasting value. For example, new development in the Village at Shirlington has built on the site's historic urban pattern with a broader mix of uses and a conscious use of programmed events to add critical mass while reinforcing a sense of place. Cultural amenities like a community theater and library, as well as a variety of local restaurants and retailers, help Shirlington feel like Shirlington, and not an interchangeable mall that might as easily be in Arizona or Illinois.

Unlike Shirlington, most suburbs don't have a "historic" pattern to build upon. Moving forward, newer suburbs, such as Reston and Rockville, will need to inject their own

Figure 15.17. At less than half an acre, Santana Row's Park Valencia accommodates a variety of community events, complementing other public spaces in the development. (Federal Realty Investment Trust)

histories and cultural traditions to further establish their own sense of place. Rockville Town Square, for example, brings people together to celebrate what is unique about the community through a range of programmed events. Community festivals and gatherings, such as the summer concert series, parades, and an arts festival, create opportunities to celebrate Rockville's cultural traditions and artistic expression. Reston, on the other hand, can draw on founding principles that stress quality of life, diversity of housing types, and provision of a range of cultural and recreational facilities. The community uses these today as a litmus test for incorporating new walkable developments.

In the end, no formula spells out how to create authenticity in suburban communities. By its nature, authenticity can mean two very different things in two neighboring towns. Suburbs can learn from and adopt some of the strategies described here, but the key remains finding ways to incorporate characteristics unique to the community—among them local terrain, climate, culture, art, building materials, resident interests, and history. New developments that work to capture these elements into their design and operation—in a sense making new places that speak with a familiar vocabulary—can foster the spirit of the community and even add new layers of meaning to it.

Conclusion

The introduction of walkable urbanism into suburban communities can raise property values and enhance a sense of community. It can create a shared new icon of the community, become a gathering point and source of pride, and add valuable new amenities that improve quality of life, expand the job market, and deliver fiscal benefits. The next generation of development in suburban communities has already begun, bringing a shift in how we envision, plan for, and build communities.

The communities highlighted in this chapter offer a limited cross section of the suburban embrace of walkable urban places. Nevertheless they suggest the strategies being employed in suburbs to promote walkability and authenticity. These vignettes show how some suburban places have taken into consideration the physical aspects of the built environment. From a social perspective, placemaking contributes to the life and identity of a community while fostering personal well-being. From a design perspective, placemaking is both a powerful concept and an economic development strategy that seems likely to grow in popularity as communities see the success of their early-adopting neighbors and decide they want more walkable urban places too.

Notes

1. "Placemaking," accessed April 2017, https://en.wiktionary.org/wiki/placemaking.
2. Project for Public Spaces blog, "Reimagining Our Streets as Places: From Transit Routes to Community Roots," accessed April 2, 2017, https://www.pps.org/reference/reimagining-our-streets-as-places-from-transit-routes-to-community-roots/.
3. Smart Growth Network, International City/County Management Association, and Environmental Protection Agency, *Getting to Smart Growth: 100 Policies for Implementation* (Smart Growth Network, 2002).
4. Ibid.
5. "Reston Master Plan," 1962, Reston Museum, accessed April 2017, https://www.restonmuseum.org/reston-history.
6. Andres Duany, Elizabeth Plater-Zyberk, and Jeff Speck, *Suburban Nation: The Rise of Sprawl and the Decline of the American Dream* (New York: North Point Press, 2000).
7. Interview with Robert Goudie, CEO Reston Town Center Association, March 13, 2017.
8. Lee Sobel, "Six Reasons for the Resurgence of Car-Free Shopping Streets," 2017, accessed June 6, 2017, www.buildabetterburb.org.

9.   William H. Whyte, *City: Rediscovering the Center* (Philadelphia: University of Pennsylvania Press, 1988).

10.   ARUP, *Cities Alive: Towards a Walking World* (London: ARUP, 2016).

11.   Ellen Dunham-Jones and June Williamson, *Retrofitting Suburbia: Urban Design Solutions for Redesigning Suburbs* (Newark, NJ: John Wiley & Sons, 2011).

12.   Alan Ward, *Reston Town Center: A Downtown for the 21st Century* (Washington, DC: National Academies Press, 2006).

CONCLUSION

Jason Beske and David Dixon

This book tells an optimistic story. Better yet, a story based on informed and reasoned optimism. Suburbs are in transition, but in this perfect storm of accelerating demographic, social, economic, technological, and environmental change, so are cities. As suburbs adapt to a more urban future, they can draw on three particular strengths:

First, while suburbs and cities face the same changing demographics and markets that are increasing demand for more walkable urban places, suburbs have much more land on which to create these places. Large, contiguous sites offered by stagnant malls and outmoded office parks are much easier to redevelop than a complex mix of smaller urban sites with multiple owners. And these suburban sites are far less expensive. The balance of investment in significant mixed-use developments will tip toward suburbs in the coming years.

Second, and closely related to this advantage, is the practical reality that, in an era when most US households don't include kids, our leading economic sectors are trying to move into urban areas, and a rapidly aging population is seeking walkable environments, cities simply do not have enough room to meet demand. A more urban generation and economy can't all fit into cities. Nor do they want to. Tens of millions of Americans prefer suburban living and working, just not necessarily in single-family subdivisions and single-use office parks. The authors intentionally selected the images in this book to demonstrate how much is happening in suburbs already. Still more exciting examples will follow over the next decade.

Third, more people (read more voters) live in suburbs than anywhere else. Suburbs have clout—potentially more than cities. After years of talking about an "urban agenda" for cities, it is time for suburbs to articulate the federal and state help—policy as much as financial—they will need to invest in the transit, streets, and technology to create the urban places essential to adapt to changing times. If banks are too big to fail, suburbs are much bigger.

As stated earlier in the book, affluent suburbs, particularly in regions with growing economies, will have an easier time leveraging these strengths to create walkable urban places. But as the Dayton Mall story tells us, less affluent suburbs in slow-growth regions can also redevelop outmoded malls and office parks to pump new life into local economies and create a new heart for their community. Meanwhile places like Rockville Town Square demonstrate that a lively new urban center can attract economic growth and become a self-fulfilling prophecy.

We are entering an urban century, but this century can be at least as much about suburbs as it is about cities.

ABOUT THE CONTRIBUTORS

Michael J. Berne, principal of MJB Consulting, uses a "psychographic" model—built on demographics, personal values, incomes, and similar factors—to track rapidly changing retail markets and develop retail strategies targeted to the unique characteristics of individual communities.

Jason Beske, AICP, is an urban planner who has focused his public- and private-sector work on the urbanization of suburban communities and the design of vital, people-oriented places. A frequent speaker and instructor at planning conferences, Jason earned his bachelor's and master's degrees in community and regional planning from Iowa State University's College of Design. He is a past chair of the American Planning Association's Urban Design and Preservation Division and a former board member of the Form-Based Codes Institute.

David Dixon, FAIA, is Stantec's Urban Places Planning & Urban Design leader. He has led significant initiatives across North America to help cities and suburbs alike create a new generation of urban places that help communities adapt to the accelerating pace of demographic, social, and economic change. David has been honored for his post-Katrina citywide master plan for New Orleans and multiple other projects by the American Planning Association, the American Institute of Architects (AIA), the Congress for New Urbanism, and other national organizations. He received the AIA's highest honor for achievement in the public sphere, the Thomas Jefferson Award. David coauthored *Urban Design for an Urban Century: Shaping More Livable, Equitable, and Resilient Cities* (Wiley, 2014).

Terry Foegler, president of Terry Foegler & Associates LLC, has led widely recognized redevelopment initiatives, including revitalization of the university district surrounding The Ohio State University's campus in Columbus and, subsequently, first as city manager

293

and then as a consultant, the planning and development of suburban Dublin, Ohio's emerging Bridge Street District.

Mark Hinshaw, an architect and urban designer, has consulted with many cities and towns on planning and urban design. He served as Bellevue, Washington's urban designer in the 1980s and is intimately familiar with the city's growth and resurgence. He has also written books and articles on urban design.

Linda E. Hollis, AICP, is a retired urban planner with more than 30 years of experience, including 14 years as a fiscal impact consultant to local governments throughout the United States, 10 years as a researcher and writer, and more than 6 years with Fairfax County, where she assisted with initiatives to transform Tysons.

Christopher B. Leinberger is a nationally recognized land use strategist, teacher, developer, researcher, and author. He is a George Washington University professor and chair of GW's Center for Real Estate and Urban Analysis. Island Press published his book *The Option of Urbanism: Investing in a New American Dream* in 2008.

Harold Madi, Stantec's Urban Places Planning & Urban Design leader for Canada, has received numerous awards for large, transformational projects across Canada. Prior to joining Stantec, he served as director of urban design for the City of Toronto. He was a charter member of the Council on Canadian Urbanism.

Simon O'Byrne, a vice president at Stantec, leads the firm's Community Development practice for Canada. An urban planner, he has been honored for significant revitalization, brownfield, and transit-oriented development projects across Canada. In 2015 he was named the Allard Chair in Business at MacEwan University.

Stewart Schwartz, executive director and a founder of the Coalition for Smarter Growth, is a leading advocate for the principles of walkable urbanism in the Washington, DC, region. The nonprofit he leads addresses land use and transportation issues in many of the region's suburbs. He is a US Navy veteran and a lawyer by training.

Chris Snyder, community development director for Miami Township, Ohio, leads his community's highly innovative planning and economic development work. He has focused his suburban community on planning for change, focusing on transformation of its unusually large commercial core into a walkable, mixed-use center.

Tianyao Sun, executive vice president of Aerotropolis Institute of China, is an urban planner who focuses his research and practice on transit-oriented development around airports, train stations, and transit stations. He has extensive large-scale urban development experience in many large cities across China and the United States.

Laurie Volk, is a co-managing director, with Todd Zimmerman, of Zimmerman/Volk Associates (ZVA), and a board member of the Congress for the New Urbanism. ZVA has developed a unique, demographics-based methodology for assessing housing demand. The firm has won recognition as a national leader in projecting housing demand for emerging and changing markets in both cities and suburbs.

Christopher Volk-Zimmerman is the director of research at Zimmerman/Volk Associates, a leading housing market research firm.

Sterling Wheeler, AICP, now retired, served as Fairfax County's chief of policy and plan development. He was lead planner for the 1994 and 2010 Tysons plans, which played a central role in transforming Tysons from an auto-oriented suburb to a walkable urban place.

Sarah Woodworth, principal of the consulting firm W-ZHA, is a real estate analyst who focuses on emerging urban markets in cities and suburbs. She is particularly known for developing innovative public/private partnership strategies that have been instrumental in launching new walkable urban centers.

Christopher Zimmerman, vice president for economic development at Smart Growth America, focuses on the economic and fiscal impact of development policies on communities. As a member of the Arlington County Board for 18 years, he was intimately involved in planning, development, housing, and transportation policy in the county.

Todd Zimmerman is a co-managing director, with Laurie Volk, of Zimmerman/Volk Associates, a leading housing market research firm. He is a former board member of the Congress for the New Urbanism.

INDEX

Page numbers in italics indicate drawings, photographs, and tables.